2020-2021 Edition

SAT Reading
New Practice Tests

PrepVantage

- All original content is Copyright PrepVantage Publishing © 2019. Unauthorized copying or distribution of any portion of this book is strictly prohibited

- Please visit PrepVantageTutoring.com for additional study materials and information regarding future book releases

ISBN-13: 9781089683421

SAT® is a registered trademark of the College Board, which does not endorse and is not affiliated with this product.

PrepVantage

Visit us at **PrepVantageTutoring.com**

SAT Reading: New Practice Tests, 2020-2021 Edition
Copyright © 2019 PrepVantage Publishing

ISBN-13: 9781089683421

All material in this book is owned exclusively by PrepVantage LLC, is reproduced under a Creative Commons license that allows international commercial distribution, or exists in the Public Domain, whether as content that appeared in the form here reproduced before 1923 or as content created by a U.S. Government official as part of his or her official duties. Unauthorized reproduction of this book is prohibited. Front cover detail photo © mslooten and licensed through Adobe Stock images as of July 2019.

Please visit https://creativecommons.org/licenses/by/4.0/ and linked pages for information on the relevant Creative Commons licenses.

Table of Contents

Test 1 ....Page 2

Answers and Explanations ....Page 18

Test 2 ....Page 32

Answers and Explanations ....Page 48

Test 3 ....Page 62

Answers and Explanations ....Page 78

Test 4 ....Page 92

Answers and Explanations ....Page 108

Test 5 ....Page 122

Answers and Explanations ....Page 140

Test 6 ....Page 154

Answers and Explanations ....Page 170

Test 7 ....Page 184

Answers and Explanations ....Page 200

Test 8 ....Page 214

Answers and Explanations ....Page 230

Test 1

Full Reading Section

2020 SAT Practice

Reading Test

65 MINUTES, 52 QUESTIONS

Turn to Section 1 of your answer sheet to answer the questions in this section.

DIRECTIONS

Each passage or pair of passages below is followed by a number of questions. After reading each passage or pair, choose the best answer to each question based on what is stated or implied in the passage or passages and in any accompanying graphics (such as a table or graph).

Questions 1-10 are based on the following passage.

This passage is adapted from Leslie Standish, "Those Things That They Were Emblems Of" (2018). In the portion of the narrative that follows, a woman named Diana has rented a small vacation bungalow on the California coast for her two daughters, Megan and Georgette.

    At the beginning, Diana had hoped that the house was far enough from the beach that the din of the elephant seals would be more or
Line less inaudible. The house was not. Through all
5 the daylight hours there was an incessant low growling and rumbling, which flared now and then into the hideous yet rhythmic guttural cries of the bull elephant seals. Work, Diana had decided, may well be impossible. Megan and Georgette
10 were not old enough to be left on their own; if they had been, Diana could have spent every morning taking a leisurely bike ride to any of a number of nearby cafés or outcroppings, just her and some none-too-urgent paperwork and the
15 silence. Instead, she kept the television blaring at all hours, a stratagem that drowned out the barbaric yawps of those elephant seals but itself made concentration impossible.
    Yet Megan and Georgette were mesmerized
20 by those enormous ugly beasts: the slimy black newborn pups, the innumerable resigned females, and especially the huge, gluttonous, ferocious bull elephant seals, with their battle scars and their great flapping noses. In the morning, the girls
25 would get dressed to go swimming. They would carefully arrange folded towels and seven-to-ten-year-old-sized deck chairs in an old wagon that had been idling in the yard when they arrived. They would take turns pulling it along while
30 Diana strolled along behind, and they would inevitably lead their paraphernalia and their mother away from anything resembling a usable beach and right to the vast expanse where the elephant seals were. They would stare for what
35 seemed like endless stretches to Diana, but for what must have seemed like mere minutes to them. And it didn't take long for them to find a favorite, either: the hugest and most hideous of all the bulls. This one had the longest and floppiest
40 proboscis of all and shifty little eyes that were perfectly dark. As Diana noticed, wincing, his chest also had a strange stencil-like scar pattern

that made it look as though he were wearing a
long necktie and a shirt with a breast pocket.
The girls called him Wilbur, after the gentle
and innocent pig from *Charlotte's Web*. Having
spent hours staring at Wilbur and his brood, the
girls would then make up adventures, conquests,
triumphs for Wilbur as evening settled over the
house.

    It was nearing bedtime one evening, on a day
when Wilbur had been strangely absent from the
beach. The girls were lounging near the blaring
television; Diana, bravely, was trying to work. She
had finally settled into her task when, of course,
commotion broke out. The television blared a
needless trumpety anthem, the one that signaled
a "Special Report." And then Georgette leapt
straight up and pointed with violent delight at the
screen. "Look!" she shouted, and Diana looked
and saw a bored-looking newscaster reading off
a script. "Oh say can you . . . seal? Townspeople
got a surprise visit today from a marine mammal
of elephantine proportions." Then there he was.
Wilbur. The program cut away to footage of
Wilbur, flopping across a parking lot and bouncing
against a jeep for no particular reason. Then more
Wilbur, crashing through a wooden fence and
wrecking some poor soul's garden. Then yet more
Wilbur, finally heaving himself over the highway
near the beach as park rangers circled around
him, waving huge red flags and trying to scare
him back home. Megan and Georgette watched,
fascinated, transfixed. Even Diana herself couldn't
help but smile, feeling that her daughters' instincts
and imagination had somehow risen beyond
the silly music and indifferent narration of the
newscast to erupt into glorious, chaotic life.

1

One of the central themes of the passage is

A) how an experience with apparently unpleasant aspects can lead to enjoyment.
B) how different generations instinctively adopt different codes of conduct.
C) whether family members can work together to overcome catastrophe.
D) whether humans can effectively safeguard the natural world.

2

In relation to her daughters, Diana would best be characterized as

A) anxious for their safety despite their carefree personalities.
B) unable to understand the nature of their emotions.
C) hopeful that conflict can serve a constructive purpose.
D) willing to accommodate one of their preoccupations.

3

As used in line 12, "leisurely" most nearly means

A) non-specific.
B) dallying.
C) undemanding.
D) lazy.

Test 1

4

An important function of the second paragraph (lines 19-50) is to

A) investigate the motivations of two characters who are drawn to grotesque sights.
B) demonstrate how characters learned to enjoy a scene that had formerly appeared to be menacing.
C) call attention to meaningful disparities in how characters react to shared conditions.
D) undermine an image of childhood innocence presented earlier in the passage.

5

As described within the passage, Diana's work is impeded by

A) her dissatisfaction with her daughters' choices.
B) the need to supervise her young daughters.
C) a strange and sudden moment of crisis.
D) her own belief that the work is ultimately insignificant.

6

Which choice provides the best evidence for the answer to the previous question?

A) Lines 8-9 ("Work . . . impossible")
B) Lines 10-15 ("if they . . . silence")
C) Lines 29-34 ("They . . . were")
D) Lines 53-56 ("The girls . . . broke out")

7

One of the important ironies of Megan and Georgette's positive response to Wilbur is that

A) Diana's dislike of Wilbur only intensifies her daughters' fascination with him.
B) Wilbur himself dislikes the presence of humans.
C) Wilbur is named after a character with radically different qualities.
D) Georgette and Megan dislike the other seals.

8

As used in line 65, "cut away to" most nearly means

A) deleted information about.
B) worked to undermine.
C) switched focus towards.
D) hurried away from.

9

As presented in the final paragraph of the passage, the newscast of Wilbur's activities calls attention to Wilbur's

A) name recognition.
B) aggression towards human spectators.
C) unexpected sensitivity.
D) destructive power.

10

Which choice provides the best evidence for the answer to the previous question?

A) Lines 62-64 ("Oh . . . proportions")
B) Lines 67-69 ("Then . . . garden")
C) Lines 69-73 ("Then . . . home")
D) Lines 73-75 ("Megan . . . smile")

Questions 11-21 are based on the following passage and supplementary material.

This passage is adapted from Samantha Wallace, "It's a Mad, Mad, Mad, Mad, but Predictable World: Scaling the Patterns of Ancient Urban Growth," an article originally published* in 2014 by EveryONE, the community blog of PLOS ONE.

With more than 7.1 billion people living across the globe, cities house more than 50% of the world's population. The United Nations Population Fund projects that by 2030 more than
5 5 billion people will live in cities across the world. The Global Heath Observatory, a program run by the World Health Organization, predicts that, by 2050, 7 out of 10 people will live in cities, compared to 2 of 10 just 100 years ago.
10 Recently, researchers developed what is called "urban scaling theory" to mathematically explain how modern cities behave in predictable ways, despite their unprecedented growth. Recent work in urban scaling research considers cities
15 "social reactors." In other words, the bigger the city, the more people and more opportunity for social interaction. Think for a moment about the social interactions that occur just on the block outside of your local coffee shop; now multiply
20 those interactions by millions. Cities magnify the number of interactions, increasing both social and economic productivity and, ultimately, encouraging urban growth itself.
    The authors of a recent PLOS ONE paper
25 sought to determine whether ancient cities "behaved" in predictable patterns similar to their modern counterparts. To do so, they developed mathematical models and tested them on archaeological settlements across the Pre-Hispanic
30 Basin of Mexico (BOM). Based on their findings, they suggest that the principles of settlement organization, which dictate city growth, were very much the same then as they are now, and may be consistent over time.
35 To test their predictions, the researchers analyzed archaeological data from over 1,500 sites in the BOM, previously surveyed in the '60s and '70s by researchers from the University of Michigan and Penn State.
40 Using low-altitude aerial photographs and primary survey reports from the original surveyors, the researchers organized the following data from approximately 4,000 sites: the settled area, the average density of potsherds—broken
45 pieces of ceramic material—within it, the count and total surface area of domestic architectural mounds, the settlement type, the estimated population, and the time period.
    The researchers were interested in examining
50 areas of the BOM that enabled social interaction between residents, so they excluded site types that did not allow social interaction—for example, isolated ceremonial centers, quarries, and salt mounds. They then grouped the remaining 1,500
55 sites into both chronological groups and size groups. For chronological grouping, each site was assigned to one of four time periods: the Formative period (1150 B.C.E.–150 B.C.E.), the Classic period (150 B.C.E.–650 C.E.), the Toltec
60 period (650–1200 C.E.), and the Aztec period (1200–1519 C.E.). By the Aztec period, the area had developed from amorphous rural settlements to booming metropolises comprising over 200,000 people. . . .
65 After separating the data into both chronological groups and size groups, the researchers applied their mathematical models and tested their predictions about urban growth in the settlements of the BOM. One aspect of city
70 development assessed by the researchers was the evolution of defined networks of roads and canals in growing cities. Because roads act as conduits, directly influencing social interaction—much like the roads leading to the aforementioned
75 coffee shop—growing cities develop increasingly defined and extensive networks to connect social hubs to one another.
    Scientists use urban scaling theory to show that population and social phenomena follow distinct,
80 mathematical patterns over time. By developing mathematical models to predict measurable changes in city growth, these researchers applied the same patterns to ancient cities and concluded

---

*See Page 30 for the citation for this text.

that the development of settlements over time in
the BOM seems analogous to the development
observed in modern cities. Researchers predict
that the same mathematical models could be
reformatted to estimate population size of
ancient cities, as well as to develop measures
for calculating socio-economic output like the
production of art and public monuments based
on the relationship between settlement size and
division of labor. Although there is still much to
be solved through the equations of urban scaling
theory, the consistency of city growth over time
has implications for both the past and the present.

11

In the first paragraph, the author of the passage calls attention to the United Nations Population Fund and the Global Health Observatory in order to

A) refute possible doubts regarding the author's own credibility.
B) underscore the need for new statistical data in population studies.
C) introduce a few ideas about future conditions.
D) establish a tone of certitude and erudition.

Typical Development of an Ancient City (BOM Site)

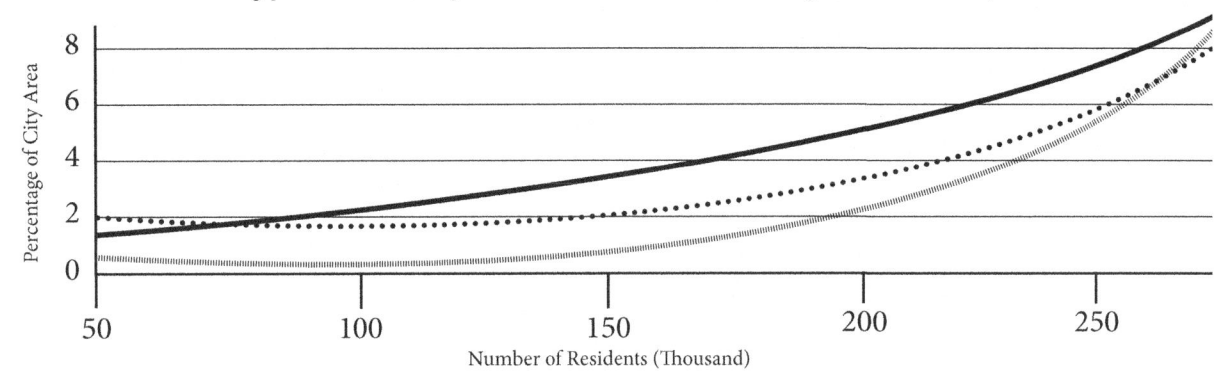

Typical Development of a Modern City (Northeastern U.S.)

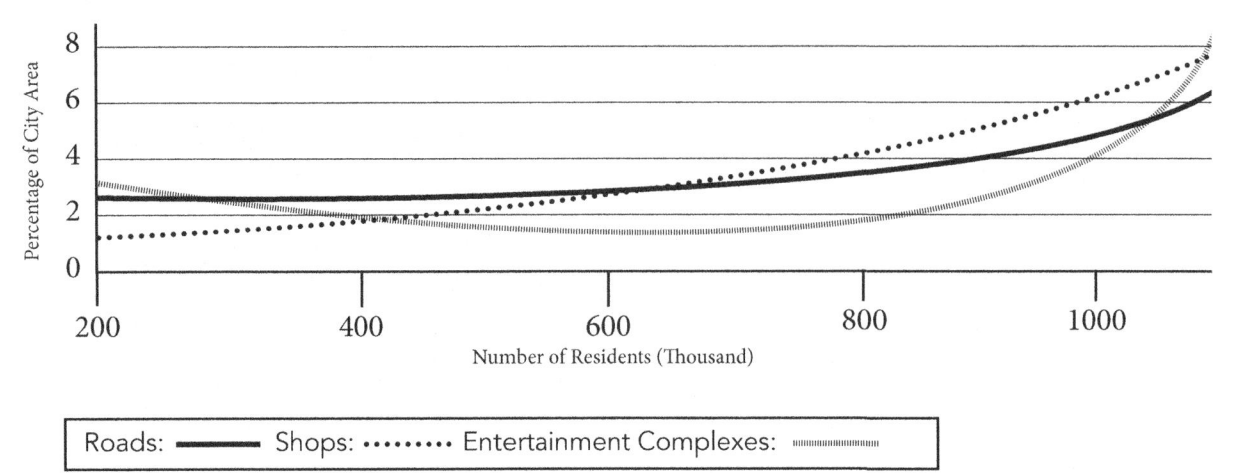

Roads: ——— Shops: ·········· Entertainment Complexes: ⊪⊪⊪⊪⊪

12

One assumption about the growth of cities that the passage addresses is that

A) roads become less important for maintaining city-wide networks as cities become more advanced.

B) a typical city will grow indefinitely in the absence of social or economic disruption.

C) mathematical models that explain ancient and modern cities are in most respects interchangeable.

D) a city lifestyle will not normally be conducive to excessively frugal or anti-social behavior.

13

Which choice provides the best evidence for the answer to the previous question?

A) Lines 20-23 ("Cities . . . itself")
B) Lines 30-34 ("Based . . . time")
C) Lines 40-43 ("Using . . . sites")
D) Lines 69-72 ("One . . . cities")

14

As used in line 32, "dictate" most nearly means

A) enshrine.
B) overrule.
C) pronounce.
D) guide.

15

The author characterizes the decades-old University of Michigan and Penn State research projects as

A) intriguing but misguided pursuits.
B) pioneering instances of mathematical modeling.
C) useful sources of information.
D) examples of rash conjecture.

16

As used in line 41, "primary" most nearly means

A) firsthand.
B) controlling.
C) underlying.
D) simplified.

17

Which of the following would be another example of a "site type" (line 51) that the PLOS ONE researchers would naturally exclude from their study?

A) A theater with several large reception rooms
B) A small temple set aside for silent prayer
C) A marketplace near a group of guild halls
D) A landscaped park frequented by aristocrats

18

On the basis of the final two paragraphs of the passage, it can be inferred that mathematical modeling is a technique that

A) remains at a stage of rudimentary development.
B) suggests solutions to recent population crises.
C) reveals linkages between the past and the present.
D) shows promise in areas beyond urban studies.

Test 1

19

The final sentence of the passage serves mainly to

A) highlight a perceived weakness of the research considered throughout the passage.
B) gesture towards future analysis while noting the significance of current findings.
C) resolve a debate in favor of the author's stance.
D) call into question the validity of specific data set.

20

The two graphs that accompany the passage support all of the following conclusions EXCEPT the idea that

A) the percentage of land area devoted to roads typically increases steadily in a modern city in the northeastern U.S.
B) the percentage of land area devoted to shops typically increases steadily in a modern city in the northeastern U.S.
C) the typical ancient city did not feature entertainment complexes at a population of 100,000.
D) the typical ancient city would feature entertainment complexes at a population of 150,000.

21

Which of the following claims in the passage is directly supported by information provided by the two graphs?

A) Lines 54-56 ("They then . . . groups")
B) Lines 65-69 ("After . . . the BOM")
C) Lines 72-77 ("Because . . . another")
D) Lines 80-86 ("By developing . . . cities")

Questions 22-32 are based on the following passage and supplementary material.

This passage is adapted from Karl Hille (Editor) et al., "Young Planets Orbiting Red Dwarfs May Lack Ingredients for Life," a 2019 news release published* by NASA.

Rocky planets orbiting red dwarf stars may be bone dry and lifeless, according to a new study using NASA's Hubble Space Telescope. Water and organic compounds, essential for life as we know
5 it may get blown away before they can reach the surface of young planets.
   This hypothesis is based on surprising observations of a rapidly eroding dust-and-gas disk encircling the young, nearby red dwarf star
10 AU Microscopii (AU Mic) by Hubble and the European Southern Observatory's Very Large Telescope (VLT) in Chile. Planets are born in disks like this one.
   Red dwarfs, which are smaller and fainter than
15 our Sun, are the most abundant and longest-lived stars in the Milky Way galaxy.
   Fast-moving blobs of material appear to be ejecting particles from the AU Mic disk. If the disk continues to dissipate at this rapid pace, it
20 will be gone in about 1.5 million years. In that short time, icy material from comets and asteroids could be cleared out of the disk. Comets and asteroids are important because they are believed to have seeded rocky planets such as Earth with
25 water and organic compounds, the chemical building blocks for life. If this same transport system is needed for planets in the AU Mic system, then they may end up "dry" and dusty—inhospitable for life as we know it.
30 "The Earth, we know, formed 'dry,' with a hot, molten surface, and accreted atmospheric water and other volatiles for hundreds of millions of years, being enriched by icy material from comets and asteroids transported from the outer solar
35 system," said co-investigator Glenn Schneider of Steward Observatory in Tucson, Arizona.

*See Page 30 for the citation for this text.

The observations are led by John Wisniewski of the University of Oklahoma in Norman, whose team is composed of 14 astronomers from the
40 U.S. and Europe.
   If the activity around AU Mic is typical of the planet-birthing process among red dwarfs, it could further reduce prospects of habitable worlds across our galaxy. Previous observations suggest
45 that a torrent of ultraviolet light from young red dwarf stars quickly strips away the atmosphere of any orbiting planets. This particular star is only 23 million years old.
   Surveys have shown that terrestrial planets are
50 common around red dwarfs. In fact, they should contain the bulk of our galaxy's planet population, which could number tens of billions of worlds. Planets have been found within the habitable zone of several nearby red dwarfs, but their physical
55 characteristics are largely unknown.
   Observations by Hubble's Space Telescope Imaging Spectrograph (STIS) and the VLT show that the AU Mic circumstellar disk is being excavated by fast-moving blobs of circumstellar
60 material, which are acting like a snowplow by pushing small particles—possibly containing water and other volatiles—out of the system. Researchers don't yet know how the blobs were launched. One theory is that powerful mass
65 ejections from the turbulent star expelled them. Such energetic activity is common among young red dwarfs.
   "These observations suggest that water-bearing planets might be rare around red dwarfs because
70 all the smaller bodies transporting water and organics are blown out as the disk is excavated," explained Carol Grady of Eureka Scientific in Oakland, California, co-investigator on the Hubble observations.
75   Conventional theory holds that billions of years ago Earth formed as a comparatively dry planet. Gravitationally perturbed asteroids and comets, rich in water from the cooler outer solar system, bombarded Earth and seeded the surface with ice
80 and organic compounds. "However, this process may not work in all planetary systems," Grady said.

22

According to the passage, which of the following is known by scientists?

A) How circumstellar material was launched from the AU Mic solar system

B) The physical characteristics of planets in the habitable zone of red dwarf solar systems

C) Whether all planets acquire water in the same way that Earth most likely did

D) The age of Au Mic

23

According to the passage, all of the following are true of red dwarf stars EXCEPT that they are

A) smaller than our Sun.

B) brighter than our Sun.

C) the most common type of star.

D) the longest-lasting type of star.

24

The author of the passage indicates that the atmospheres of planets that surround red dwarfs would be eroded by

A) comets and asteroids.

B) UV radiation from stars.

C) the gravity of nearby stars.

D) water and ice.

Celestial Bodies in the Milky Way Galaxy (Estimated)

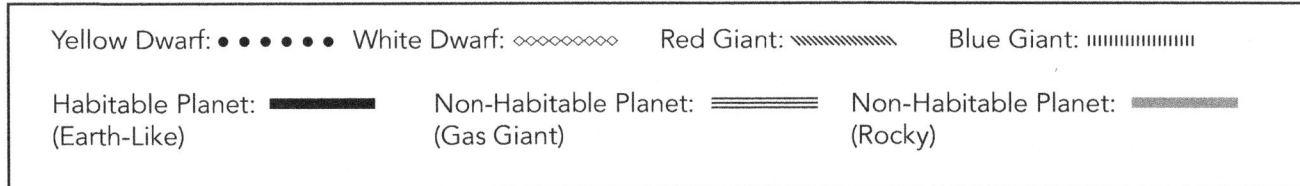

Y-axis: Total Number of Celestial Bodies: Billions (Estimate), 0 to 16
X-axis: Age Range: Billions of Years (Oldest to Youngest Celestial Bodies, Estimate), 0 to 16

Legend:
- Yellow Dwarf: • • • • •
- White Dwarf: ◊◊◊◊◊◊◊
- Red Giant: 〰〰〰〰
- Blue Giant: ||||||||||||
- Habitable Planet (Earth-Like): ▬▬▬
- Non-Habitable Planet (Gas Giant): ≡≡≡
- Non-Habitable Planet (Rocky): ▬▬▬

25

Which choice provides the best evidence for the answer to the previous question?

A) Lines 7-13 ("This hypothesis . . . this one")
B) Lines 20-22 ("In that . . . disk")
C) Lines 41-47 ("If the activity . . . planets")
D) Lines 77-80 ("Gravitationally . . . compounds")

26

As used in line 65, the word "turbulent" functions to

A) emphasize the high amount of energy emitted from AU Mic.
B) imply that AU Mic exhibits dangerous surface conditions.
C) indicate that AU Mic is different from other stars.
D) show that AU Mic is destructive to nearby celestial bodies.

27

As used in line 77, "perturbed" most nearly means

A) bothered.
B) affected.
C) weakened.
D) damaged.

28

It can be inferred from the passage that life would be more likely to develop on rocky planets if they

A) had more energetic orbiting activity.
B) were not formed in the disk of a solar system.
C) had ice from comets and asteroids as surface matter components.
D) exhibited greater gravitational pull.

29

Which choice provides the best evidence for the answer to the previous question?

A) Lines 7-13 ("This hypothesis . . . this one")
B) Lines 22-26 ("Comets . . . life")
C) Lines 49-52 ("Surveys . . . worlds")
D) Lines 63-67 ("Researchers . . . red dwarfs")

30

Which of the following offers a possible explanation for the age range of blue giant stars, as indicated by the graph?

A) Yellow dwarf stars can collapse to form blue giant stars.
B) Blue giant stars can collapse to form white dwarf stars.
C) The presence of a blue giant causes the atmosphere of a gas giant planet to evaporate.
D) Earth-like habitable planets have never been traced to the solar systems of blue giant stars.

31

The passage and the graph indicate that the formation of a habitable and Earth-like planet often involves

A) the presence of a white dwarf.
B) the presence of a red giant.
C) the transformation of a non-habitable rocky planet.
D) the transformation of a gas giant planet.

32

Given the information in lines 14-16 in the passage, which of the following additional facts would explain why the graph does NOT consider red dwarf stars?

A) Within the Milky Way, red dwarf stars are more common than Earth-like habitable planets.
B) Red dwarf stars have shorter lifespans than blue giant stars.
C) Relatively few red dwarf stars have been captured in telescope images.
D) There are over 100 billion stars in the Milky Way.

Test 1

Questions 33-42 are based on the following passages.

Passage 1 is adapted from *The Principles of Scientific Management* (1911) by Frederick Winslow Taylor. Passage 2 is adapted from *Life in a Railway Factory* (1915) by Alfred Williams.

Passage 1

It would seem to be so self-evident that maximum prosperity for the employer, coupled with maximum prosperity for the employee, ought to be the two leading objects of management, that even to state this fact should be unnecessary. And yet there is no question that, throughout the industrial world, a large part of the organization of employers, as well as employees, is for war rather than for peace, and that perhaps the majority on either side do not believe that it is possible so to arrange their mutual relations that their interests become identical.

The majority of these men believe that the fundamental interests of employees and employers are necessarily antagonistic. Scientific management, on the contrary, has for its very foundation the firm conviction that the true interests of the two are one and the same; that prosperity for the employer cannot exist through a long term of years unless it is accompanied by prosperity for the employee, and vice versa; and that it is possible to give the workman what he most wants—high wages—and the employer what he wants—a low labor cost—for his manufactures.

It is hoped that some at least of those who do not sympathize with each of these objects may be led to modify their views; that some employers, whose attitude toward their workmen has been that of trying to get the largest amount of work out of them for the smallest possible wages, may be led to see that a more liberal policy toward their men will pay them better; and that some of those workmen who begrudge a fair and even a large profit to their employers, and who feel that all of the fruits of their labor should belong to them, and that those for whom they work and the capital invested in the business are entitled to little or nothing, may be led to modify these views.

Passage 2

We hear a great deal about the "discontent" of the workers, and a degree of censure and reproach is usually conveyed with the expression. It is not half general enough. The average working man is too content. He is often lazily apathetic. Is the mineowner, the manufacturer, or the railway magnate content? Of course he is not. Strength is in action. When I hear of a man's being satisfied I know that he is done for. He might as well be dead. I wish the workers were more discontented, though I should in every case like to see their discontent rationally expressed and all their efforts intelligently directed. They waste a fearful amount of time and energy through irresolution and uncertainty of objective.

The selfishness, cruelty, and arrogance of the capitalist and his agents force the workers into rebellion. The swaggering pomposity and fantastic ceremony of officials fill them with deserving contempt. Their impudence is amazing. I have known a foreman of the shed to attack a man by reason of the decent clothes he had on and forbid him to wear a bowler hat. Not only in the workshop but even at home in his private life and dealings he is under the eye of his employer. His liberty is tyrannically restricted. In the town he is not allowed to supplement his earnings by any activity except such as has the favour of the works' officials. He must not keep a coffee-shop or an inn, or be engaged in any trading whatever. He may not even sell apples or gooseberries. And if he happens to be the spokesman of a labourers' union or to be connected with any other independent organisation, woe betide him! The older established association—such as that of the engineers—is not interfered with. It is the unprotected unskilled workman that must chiefly be terrorised and subjugated.

The worker is everywhere exploited. The speeding-up of late years has been general and insistent. New machinery is continually being installed in the sheds. This is driven at a high rate and the workman must keep pace with it.

33

As used in line 4, "objects" most nearly means

A) items.
B) goals.
C) challenges.
D) lessons.

34

Passage 1 states that, according to scientific management,

A) employees and employers cannot both benefit under modern conditions.
B) the challenges of employee-to-employee relations are explained by workplace grudges.
C) the challenges of employee-to-employee relations can be traced to greedy employers.
D) it is possible to pay workers a good wage while employers enjoy high profits.

35

Which choice provides the best evidence for the answer to the previous question?

A) Lines 6-9 ("And yet . . . for peace")
B) Lines 22-25 ("it is possible . . . manufacturers")
C) Lines 28-31 ("that some . . . wages")
D) Lines 33-36 ("and that some . . . to them")

36

The primary point of Passage 2 is that

A) business owners are inherently tyrannical.
B) workers in low-wage positions are being replaced by machines.
C) workers must rise up and express discontent with the unfair status quo.
D) workers are not permitted to have secondary jobs or to own their own businesses.

37

According to Passage 2, which of the following contributes to poor working conditions?

A) Employees having to keep up with the productivity of machines
B) Infighting between employees
C) Long working hours
D) A false belief that employees' and employers' goals are inherently antithetical

38

As used in line 57, the word "fantastic" serves primarily to

A) show how extreme the vicious and disingenuous behavior of employers is.
B) suggest how enjoyable and fulfilling work-related ceremonies are.
C) emphasize the imaginary nature of some disputes.
D) demonstrate how altruistic workers are in a manner that places them in contrast to their employers.

39

Which of the following best supports the notion that the author of Passage 2 believes that contentment leads to inaction?

A) Lines 47-49 ("When I . . . discontented")
B) Lines 50-52 ("I should . . . directed")
C) Lines 55-57 ("The selfishness . . . rebellion")
D) Lines 74-77 ("The older . . . subjugated")

40

Which of the following is seen by both the author of Passage 1 and the author of Passage 2 as a source of tension between employers and employees?

A) Workers operating an inn of their own
B) Workers operating a produce shop
C) Antagonism involving desired wages
D) Low worker productivity over the long term

41

One key difference between the passages is that

A) Passage 1 advocates for mutual benefit, while Passage 2 sees the employee-employer relationship as more adversarial.
B) Passage 1 sees the employee-employer relationship as adversarial, while Passage 2 advocates a cooperative approach.
C) Passage 1 argues that unions are unnecessary, while Passage 2 sees unions as vital to workers' rights.
D) Passage 1 advocates for peaceful interactions, while Passage 2 advocates for a violent uprising of the working class.

42

Regarding blame for employee-employer conflicts,

A) Passage 1 blames employers for being greedy, while Passage 2 blames employees for complacency.
B) Passage 1 blames workers and employers for not finding common cause, while Passage 2 blames established unions for overshadowing newer unions of unskilled workers.
C) Passage 1 blames workers and employers for not working in unison, while Passage 2 blames employees for inaction and employers for cruel treatment of workers.
D) Passage 1 blames workers and employers for not cooperating, while Passage 2 blames employees for not keeping up with machines and employers for detrimental labor practices.

Questions 43-52 are based on the following passage.

This passage is adapted from "Brain-activated muscle stimulation restores monkeys' hand movement after paralysis," a 2012 news release* from the National Institutes of Health.

   An artificial connection between the brain and muscles can restore complex hand movements in monkeys following paralysis, according to a study funded by the National Institutes of Health.
   In a report in the journal *Nature*, researchers describe how they combined two pieces of technology to create a neuroprosthesis, "a device that replaces lost or impaired nervous system function." One piece is a multi-electrode array implanted directly into the brain which serves as a brain-computer interface (BCI). The array allows researchers to detect the activity of about 100 brain cells and decipher the signals that generate arm and hand movements. The second piece is a functional electrical stimulation (FES) device that delivers electrical current to the paralyzed muscles, causing them to contract. The brain array activates the FES device directly, bypassing the spinal cord to allow intentional, brain-controlled muscle contractions and to restore movement.
   The research team was led by Lee E. Miller, Ph.D., professor of physiology at Northwestern University's Feinberg School of Medicine in Chicago. Prior to testing the neuroprosthesis, Dr. Miller's group recorded the brain and muscle activity of two healthy monkeys as the animals performed a task requiring them to reach out, grasp a ball, and release it. The researchers then used the data from the brain-controlled FES device to determine the patterns of muscle activity predicted by the brain activity.
   To test the device, the researchers gave monkeys an anesthetic to locally block nerve activity at the elbow, causing temporary paralysis of the hand. With the aid of the neuroprosthesis, both monkeys regained movement in the paralyzed hand, could pick up and move the ball in a nearly routine manner and complete the task as before. Dr. Miller's research team also performed grip strength tests, and found that their system restored precision grasping ability. The device allowed voluntary and intentional adjustments in force and grip strength, which are keys to performing everyday tasks naturally and successfully.
   This new research moves beyond earlier work from Dr. Miller's group showing that a similar neuroprosthesis restores monkeys' ability to flex or extend the wrist despite paralysis. "With these neural engineering methods, we can take some of the important basic physiology that we know about the brain, and use it to connect the brain directly to muscles," Dr. Miller said. "This connection from brain to muscles might someday be used to help patients paralyzed due to spinal cord injury perform activities of daily living and achieve greater independence."
   In 2008, a team led by Eberhard Fetz, Ph.D. at the University of Washington in Seattle coupled the activity of single neurons to an FES device similar to the one used for Miller's study. Monkeys learned to activate individual neurons to control the FES device and move a joystick, and could adapt neurons previously unassociated with wrist movement to complete the task. The investigators suggest that this process of learning and adaption plays an important role in how the BCI translates the brain's activity patterns into adaptive control of the FES device.
   The unique design of the ball grasp-and-release task used with the animals in this study is a further contribution to advanced neuroprosthetic testing and development. Daofen Chen, Ph.D., a program director at NIH's National Institute of Neurological Disorders and Stroke (NINDS), described how researchers in the field are striving toward devices that will go beyond simple arm movements and allow fine hand and finger movements. "We've learned a lot from non-human primate studies focused on understanding neural control of arm and wrist movements," said Dr. Chen. "Dr. Miller's study builds on those efforts and focuses on the complex hand and finger movements needed to grasp an object."

---

*See Page 30 for the citation for this text.

... FES devices in current clinical use take advantage of the patient's residual muscle activity. For example, a prosthetic arm can use sensors built into the shoulder, sensing a shrugging motion that is used to stimulate muscles to open or close the hand. However, this is a less precise and less natural method of control, and it is not an option for patients with higher level spinal cord injuries and little or no shoulder and arm movement. For these patients, the creation of a brain-controlled FES device that connects brain activity directly to muscle stimulation would provide an opportunity to restore hand function.

43

Which choice best summarizes the passage?

A) Research on paralysis shows that any curative procedure will be successfully performed on primates alone.

B) Dr. Miller's medical team believes that one day functional electrical stimulation devices will be able to deliver current to paralyzed primates.

C) Hand movement restoration has been successfully achieved in human subjects since 2008.

D) Primate studies on restoring hand movements after paralysis have paved the way for medical breakthroughs.

44

In presenting the research described in the passage, the author indicates that

A) people will not respond well to the treatments that have been derived from Dr. Miller's research.

B) eminent scientists have taken an interest in the author's chosen research topic.

C) Dr. Miller's work enabled a theoretical advance.

D) paralysis will soon be medically eliminated.

45

As used in line 11, "interface" most nearly means

A) interaction.

B) recreation.

C) conversation.

D) pairing.

46

The passage's discussion of Dr. Miller suggests that

A) the FES device was exclusively used by Dr. Miller's team.

B) other scientists failed to activate individual neurons in primates.

C) Dr. Miller's team's new and more sophisticated research was based on previous work.

D) standard FES devices can function even if a subject has no muscle activity.

47

Which choice provides the best evidence for the answer to the previous question?

A) Lines 32-35 ("To . . . hand")

B) Lines 39-41 ("Dr. Miller's . . . ability")

C) Lines 46-49 ("This . . . paralysis")

D) Lines 70-73 ("The unique . . . development")

48

The second paragraph (lines 5-20) serves mainly to

A) give an overview of the mechanisms that can restore hand movement.
B) hint at the ethical implications of primate experiments.
C) discourage researchers from tackling neuroprosthetic experiments in the absence of advanced technology.
D) provide a purely conceptual explanation of a well-known experiment.

49

It can reasonably be inferred that an artificial connection between the brain and the muscles

A) may improve the quality of some people's lives in the future.
B) will eventually cease to operate properly in any given test subject.
C) should be replaced by a natural form of bodily cooperation.
D) will function properly in all prospective cases once new technology emerges.

50

As used in line 51, "basic" most nearly means

A) dependent.
B) fundamental.
C) easy.
D) unrefined.

51

According to the passage, one of the primary goals of scientists working in the field of neuroprosthetics is to

A) perfect the hand dexterity of patients with paralysis.
B) reduce paralysis in primates.
C) facilitate the mass production of FES devices.
D) popularize neuroprosthesis among medical institutions.

52

Which choice provides the best evidence for the answer to the previous question?

A) Lines 28-31 ("The researchers . . . activity")
B) Lines 42-45 ("The device . . . successfully")
C) Lines 58-61 ("In 2008 . . . study")
D) Lines 76-79 ("researchers . . . movements")

STOP

If you finish before time is called, you may check your work on this section only.
Do not turn to any other section.

Answer Key: Test 1

Passage 1	Passage 2	Passage 3	Passage 4	Passage 5
1. A	11. C	22. D	33. B	43. D
2. D	12. D	23. B	34. D	44. B
3. C	13. A	24. B	35. B	45. A
4. C	14. D	25. C	36. C	46. C
5. B	15. C	26. A	37. A	47. C
6. B	16. A	27. B	38. A	48. A
7. C	17. B	28. C	39. A	49. A
8. C	18. C	29. B	40. C	50. B
9. D	19. B	30. A	41. A	51. A
10. B	20. C	31. C	42. C	52. D
	21. C	32. D		

Question Types

Major Issue
1-2, 22-23, 36, 43-44

Passage Details
4, 7, 11, 15, 17-19, 37, 48-49

Command of Evidence
5-6, 9-10, 12-13, 21, 24-25, 28-29, 34-35, 39, 46-47, 51-52

Word in Context
3, 8, 14, 16, 26-27, 33, 38, 45, 50

Graphics and Visuals
20-21, 30-32

Passage Comparison
40-42

Answer Explanations
Test 1, Pages 2-17

Passage 1, Pages 2-4

1. A is the correct answer.

At first, Diana is dismayed by the presence of the elephant seals and the noise they cause. However, by the end of the passage she has come to feel some affection for one of the seals, observing how this animal contributes to a sense of "glorious, chaotic life" (line 78). This content shows a movement from focusing on the unpleasant to feeling appreciation; choose A to support this information. Be careful not to choose D, since the passage does NOT explicitly focus on preserving nature (despite its natural beach setting). B is too broad in scope (since a few characters, NOT entire generations, are considered), while C ("catastrophe") assumes an inappropriately strong negative when in fact the passage mostly considers differences of opinion.

2. D is the correct answer.

Diana's two daughters become fascinated with one of the seals, and she patiently accommodates this interest by taking them to the beach and listening to their stories about the seal (lines 45-50). Choose D to support this content. Be careful not to choose B, since while Diana does not share their affection for the seal, it is an interest (NOT an emotion) that she finds herself unable to understand at first. A and C can also be eliminated since the passage does not contain any open conflict or explicit threats to safety, despite the possibly negative theme of differences of opinion.

3. C is the correct answer.

In line 12, "leisurely" refers to Diana imagining a pleasant and relaxing bicycle ride, one associated with "none-too-urgent" (line 14) and mostly soothing activities. Choose C to reflect this meaning. A (inappropriately implying generality or lack of clarity), B (inappropriately and negatively implying delaying or hesitating), and D (inappropriately implying a failure to use adequate effort) all introduce improper contexts and should thus be eliminated.

Answer Explanations, Test 1

4. C is the correct answer.

The second paragraph describes how the young girls respond to one particular seal with affection and curiosity, while Diana responds to the same seal with discomfort and unease. Choose C to reflect this gap between how different characters react to the same condition of being close to the seals. Be careful not to choose A, since the girls are indeed attracted to a somewhat grotesque animal, but this passage does NOT focus on exploring their motivations for that response. B and D can be rejected since the seal was never presented as menacing, and the paragraph does NOT undermine the concept of the girls' innocence, despite the seal's grotesque (negative) appearance.

5. B is the correct answer.

Lines 10-14 describe how Diana could have organized her time had her daughters been older and more independent: "if they had been, Diana could have spent every morning taking a leisurely bike ride to any of a number of nearby cafés or outcroppings, just her and some none-too-urgent paperwork and the silence." This information implies that her work is delayed due to the need to supervise her daughters; choose B to support this content. A and D can be eliminated since Diana does not question her daughters' choices, nor does she seem to find her work completely unimportant. C can also be ruled out since the passage does not describe a moment of crisis; instead, Diana's work is impeded by a routine and predictable inconvenience.

6. B is the correct answer.

See the previous answer explanation for analysis of the correct line reference. A describes Diana's resignation to how the noise will prevent her from being productive, while C describes how her daughters inevitably want to spend their days near the seals. D describes how the girls disrupt Diana in a rare moment of productivity. None of these other answers describe Diana's need to supervise her daughters (who are mentioned in OTHER contexts), so all choices except for B should all be eliminated.

7. C is the correct answer.

Despite the seal's rugged and grotesque appearance, the girls name him "Wilbur, after the gentle and innocent pig from *Charlotte's Web*" (lines 45-46). There is a clear contradiction in demeanor between the seal and the animal he is named after; choose C to support this content. Be careful not to choose A, since while Diana does dislike Wilbur, there is no evidence that her daughters are aware of this dislike. B and D can also be dismissed since the passage never states that Wilbur dislikes humans, or that the girls dislike other seals; Diana's OWN dislike is the true topic.

8. C is the correct answer.

In line 65, "cut away to" refers to the television program switching to a different visual image (namely from a newscaster to a huge elephant seal). Choose C to reflect this meaning. A (inappropriately implying a removal of information), B (inappropriately implying subversion or working to remove from power), and D (inappropriately implying running away) all introduce improper contexts and should thus be eliminated.

Answer Explanations, Test 1

9. D is the correct answer.

Lines 67-69 describe Wilbur "crashing through a wooden fence and wrecking some poor soul's garden," an action which shows the seal's destructive power. Choose D to support this content. Be careful not to choose B, since Wilbur is show destroying inanimate objects but NOT spectators. A and C can also be eliminated since there is no evidence that Wilbur himself recognizes his name or shows any type of sensitivity; instead, a few of the human characters recognize Wilbur and experience a moment of emotion.

10. B is the correct answer.

See the previous answer explanation for analysis of the correct line reference. A quotes the dialogue spoken by the newscaster, while C describes footage of rangers trying to frighten Wilbur away. D describes the reaction of the young girls to the news story and Diana's surprising reaction to their response. While some of these choices do occur in the broad context of the news program, none of these other answers describe the seal's destructive capacity, and all should be eliminated as failing to align with an answer to the previous question.

Passage 2, Pages 5-8

11. C is the correct answer.

In the first paragraph, both the United Nations Population Fund and the Global Health Observatory are mentioned immediately before the author cites future projections which these organizations have provided. Therefore, the primary purpose of this content is to introduce ideas about future conditions; choose C. Be careful not to choose D, since the reference to well-established organizations DOES imply expertise, but given that these are future predictions, certainty about them is not possible. A and B can both be dismissed since no doubts have been raised about the author's OWN credibility (since the author is not mentioned directly in the opening), and there is no reference to collecting new statistical information (since, instead, statistical information that was collected PREVIOUSLY is referenced).

12. D is the correct answer.

In lines 20-23, the author notes that "Cities magnify the number of interactions, increasing both social and economic productivity." This statement supports an assumption that, conversely, an urban lifestyle will typically NOT support anti-social or low-expense habits; choose D as appropriate. A can be dismissed since roads are mentioned as significant factors that enable networks and social activity, while B can be eliminated because the passage focuses on establishing patterns of growth in cities, NOT on arguing that cities will grow indefinitely (which may not be the case because a city's area and population could remain limited). C should be eliminated because the passage suggests that comparable models could be used to analyze ancient and modern cities, but that the models would have to be "reformatted" (line 87), which indicates that they are not interchangeable in a straightforward way.

Answer Explanations, Test 1

13. A is the correct answer.

See the previous answer explanation for analysis of the correct line reference. B summarizes the findings of the study before delving into more detail, while C describes the methodology of the study. D specifies one type of data which was analyzed in the study. Only B references urban growth (as opposed to research methods) as its key topic, but the idea raised by this answer (stability and unchanging patterns) does not align with any of the content in the answers to the previous question.

14. D is the correct answer.

In line 32, "dictate" refers to the way in which the principles of settlement influence the growth of a city. Choose D to reflect this meaning. A (inappropriately implying to intentionally elevate or establish as law), B (inappropriately implying one opinion dominating another), and C (inappropriately implying the communication of a decision or a judgment) all introduce incorrect contexts and therefore should be eliminated.

15. C is the correct answer.

The author describes how, in this recent study, archaeological data collected in the 1960s and 1970s was re-purposed and served a useful function for those looking to study patterns of urban growth (lines 35-39). It is therefore accurate to say that the author views the studies from the University of Michigan and Penn State as sources of useful information; choose C as appropriate. Be careful not to choose B, since the original archaeological studies provided data on which modeling was later based but did NOT include any modeling themselves. A and D can also be eliminated, since the author's tone towards these studies is positive while both of these answers refer to the studies in negative ways.

16. A is the correct answer.

In line 41, "primary" refers to the status of the survey reports as the original reports written directly by the surveyors. Choose A to reflect this meaning. B (inappropriately implying dominating or influencing), C (inappropriately implying something that is influential but not directly stated) and D (inappropriately implying something having been reduced to essentials) all introduce incorrect contexts and therefore should be eliminated.

17. B is the correct answer.

In the study, researchers excluded "site types that did not allow social interaction" (lines 51-52). Of the possible answer choices, a temple focused on silent prayer is the only one where social interactions would NOT take place since the activity involved is not based on communication. Therefore, choose B; all of the others refer to sites where social interactions (whether for leisure and entertainment or for commerce) would take place, and these should therefore be eliminated.

Answer Explanations, Test 1

18. C is the correct answer.

The final paragraphs of the passage explain that models of growth in both ancient and modern cities are relatively constant, a fact which implies that mathematical models can reveal connections between the past and the present. Choose C as the best option. A can be eliminated because the models can successfully be used to study complex patterns and are thus not basic or "rudimentary," while B distorts the focus on similarities between past and present to indicate that the models can solve problems, NOT simply reveal connections. D can be eliminated as beyond the scope of the passage, since nothing contained in the passage refers to these models having implications outside of urban studies.

19. B is the correct answer.

The final sentence of the passage indicates that more research remains to be done while gesturing towards a hopeful potential for the information remaining to be uncovered. Choose B as appropriate. A and C can be eliminated since the sentence acknowledges work remaining to be done, NOT a methodological weakness, while the mostly factual passage has NOT focused on a central debate. D can also be eliminated since the validity of the data is not being called into question here; the author is pointing out that future work can be performed, not that PAST work is unreliable.

20. C is the correct answer.

The two graphs show that the percentage of land devoted to roads and shops grows steadily as the population of the city grows; they also show that an ancient city of 150,000 residents would typically include a relatively small number of entertainment complexes by percentage of area. On account of this data, A, B, and D can all be eliminated. C can be identified as correct because an ancient city of 100,000 residents WOULD typically have a small number of entertainment complexes (since the line on the graph does not dip below zero).

21. C is the correct answer.

Lines 70-72 indicate that the surface area of roads would steadily increase along with the growth of a city's population, and since the graphs plot the growth of land area devoted to roads alongside population growth, this claim from the passage is directly supported by the data in the graphs. Choose C as appropriate. A and B can be eliminated since chronological information is NOT included in the graphs and since these answers consider research methodology instead of modeled findings (the true focus of the graphs). D can also be eliminated since it describes the accuracy of models, a factor that is not clearly evaluated in the graphs.

Passage 3, Pages 8-11

22. D is the correct answer.

The author states that "This particular star [Au Mic] is only 23 million years old" (lines 47-48), which reveals that scientists know how old Au Mic is. Choose D. All of the other answers describe conditions which

Answer Explanations, Test 1

scientists remain uncertain about or hope to explore in the future, as indicated in the author's analysis in the later portions of the passage (lines 41-74). As a result, A, B, and C can all be eliminated.

23. B is the correct answer.

The passage states that "Red dwarfs, which are smaller and fainter than our Sun, are the most abundant and longest-lived stars in the Milky Way galaxy" (lines 14-16). This content reveals that red dwarfs are NOT brighter than the sun; since B is the only answer indicating incorrect information, choose B as appropriate. A, C, and D all represent information which is reflected in the same lines of the passage.

24. B is the correct answer.

In lines 41-47, the author explains that "If the activity around AU Mic is typical of the planet-birthing process among red dwarfs, it could further reduce prospects of habitable worlds across our galaxy. Previous observations suggest that a torrent of ultraviolet light from young red dwarf stars quickly strips away the atmosphere of any orbiting planets." This content indicates that the UV radiation from stars such as red dwarfs can erode the atmosphere of nearby planets; choose B as appropriate. Be careful not to choose C, since activity from nearby stars can impact the atmosphere of a planet, but this occurrence is due to radiation, NOT gravity. A and D can be eliminated since comets, asteroids, water, and ice are not known to impact the atmosphere of a given planet; at most, these factors are linked to Earth in the final paragraph (lines 75-82) not to exoplanets that are associated with red dwarfs.

25. C is the correct answer.

See the previous answer explanation for analysis of the correct line reference. A identifies an observation about a specific red dwarf star and the tools used to make that observation, while B describes a change that might occur in the disc over time. D explains how Earth evolved from a "dry" planet to one that could support life. None of these other answers describe how the atmospheres of surrounding planets are impacted by red dwarf stars (and some in fact refer to other features of the universe), and therefore all should be eliminated.

26. A is the correct answer.

In line 65, "turbulent" is used to describe how AU Mic emits energy, leading to circumstellar material being ejected from the star. Choose A as appropriate. B and C can both be eliminated, since AU Mic is too far away from life forms to be a source of danger and is behaving in a way common to young stars. D can also be eliminated, since the volatile activity emanating from AU Mic may actually have functional impacts for other celestial bodies and should thus not take a strongly negative description.

27. B is the correct answer.

In line 77, "perturbed" refers to the way in which asteroids and comets were impacted by gravity so that they reached Earth. Choose B to reflect a context of being moved or affected. A (inappropriately implying irritation or annoyance), C (inappropriately implying a reduction in strength or power) and D (inappropriately implying something that has been harmed) all introduce incorrect contexts and therefore should be eliminated.

Answer Explanations, Test 1

28. C is the correct answer.

Lines 22-26 state that "Comets and asteroids are important because they are believed to have seeded rocky planets such as Earth with water and organic compounds, the chemical building blocks for life." This content implies that rocky planets would be more likely to develop conditions necessary for life if they received ice from comets; choose C as the best answer. A and D can both be eliminated since the passage does not provide any evidence that gravity or orbiting activity influences a planet's ability to support life (since even though "habitable worlds" are considered as a topic in lines 41-55, the precise qualities of these worlds remain unknown). B can also be eliminated since, despite scientific interest in the possibility of life beyond Earth, it is not yet definitively known whether hospitable planets can develop in the disc of a solar system.

29. B is the correct answer.

See the previous answer explanation for analysis of the correct line reference. A provides information about the test case that led to the development of a broader hypothesis, while C explains that many planets exist relatively close to red dwarf stars. D explains a research question which remains unsolved, as well as one possible answer. None of these other answers demonstrate the connection between comets and the qualities necessary to sustain life, and therefore they should all be eliminated.

30. A is the correct answer.

The graph shows that yellow dwarf stars range in age from approximately 4 to 12 billion years old, while blue giant stars range in age from 0 to 1 billion years old. Since there are no yellow dwarf and blue giants of the same age, and all of the blue giant stars are younger than the yellow dwarf stars, it is possible to hypothesize that blue giant stars can form from yellow dwarfs. Choose A as most appropriate to this information. B can be eliminated since all blue giant stars are younger than white dwarf stars; this answer primarily may help to explain how white dwarf stars develop but does NOT clearly explain the formation and lifespan of blue giants. C and D can be eliminated since they raise factors that are here irrelevant; the graph does not document the presence of atmosphere, nor which planets are located in the solar system of which stars.

31. C is the correct answer.

The passage explains that "The Earth, we know, formed 'dry' " (line 30) and gradually became hospitable to life. This information is confirmed by the graph, which shows that habitable planets range in age from approximately 3 to 7 billion years old while inhospitable rocky planets range in age from 2 to 5 billion years old; this situation indicates that rocky planets may eventually become habitable. Choose C as appropriate. D can be eliminated since there are gas giants which are much older than habitable planets, making it unlikely for gas giants to become habitable over time. A and B can also be eliminated since the passage and the graph do not indicate a connection between habitable planets and the presence of yellow dwarf or red giant stars.

32. D is the correct answer.

Lines 14-16 specify that red dwarf stars are the most abundant type of stars; if there are more than 100 billion stars in the Milky Way, there are likely to be more than 16 billion red dwarfs. Since the graph only shows celestial bodies numbering up to 16 billion, this arrangement could plausibly explain why red dwarfs are not included. Choose D as the best option. A and B can be eliminated since greater frequency and shorter lifespan would not prevent red dwarfs from being documented on the graph, since both prevalence and age ARE directly considered. C can also be eliminated since telescope images are not necessarily required for age and number of celestial bodies to be documented; method of documentation is not considered in the graph and it is entirely possible that methods that do NOT involve telescope observation would yield information about age and prevalence.

Passage 4, Pages 12-14

33. B is the correct answer.

In line 4, "objects" refers to conditions of "prosperity" (lines 2-3) desired by both employers and employees, and thus indicates possible accomplishments or achievements. Choose B to reflect this meaning. A (inappropriately implying material goods), C (inappropriately implying hurdles or obstacles), and D (inappropriately implying knowledge acquired through experience) all introduce incorrect contexts and therefore should be eliminated.

34. D is the correct answer.

In lines 22-25, the author points out that workers want high wages while employers want low costs, and that these two goals are not mutually exclusive. Choose D as the best answer. B and C can be eliminated since the author of Passage 1 (who seeks a sense of compromise) does not blame workplace conflict on either side being selfish or malicious. A can also be eliminated since the main argument of Passage 1 is that both employers and employees could benefit from the SAME system of scientific management.

35. B is the correct answer.

See the previous answer explanation for analysis of the correct line reference. A describes the antagonism which typically exists between employers and workers, while C describes a viewpoint held by employers but which the author would like to see altered. D describes a view which the author thinks that workers may hold but which he believes to be incorrect. Though relevant to scientific management as a topic, these answers do not convey the author's primarily POSITIVE view of scientific management by indicating that high wages and strong profits can coexist, and therefore they should all be eliminated.

36. C is the correct answer.

The author of Passage 2 argues that "The worker is everywhere exploited" (line 78) and believes that workers must fight back against unfair conditions. Choose C as appropriate. A and B can be eliminated since the author mostly considers the perspective of workers (who are exploited by large business owners and THEMSELVES hope to run fair businesses) and expresses concerns about workers having to keep pace with new machines, NOT about workers being replaced by such machines. Be careful not to choose D, since the author does note the injustice of workers being restricted in their lives outside of work, but this arrangement is NOT the primary focus of the passage.

Answer Explanations, Test 1

37. A is the correct answer.

At the end of Passage 2, the author expresses concern that technological advances are producing faster and faster machines which workers have to keep pace with. Choose A to reflect this content. B and C can be eliminated since the author does not discuss working hours or infighting (which, though possible outcomes of oppression by employers, are not EXPLICITLY considered in the passage). Be careful not to choose D, since the author of Passage 1 believes that workers and employers can both achieve their goals, but it is not clear whether the author of Passage 2 (who instead focuses on conflict and disadvantages) would agree.

38. A is the correct answer.

In line 57, the author is arguing that employers behave in cruel, unjust, and purposefully confusing ways towards their employees; the word "fantastic" is used to support this argument. Choose A as appropriate. B and C can both be eliminated as illogical since the author disapproves of work-related ceremonies and thinks that disputes between workers and employers are valid and real. D can also be ruled out since the author depicts workers as exploited but NOT necessarily as altruistic.

39. A is the correct answer.

In lines 47-49, the author of Passage 2 explains that "When I hear of a man's being satisfied I know that he is done for. He might as well be dead. I wish the workers were more discontented." This content shows that the author believes that contentment leads to inaction; choose A as the best answer. B describes how the author would like to see workers express their discontent, while C describes the roots of injustice towards workers. D indicates a distinction between different types of employee associations and explains that older associations are tolerated by employers but NOT that workers become complacent as a result. None of these other answers display the author's belief that contentment leads to inaction, and therefore they should all be eliminated.

40. C is the correct answer.

The authors of both passages agree that workers generally desire the highest wages possible and that this desire can be a source of conflict with employers. Choose C to reflect this information. A and B can both be eliminated since the activities mentioned in these choices are discussed only by the author of Passage 2. D can be eliminated since the authors find the expectations of employers who would naturally desire HIGH productivity problematic and often sympathize with workers,

41. A is the correct answer.

The author of Passage 1 believes that the interests of workers and employers are essentially aligned, but that conflict arises out of misunderstanding (lines 1-12). In contrast, the author of Passage 2 believes that workers are oppressed by employers and should organize to fight back (lines 55-57). Choose A to reflect this content. B can be eliminated since this answer understates the awareness of conflict present in Passage 1 and avoids the sense of ongoing difficulty or struggle (as opposed to cooperation) present in Passage 2. Be careful not to choose C, since while Passage 2 does advocate for unions, Passage 1 does not mention them. D can also

Answer Explanations, Test 1

be eliminated since while Passage 2 is relatively antagonistic in tone, it still advocates for rational resistance, NOT violent uprising.

42. C is the correct answer.

The author of Passage 1 argues that conflict is created because workers and employers fail to see their mutual interest and work together, while the author of Passage 2 argues that injustice occurs due to exploitation by the employers and passivity on the part of the workers. Choose C to reflect this content. A can be eliminated because it mis-characterizes the argument of Passage 1 (which does not primarily blame employers for being greedy but DOES point out that they do not always coexist well with workers), while D can be eliminated because it mis-characterizes Passage 2 (since the author does mention the increasing speed of machinery but NOT in order to blame workers for failing to keep up). Be careful not to choose B, since Passage 2 does mention that established unions are treated differently from unions of unskilled workers but mostly criticizes employers, NOT the groups for workers themselves.

Passage 5, Pages 15-17

43. D is the correct answer.

The passage describes a study relevant to primates and designed to investigate whether hand movements can be restored after paralysis. The success of the experiments provides grounds for progress towards "devices that will go beyond simple arm movements and allow fine hand and finger movements" (lines 77-79) in humans. Choose D to support this content. A can be dismissed since the passage clearly states that the researchers hope that the findings will translate to use by human subjects, while B can be rejected since the research is designed to develop treatment protocols for humans, NOT primates. C can also be dismissed, since hand movement (despite some promising findings) has NOT yet been successfully restored in human subjects.

44. B is the correct answer.

The passage cites "Daofen Chen, Ph.D., a program director at NIH's National Institute of Neurological Disorders and Stroke (NINDS)" (lines 73-75) as a scientist who is interested in the findings from Dr. Miller's research, suggesting that well-known scientists from an institute are interested in this research area. Choose B to support this content. A can be eliminated since no contra-indications that construe the research as flawed are identified in the passage, while C can be ruled out because the research entails tangible findings, not just theoretical developments. Be careful not to choose D, since this answer wrongly states that promising yet incomplete results will provide a broad and definitive remedy for paralysis.

45. A is the correct answer.

In line 11, "interface" refers to a site where the brain and a device which can be "implanted" (line 10) come into physical contact. Choose A to reflect this meaning. B (inappropriately implying activities engaged in for pleasure or relaxation), C (inappropriately implying a verbal exchange), and D (inappropriately implying the creation of a relationship between two things) all introduce improper contexts and should thus be eliminated.

Answer Explanations, Test 1

46. C is the correct answer.

Lines 46-49 describe the relationship between Dr. Miller's latest work and earlier studies: "This new research moves beyond earlier work from Dr. Miller's group showing that a similar neuroprosthesis restores monkeys' ability to flex or extend the wrist despite paralysis." Choose C to reflect this content. A and B both shift the focus to issues that would involve COMPARISON involving outside scientists, when in fact Dr. Miller's work alone is considered in the relevant evidence. D raises an issue ("muscle activity") that is indeed relevant to the passage, but wrongly indicates that FES devices (which aid muscle stimulation) operate without muscle activity and suggests a comparison ("standard" devices) that the evidence choices avoid.

47. C is the correct answer.

See the previous answer explanation for analysis of the correct line reference. A describes how the researchers simulated paralysis in the monkeys, while B highlights an additional result identified in the study. D describes how the progress of the study can contribute to further research. Though relevant to Dr. Miller's work, these answers do not directly align with content in the previous question; only C properly indicates that Dr. Miller's work had meaningful precedents that were themselves created by Dr. Miller.

48. A is the correct answer.

The second paragraph provides an overview of the process by which the researchers were able to restore the monkeys' ability to perform complex hand movements, with particular attention to the use of a "multi-electrode array" (line 9) and a FES device (line 15); choose A to support this content. B and C can both be eliminated since this paragraph does NOT engage with any ethical implications or the limits of current technology, which is mostly described as practical or useful. D can also be eliminated since the author is here describing the practical configuration of the experiment, so that characterizing the information in the paragraph as "conceptual" or theoretical would be inaccurate.

49. A is the correct answer.

The passage describes how research has shown that an artificial connection between the brain and the muscles can restore some complex muscle functions in primates (lines 1-4), which are reasonably similar to humans (lines 53-57). It is reasonable to infer that if this same technology can be applied to human subjects, it may restore some muscle functions and thereby increase quality of life. Choose A to support this content. B and D should both be dismissed since nothing in the passage indicates that these artificial connections, which remain untested in terms of human subjects, would consistently fail (too negative) or consistently perform flawlessly (too positive). C can be dismissed as illogical since these connections are designed for people for whom natural bodily cooperation between brain and muscles no longer exists.

50. B is the correct answer.

In line 51, "basic" refers to knowledge, particularly things "that we know about the brain" (lines 51-52), that serves as the foundation of other meaningful understanding. Choose B to reflect this meaning. A (inappropriately implying reliance on something else), C (inappropriately implying something simple or unchallenging), and

Answer Explanations, Test 1

D (inappropriately implying something that is not yet well-developed) all introduce improper contexts and should thus be eliminated.

51. A is the correct answer.

Lines 76-79 state that "researchers in the field are striving toward devices that will go beyond simple arm movements and allow fine hand and finger movements." This content suggests that scientists hope to give individuals suffering from paralysis a sophisticated range of motion; choose A to support this information. B can be dismissed since, while studies were performed on primates, the ultimate goal is to advance quality of life for humans experiencing paralysis (lines 53-57). C and D can also be eliminated since there is no specific discussion of mass production or popularizing devices within the medical community, even though the researchers involved do have a broad hope that their devices will have practical uses.

52. D is the correct answer.

See the previous answer explanation for analysis of the correct line reference. A describes one stage of data analysis connected to the experiment, while B describes some of what the devices made possible and why these attributes are important. C gives an overview of a different but related research study. Instead of providing main goals, these answers mainly describe experimental stages and background; only D properly relates to the topic of the previous question.

NOTES

- Passage 2 on Pages 5-6, "It's a Mad, Mad, Mad, Mad, but Predictable World: Scaling the Patterns of Ancient Urban Growth," is adapted from the article of the same name by Samantha Wallace and published by EveryONE, the community blog of PLOS ONE. 21 February 2014, PLOS ONE. https://blogs.plos.org/everyone/2014/02/21/mad-mad-mad-mad-predictable-world-scaling-patterns-ancient-urban-growth/. Accessed 28 July 2019.

- Passage 3 on Pages 8-9, "Young Planets Orbiting Red Dwarfs May Lack Ingredients for Life," is adapted from the article of the same name by Karl Hille et al. and published by NASA. 8 January 2019, NASA. https://www.nasa.gov/feature/goddard/2019/young-planets-orbiting-red-dwarfs-may-lack-ingredients-for-life. Accessed 28 July 2019.

- Passage 5 on Pages 15-16, "Brain-activated muscle stimulation restores monkeys' hand movement after paralysis," is adapted from the article of the same name published by the National Institutes of Health. 18 April 2012, NIH. https://www.nih.gov/news-events/news-releases/brain-activated-muscle-stimulation-restores-monkeys-hand-movement-after-paralysis. Accessed 28 July 2019.

About the Figures: The various visual resources that accompany the passages in this section are primarily meant to facilitate critical thinking skills and may not reflect historical data.

Test 2
Full Reading Section
2020 SAT Practice

Test 2

Reading Test

65 MINUTES, 52 QUESTIONS

Turn to Section 1 of your answer sheet to answer the questions in this section.

DIRECTIONS

Each passage or pair of passages below is followed by a number of questions. After reading each passage or pair, choose the best answer to each question based on what is stated or implied in the passage or passages and in any accompanying graphics (such as a table or graph).

Questions 1-10 are based on the following passage.

This passage is adapted from Anne Brontë, *The Tenant of Wildfell Hall* (1848). The narrator, Gilbert Markham, is a young gentleman who is paying a visit to a new acquaintance, Mrs. Graham; Arthur is Mrs. Graham's child, and Rose is Gilbert's own sister.

It was about the close of the month, that, yielding at length to the urgent importunities of Rose, I accompanied her in a visit to Wildfell
Line Hall. To our surprise, we were ushered into a
5 room where the first object that met the eye was a painter's easel, with a table beside it covered with rolls of canvas, bottles of oil and varnish, palette, brushes, paints, &c. Leaning against the wall were several sketches in various stages of
10 progression, and a few finished paintings—mostly of landscapes and figures.
 "I must make you welcome to my studio," said Mrs. Graham; "there is no fire in the sitting-room to-day, and it is rather too cold to show you into a
15 place with an empty grate."
 And disengaging a couple of chairs from the artistical lumber that usurped them, she bid us be seated, and resumed her place beside the easel—not facing it exactly, but now and then glancing
20 at the picture upon it while she conversed, and giving it an occasional touch with her brush, as if she found it impossible to wean her attention entirely from her occupation to fix it upon her guests. It was a view of Wildfell Hall, as seen at
25 early morning from the field below, rising in dark relief against a sky of clear silvery blue, with a few red streaks on the horizon, faithfully drawn and coloured, and very elegantly and artistically handled.
30 "I see your heart is in your work, Mrs. Graham," observed I: "I must beg you to go on with it; for if you suffer our presence to interrupt you, we shall be constrained to regard ourselves as unwelcome intruders."
35 "Oh, no!" replied she, throwing her brush on to the table, as if startled into politeness. "I am not so beset with visitors but that I can readily spare a few minutes to the few that do favour me with their company."
40 "You have almost completed your painting," said I, approaching to observe it more closely, and surveying it with a greater degree of admiration and delight than I cared to express. "A few more touches in the foreground will finish it, I should

Test 2

45 think. But why have you called it Fernley Manor, Cumberland, instead of Wildfell Hall?" I asked, alluding to the name she had traced in small characters at the bottom of the canvas.

But immediately I was sensible of having
50 committed an act of impertinence in so doing, for she coloured and hesitated, but after a moment's pause, with a kind of desperate frankness, she replied:—

"Because I have friends—acquaintances at
55 least—in the world, from whom I desire my present abode to be concealed, and as they might see the picture, and might possibly recognise the style in spite of the false initials I have put in the corner, I take the precaution to give a false name
60 to the place also, in order to put them on a wrong scent, if they should attempt to trace me out by it."

"Then you don't intend to keep the picture?" said I, anxious to say anything to change the subject.

65 "No, I cannot afford to paint for my own amusement."

"Mamma sends all her pictures to London," said Arthur, who had presently joined us; "and somebody sells them for her there, and sends us
70 the money."

In looking round upon the other pieces, I remarked a pretty sketch of Linden-hope from the top of the hill; another view of the old hall basking in the sunny haze of a quiet summer
75 afternoon; and a simple but striking little picture of a child brooding, with looks of silent but deep and sorrowful regret, over a handful of withered flowers, with glimpses of dark low hills and autumnal fields behind it, and a dull beclouded
80 sky above.

1

Within the passage, Mrs. Graham is characterized as someone who

A) had once chosen to reside in London.

B) is purposefully impolite toward her visitors.

C) longs to have more exposure to sophisticated culture.

D) does not frequently have visitors.

2

As used in line 15, "empty" most nearly means

A) meaningless.

B) weakened.

C) vacant.

D) nullified.

3

The narrator mentions in the third paragraph (lines 16-29) that Mrs. Graham's painting is of Wildfell Hall in order to

A) provide information that anticipates a question that is asked later in the passage.

B) answer a question that has been on the narrator's mind for some time.

C) add visual imagery to the paragraph.

D) clarify the setting of the narrative.

4

As used in line 42, "surveying" most nearly means

A) scrutinizing.

B) observing.

C) polling.

D) measuring.

Test 2

5

The narrator, Gilbert Markham, regards himself as an unwelcome intruder because

A) he invited himself to Wildfell Hall.
B) Mrs. Graham did not light a fire in the sitting room for him.
C) Mrs. Graham continues to work on her painting while Markham is present.
D) Arthur joins Markham's conversation with Mrs. Graham.

6

Which choice provides the best evidence for the answer to the previous question?

A) Lines 4-6 ("To our . . . easel")
B) Lines 12-15 ("I must . . . grate")
C) Lines 17-24 ("she bid us . . . guests")
D) Lines 67-70 ("Mamma . . . money")

7

Which of the following is NOT a way in which Mrs. Graham stays anonymous regarding her artwork?

A) Using false initials for her artist's signature
B) Using false place names to title her landscape pieces
C) Having an intermediate sell her work for her
D) Painting only landscapes rather than human subjects

8

On the basis of the episode depicted in the passage, it is reasonable to infer that the narrator regards Mrs. Graham as

A) an adept painter.
B) an impolite hostess.
C) a paranoid artist.
D) a sorrowful woman.

9

After asking why Mrs. Graham's painting is called Fernley Manor, the narrator

A) pressures Mrs. Graham for an answer.
B) expresses admiration for Mrs. Graham's work.
C) asks if Mrs. Graham profits from her work.
D) regrets asking the question itself.

10

Which choice provides the best evidence for the answer to the previous question?

A) Lines 40-43 ("You have . . . express")
B) Lines 49-51 ("I was . . . hesitated")
C) Lines 51-53 ("but after . . . replied")
D) Line 62 ("Then . . . picture?")

Questions 11-21 are based on the following passage and supplementary material.

This passage is an excerpt from Anne Douglass, "Why your child's preschool teacher should have a college degree" (2018). Originally published* by The Conversation.

　　How much education does a preschool teacher need?
　　When the District of Columbia announced in March that it would require an associate's degree for all lead teachers at child care centers who work with children up to age 5, the reaction was widely negative. Journalist Matthew Yglesias tweeted that the requirement seemed "ill-advised," while Senator Ben Sasse, a Republican from
10　Nebraska, described it as "insanely stupid."
　　As the founding executive director of the Institute for Early Education Leadership and Innovation at the University of Massachusetts Boston, I can tell you that there is nothing "ill-
15　advised" or "insanely stupid" about the D.C. requirement. From an educational standpoint, it makes a lot of sense.
　　The science of brain development shows a clear connection between positive early
20　educational experiences and later success in life. The foundation for literacy, mathematics, and science develops rapidly in infancy and continues throughout early childhood. The competencies early educators must have to guide
25　this development effectively, as outlined in a 2015 Institute of Medicine report, are extensive. They include a "sophisticated understanding of the child's cognitive and socioemotional development [and] knowledge of a broad range of subject-
30　matter content areas."
　　Young children are natural scientists and innovators who test ideas and evaluate results. It requires skill, experience, and knowledge to structure learning experiences and ask questions
35　that guide the development of children's creative problem solving and conceptual thinking.
　　Despite this, currently only 45 percent of early educators who teach children ages 3 to 5 hold a bachelor's degree in early education. An
40　additional 17 percent hold an associate's degree. No state requires early educators to have these degrees. Although 10 require center-based lead teachers to complete a vocational program or earn the Child Development Associate Credential,
45　most just require a high school diploma. Notable exceptions are federally funded Head Start programs and Military Child Care, both of which require lead teachers to have bachelor's degrees.
　　I'd contend that these low, inconsistent, and
50　uneven requirements are holding the field—and the families it serves—back. The majority of children in the United States under the age of 5—or 61 percent, to be precise—are cared for in child care and preschool settings. Many spend between
55　40 and 50 hours each week in care. Given this, it would seem ill-advised not to expect the lead teachers for these children to study the science of early learning and bring these quality teaching practices into their classrooms.
60　Critics rightly point out that there is a lack of conclusive evidence that teachers with college degrees improve educational outcomes for young children. All we have at this point are studies that examine the impact of early education
65　itself, not teachers' credentials, on a child's later performance. Still, nearly every rigorous study of this sort shows a positive correlation between teachers with bachelor's degrees in early education and the most successful early childhood
70　programs. That is, students in such programs tend to do better in school.
　　The groundbreaking Perry Preschool Project measured whether children living in poverty and at high risk for poor school performance would
75　do better academically if they attended a high-quality preschool. The study tracked participants' progress through age 40. By then, those who had attended the preschool program "had higher earnings, committed fewer crimes, were more
80　likely to hold a job, and were more likely to have graduated from high school than adults who did not have a preschool education." Although the study was not meant to measure the performance of teachers with a degree in early education versus

---
*See Page 60 for the citation for this text.

85 those without one, the Perry researchers noted that the classrooms they studied were all run by teachers with bachelor's degrees. And they concluded that the teachers' "early childhood training was most relevant to their classroom
90 practices."

11

The main purpose of the passage is to

A) present a stance in favor of a requirement.
B) rebut a critique of a recent requirement.
C) describe the benefits of a law.
D) question the validity of a set of data.

12

The author includes the background content in lines 11-14 ("As the . . . Boston") in order to

A) lend credibility to her subject-matter expertise.
B) emphasize her level of education.
C) promote the merits of her organization.
D) undermine the credibility of her critics.

13

Which choice provides the best evidence for the claim that preschool teachers need "a sophisticated understanding of the child's cognitive and socioemotional development" (lines 27-28)?

A) Lines 16-17 ("From an . . . sense")
B) Lines 18-21 ("The science . . . life")
C) Lines 31-36 ("Young . . . thinking")
D) Lines 54-55 ("Many . . . care")

14

According to the author, early childhood development is a continuation of infant development in that

A) motor skills become more refined.
B) the precursors to math, science, and language skills continue to develop.
C) preschoolers use their newly acquired language skills to socialize.
D) preschoolers begin to develop a sense of ethics and empathy.

15

Which choice provides the best evidence for the answer to the previous question?

A) Lines 3-7 ("When . . . negative")
B) Lines 14-16 ("there is . . . requirement")
C) Lines 21-23 ("The foundation . . . childhood")
D) Lines 63-66 ("All we . . . performance")

16

As used in line 34, "structure" most nearly means

A) support.
B) design.
C) alter.
D) teach.

17

As used in line 66, "performance" most nearly means

A) success.
B) show.
C) productivity.
D) production.

Test 2

Results of a 2018 Opinion Poll of 833 Adults in the Washington D.C. Metro Area

1. Should there be a minimum education level requirement for preschool teachers?

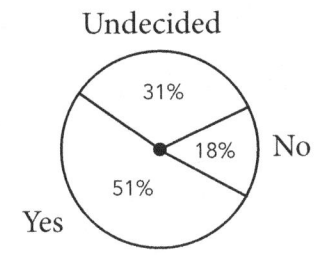

Undecided 31%
No 18%
Yes 51%

2. Should all preschool teachers possess at least an associate's degree?

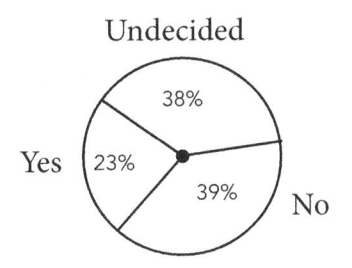

Undecided 38%
Yes 23%
No 39%

3. Does advanced coursework or training in early childhood learning make a preschool teacher more effective?

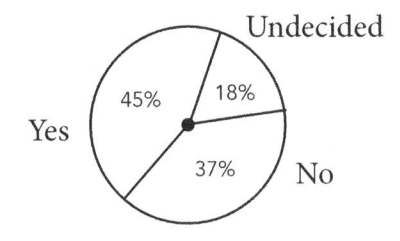

Undecided 18%
Yes 45%
No 37%

18

According to the passage, critics of requiring preschool teachers to have bachelor's degrees argue that

A) daycare staff play only a supervisory, rather than an educational, role.
B) such degrees do not provide teachers with useful classroom techniques.
C) such degrees are too expensive for most teachers to attain.
D) such degrees may not have an effect on student outcomes.

19

According to the graphics, which groups featured almost equal numbers of poll participants?

A) "Undecided," Question 1; "Undecided," Question 2
B) "Yes," Question 1; "No," Question 2
C) "Yes," Question 2; "Undecided," Question 3
D) "Undecided," Question 2; "No," Question 3

20

Which of the following groups would most likely include "Matthew Yglesias" (line 7) and "Ben Sasse" (line 9) had these two individuals taken part in the poll?

A) "No," Question 1
B) "No," Question 2
C) "No," Question 3
D) "Undecided," Question 3

21

How does the information provided in the graphics relate to the author's argument in lines 55-59 ("Given . . . classrooms")?

A) The information indicates that several but not all of the participants in the poll would agree with the author's argument.
B) The information indicates that the author has overestimated the level of public support for her argument.
C) The information indicates that public acceptance of the author's argument will grow significantly in the near future.
D) The information indicates that the author has drawn a false correlation between advanced training and optimal teaching outcomes.

Questions 22-31 are based on the following passages.

Passage 1 is adapted from Caitlin MacDonough MacKenzie, "Bumble and Bumble: what's black and yellow and maybe more than one species?" (2018), an article* that appeared on the PLOS Ecology Community blog. Passage 2 is adapted from Jonathan B. Koch et al., "Phylogeny and population genetic analyses reveal cryptic speciation in the Bombus fervidus species complex" (2018), a PLOS Research journal article* referenced in Passage 1.

Passage 1

As a master's student, Dr. Jon Koch and his insect net chased bumble bees all over the western United States. He was studying bumble bee decline, but hit a weird hurdle: a messy species boundary between two bumble bees.

Taxonomists and field guides were torn on whether Bombus fervidus was or was not Bombus californicus. These two "species" in the Bombus fervidus species complex were nearly morphologically identical, except for their color patterns: B. fervidus is noted as usually mostly yellow with a little black, while B. californicus sports mostly black with some yellow in variable detail. They were maybe different species, maybe hybridizing, or maybe the same thing with different color morphs. As Jon explained to me, "If we don't know what the species are, how will we manage them? Bumble bees are differentially sensitive to land use change, disease, etc. The bumble bees in the Bombus fervidus species complex are found to be impacted by one disease, Nosema bombi, but perhaps differently. Therefore, it is important to recognize what the species boundaries are because estimates of infection prevalence might be not be done correctly due to the inability to tell the species apart."

Jon wanted to bring some clarity to the species complex by providing some new molecular evidence with broader taxa sampling. His new PLOS ONE paper, "Phylogeny and population genetic analyses reveal cryptic speciation in the Bombus fervidus species complex (Hymenoptera: Apidae)" delivers on the broader taxa sampling—320 specimens from 53 sites—but the clarity is a bit of a cliffhanger.

During the fieldwork, Jon and his coauthors keyed out identifications for their bees based on the setal color, and also took a tarsal clipping from the mid-leg for DNA extraction and microsatellite genotyping. When they compared field identification to the genotypes, they had an ID rate of just under 94%. Jon and I agree that that's a pretty good record for fieldwork with cryptic species, but he adds, "it's also cool to think that 6.2% of the time we were wrong! These bees are great at fooling us."

Passage 2

Cryptic speciation is the process in which organisms share a nearly identical phenotype but belong to different species. It is a common phenomenon observed across the understudied and numerically dominant insects, and can pose a significant hurdle to effective conservation and management. Biodiversity is rapidly declining on a global scale primarily due to resource extraction activities associated with economic growth and expansion. In fact, it is estimated that the contemporary extinction rate is 1,000 times higher than what has been experienced prior to the global effects of humanity's economic and developmental activities. A major impediment to the effective conservation of biodiversity includes the lack of consensus among scientists and conservation practitioners on the taxonomic resolution appropriate to a conservation or management goal. Without an operational unit that considers the ecology and evolutionary history of a species, efforts to promote species conservation will remain daunting.

Bumble bees are one of the most important native pollinators of North America, contributing to the ecosystem services required by wild and economically important flowering plant species. They are dominant pollinators of the northern hemisphere, specifically in alpine and temperate ecosystems. Furthermore, wild bumble bee populations have been found to enhance crop productivity through effective pollination.

*See Page 60 for the citations for these texts.

However, the global decline of wild bumble bee populations due to disease, pesticides, urbanization, and agricultural intensification have prompted state, national, and international efforts to document the diversity and distribution of these iconic bee fauna.

Concurrent efforts to conserve bumble bees are dependent on recognizing operational units, whether they are species, taxonomic, evolutionary, or otherwise... Due to the spatial cohabitation of aposematic setal coloration patterns, bumble bees have proven to be difficult to identify to species by both novice and seasoned taxonomists. The dependence on setal coloration patterns to delineate between closely related species has caused debate on the species status of many of these taxonomic groups. Contemporary phylogenetic investigations using both single and multiple genetic loci, as well as morphology-based taxonomic studies, have resolved some cryptic species complexes across bumble bee subgenera. It has been demonstrated with a single gene, Cytochrome c oxidase I (COI), that bumble bees exhibiting nearly identical aposematic coloration patterns have been found to be separate species.

22

As used in line 2, "chased" most nearly means

A) exhausted.
B) approximated.
C) surpassed.
D) investigated.

23

It can be inferred from Passage 1 that incorrect taxonomic classification

A) can increase error in epidemiological studies.
B) can result in species hybridization.
C) can cause population decline among bees.
D) stems from faulty evidence in genetic studies.

24

Which choice provides the best evidence for the answer to the previous question?

A) Lines 3-5 ("He was . . . bumble bees")
B) Lines 24-26 ("estimates of . . . apart")
C) Lines 27-29 ("Jon . . . sampling")
D) Lines 44-46 ("it's also . . . fooling us")

25

According to Passage 2, wild bumble bee populations are shrinking due to

A) pathogens and human activities.
B) pathogens and natural predators.
C) human activities and natural predators.
D) misguided species conservation efforts.

26

According to Passage 2, it is difficult to identify species of bumble bees because

A) all species share a Cytochrome c oxidase I (COI) gene.
B) scientists have been overly reliant on setal coloration patterns.
C) species hybridization is increasingly prevalent.
D) bumble bee species differ only morphologically rather than genetically.

27

Which choice provides the best evidence for the answer to the previous question?

A) Lines 60-65 ("A major . . . goal")
B) Lines 84-87 ("Concurrent . . . otherwise")
C) Lines 91-94 ("The dependence . . . groups")
D) Lines 94-99 ("Contemporary . . . subgenera")

28

As used in line 92, "delineate" most nearly means

A) hybridize.
B) differentiate.
C) illustrate.
D) segregate.

29

Which choice best states the relationship between the two passages?

A) Passage 1 calls into question an assumption integral to Passage 2.
B) Passage 1 defines terms that are central to the analysis undertaken in Passage 2.
C) Passage 1 explains the purpose of the research of which Passage 2 is a part.
D) Passage 1 outlines a problem while Passage 2 proposes a solution.

30

Based on the passages, both authors would agree with which of the following claims?

A) The species designation of most bumble bees can be better identified via a multi-pronged approach.
B) Setal coloration alone is sufficient to differentiate between bumble bee species.
C) Bumble bees will most likely be extinct within the next 100 years as a result of human activity.
D) Pesticides are the primary threat to present-day bumble bee populations.

31

It can be reasonably inferred from the passages that the two authors are

A) competitors in the same scientific field.
B) student and teacher.
C) employer and employee.
D) colleagues on good terms.

Questions 32-41 are based on the following passage.

This passage is adapted from W.E.B. du Bois, *Darkwater: Voices from within the Vale* (1920).

There are no races, in the sense of great, separate, pure breeds of men, differing in attainment, development, and capacity. There are great groups—now with common history, [5] now with common interests, now with common ancestry; more and more common experience and present interest drive back the common blood and the world today consists, not of races, but of the imperial commercial group of master [10] capitalists, international and predominantly white; the national middle classes of the several nations, white, yellow, and brown, with strong blood bonds, common languages, and common history; the international laboring class of all colors; [15] the backward, oppressed groups of nature-folk, predominantly yellow, brown, and black.

Two questions arise from the work and relations of these groups: how to furnish goods and services for the wants of men and how [20] equitably and sufficiently to satisfy these wants. There can be no doubt that we have passed in our day from a world that could hardly satisfy the physical wants of the mass of men, by the greatest effort, to a world whose technique supplies [25] enough for all, if all can claim their right. Our great ethical question today is, therefore, how may we justly distribute the world's goods to satisfy the necessary wants of the mass of men.

What hinders the answer to this question? [30] Dislikes, jealousies, hatreds,—undoubtedly like the race hatred in East St. Louis; the jealousy of English and German; the dislike of the Jew and the Gentile. But these are, after all, surface disturbances, sprung from ancient habit more [35] than from present reason. They persist and are encouraged because of deeper, mightier currents. If the white workingmen of East St. Louis felt sure that Negro workers would not and could not take the bread and cake from their mouths, their [40] race hatred would never have been translated into murder. If the black workingmen of the South could earn a decent living under decent circumstances at home, they would not be compelled to underbid their white fellows.

[45] Thus the shadow of hunger, in a world which never needs to be hungry, drives us to war and murder and hate. But why does hunger shadow so vast a mass of men? Manifestly because in the great organizing of men for work a few of the [50] participants come out with more wealth than they can possibly use, while a vast number emerge with less than can decently support life. In earlier economic stages we defended this as the reward of Thrift and Sacrifice, and as the punishment of [55] Ignorance and Crime. To this the answer is sharp: Sacrifice calls for no such reward and Ignorance deserves no such punishment. The chief meaning of our present thinking is that the disproportion between wealth and poverty today cannot be [60] adequately accounted for by the thrift and ignorance of the rich and the poor.

Yesterday we righted one great mistake when we realized that the ownership of the laborer did not tend to increase production. The world at large [65] had learned this long since, but black slavery arose again in America as an inexplicable anachronism, a wilful crime. The freeing of the black slaves freed America. Today we are challenging another ownership—the ownership of materials which go [70] to make the goods we need. Private ownership of land, tools, and raw materials may at one stage of economic development be a method of stimulating production and one which does not greatly interfere with equitable distribution. [75] When, however, the intricacy and length of technical production increased, the ownership of these things becomes a monopoly, which easily makes the rich richer and the poor poorer. Today, therefore, we are challenging this ownership; [80] we are demanding general consent as to what materials shall be privately owned and as to how materials shall be used.

32

According to the author, the main ethical issue at the time of the composition of the passage was

A) whether goods should be privately or publicly owned.
B) how to decrease wealth inequality between the master industrialists and the lower classes of society.
C) how to decrease racial hatred in the United States.
D) how to distribute resources to best meet the needs of the population.

33

Over the course of the passage, the focus shifts from

A) general context to social issues, and finally to a demand.
B) historical context to questions, and finally to a counterargument.
C) social issues to philosophical issues, and finally to psychological issues.
D) a thesis to examples, and finally to a conclusion.

34

As used in line 21, "passed" most nearly means

A) changed.
B) overcome.
C) defeated.
D) transferred.

35

According to the author, racial hatred persists as a result of

A) undiminished anti-Semitism.
B) historical oppression by governing authorities.
C) underlying concerns about economic resources.
D) private ownership of goods.

36

Which choice provides the best evidence for the answer to the previous question?

A) Lines 1-3 ("There are no . . . capacity")
B) Lines 37-44 ("If the white . . . white fellows")
C) Lines 52-55 ("In earlier . . . Crime")
D) Lines 76-78 ("the ownership . . . poor poorer")

37

As used in line 47, "shadow" most nearly means

A) follow.
B) darken.
C) cover.
D) afflict.

38

The author's attitude toward the theories traced to earlier economic stages (lines 52-55) can best be described as

A) full agreement.
B) cautious agreement.
C) full disagreement.
D) ambivalence.

39

The author discusses American slavery in order to

A) argue in favor of aiding enslaved peoples around the world.
B) explain the basis of racial hatred in America.
C) establish that ownership does not promote a healthier economy.
D) describe the basis of wealth discrepancy in America.

40

Which choice provides the best evidence for the answer to the previous question?

A) Lines 11-15 ("the national . . . black")
B) Lines 57-61 ("The chief . . . the poor")
C) Lines 62-64 ("Yesterday . . . production")
D) Lines 64-67 ("The world . . . crime")

41

According to the author, the evident effect of monopolies is to promote

A) free trade.
B) wealth disparity.
C) modern equivalents of slavery.
D) racial prejudice.

Questions 42-52 are based on the following passage and supplementary material.

This passage is adapted from "USGS Finds 28 Types of Cyanobacteria in Florida Algal Bloom," a 2017 news release* from the U.S. Geological Survey.

Twenty-eight species of cyanobacteria were identified in an extensive algal bloom, which occurred in the summer of 2016 in southern
Line Florida's Lake Okeechobee, the St. Lucie Canal
5 and River, and the Caloosahatchee River. As the guacamole-like sludge created by the bloom began to stick together, it formed a thick, floating mat that coated river and coastal waters and shorelines—affecting tourism, killing fish, and, in
10 some cases, making people sick.

The culprit causing the bloom was a well-known species of cyanobacteria called Microcystis aeruginosa. However, water samples collected by state and federal agencies before and
15 during the disruptive bloom on Lake Okeechobee and the Okeechobee waterway were analyzed by the USGS and found to contain 27 other species of cyanobacteria.

Cyanobacteria, also known as blue-green algae,
20 are naturally occurring microscopic organisms that, under the right conditions, can undergo explosive population growth, resulting in a harmful algal bloom.

While Microcystis aeruginosa was the most
25 abundant cyanobacteria found, other species were present before, during, and after last summer's Florida bloom.

"It's not just a single organism out there that has the potential to cause a harmful algal
30 bloom," said Barry Rosen, USGS Biologist and lead author of the study. "There are a multitude of species, each with its own ability to create blooms, all of which can cause oxygen deprivation in water that can kill fish, and many with the
35 ability to create toxins harmful to wildlife, or to people."

Hepatoxins formed by Microcystis aeruginosa are well known to have the potential to cause liver damage, but several other cyanobacteria
40 present in this bloom can create equally or even more dangerous toxins. For instance, some of the cyanobacteria can produce cylindrospermopsin, which can damage the liver or kidneys, while other species produce neurotoxins, like anatoxin
45 and saxitoxin. Saxitoxin is one of the most potent natural toxins in the world.

As bad as these four toxins can be, simple skin contact with them is normally not enough to cause harm to humans (as they have to be ingested),
50 but only a small amount is needed to jeopardize a person's health.

"One of the main human risks with these toxins is if a drinking water treatment plant unknowingly pulls some of the bloom into the facility," said
55 Rosen. "If that happens, the water often isn't treated properly and the toxins can make it into finished drinking water."

This type of water contamination has become more common over the years and guidelines
60 have been developed to help drinking water treatment plants mitigate possible drinking water contamination from toxic blooms.

Even though cyanobacteria are a natural and vital part of the food web, the extreme quantities
65 found in a harmful algal bloom can cause negative effects on human health, aquatic ecosystems, and local economies.

The total economic impact of an algal bloom can be difficult to estimate, but according to the
70 EPA, harmful algal blooms can influence property values, hamper commercial fishing, and slow down recreational business and tourism—which loses close to $1 billion each year across the United States due to blooms preventing fishing
75 and boating activities.

"We have a good idea of the conditions which make a bloom more likely—warmer water, excess nutrients from runoff from homeowners' yards or farmers' fields when they fertilize, and
80 slow moving water, to name a few," said Rosen. "What we don't understand is why under similar conditions sometimes we have a bloom, and sometimes we don't."

What triggers one species to bloom over

---

*See Page 60 for the citation for this text.

85 another is also unknown.
   "It is likely that no two blooms are exactly alike, and there probably isn't one single set of circumstances that can lead to a bloom." Rosen said. "The complicated part scientists are dealing
90 with is having dozens of different organisms with the potential to bloom, yet they all have their own specific parameters needed to make it just right for them."
   In time and with more knowledge of the factors
95 that contribute to these blooms, scientists are hopeful they'll be able to provide information that will help land managers to reduce bloom occurrence and potentially forecast when bloom events are going to happen.

42

According to the information presented in the passage, cyanobacterial toxins affect all of the following EXCEPT the

A) nervous system.
B) liver.
C) kidneys.
D) stomach.

43

As used in line 22, "explosive" most nearly means

A) rapid.
B) combustible.
C) fateful.
D) unpredictable.

44

The author's opinion regarding the prospect of eliminating cyanobacteria from the environment would most likely be one of

A) disapproval.
B) agreement.
C) indecision.
D) relief.

45

Which choice provides the best evidence for the answer to the previous question?

A) Lines 5-10 ("As the . . . sick")
B) Lines 63-64 ("cyanobacteria . . . food web")
C) Lines 64-67 ("the extreme . . . economies")
D) Lines 68-69 ("The total . . . estimate")

46

The main point of the sixth paragraph (lines 37-46) is that

A) M. aeruginosa is the most harmful species of aquatic bacteria.
B) M. aeruginosa is harmful but other species are similarly threatening.
C) hepatoxins are the most deadly toxins produced by bloom species.
D) saxitoxin is the most deadly toxin produced by bloom species.

47

The author includes the content in the seventh paragraph (lines 47-51) in order to

A) explain terms used elsewhere in the passage.
B) allay the reader's probable concerns about bacterial toxins.
C) underscore how sensitive humans are to bacterial toxins.
D) transition from the topic of toxins to the topic of how they are ingested by people.

48

As used in line 54, "pulls" most nearly means

A) flushes out.
B) attracts.
C) introduces.
D) forces.

Algal Bloom Outbreaks in the Contiguous United States

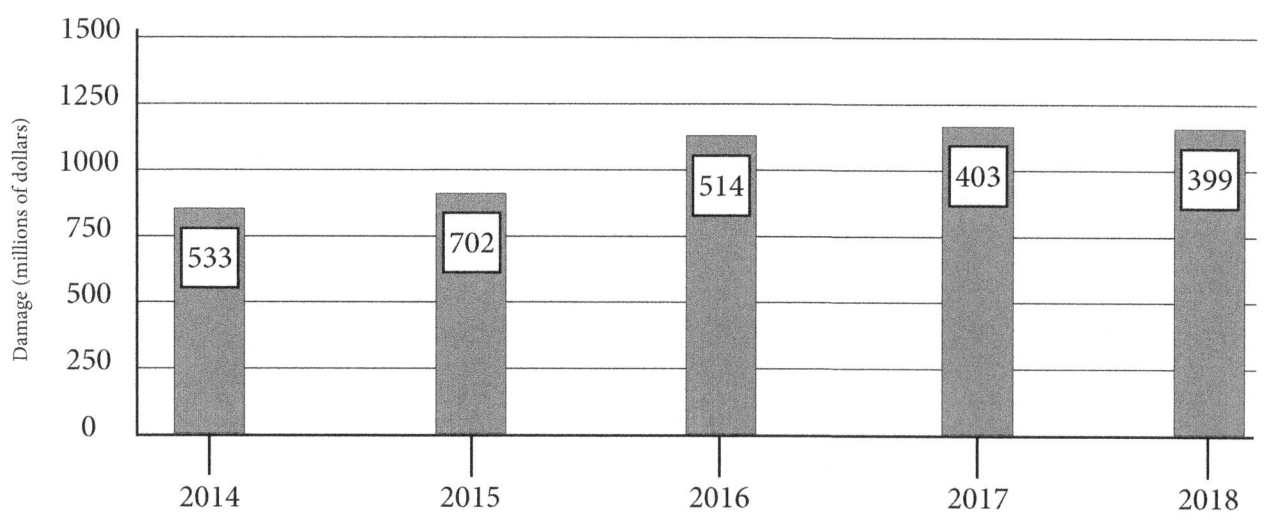

Year	Damage (millions of dollars)	Outbreaks
2014	~850	533
2015	~900	702
2016	~1120	514
2017	~1150	403
2018	~1140	399

NOTE: Each boxed number represents the number of recorded outbreaks for the relevant year.

49

Which of the following best supports the idea that certain environmental circumstances sometimes but not always lead to bacterial blooms?

A) Lines 13-18 ("However . . . of cyanobacteria")
B) Lines 76-80 ("We have . . . said Rosen")
C) Lines 81-83 ("What we . . . we don't")
D) Lines 84-85 ("What triggers . . . unknown")

50

The tone of the fourteenth paragraph (lines 86-93) is

A) persuasive.
B) hopeful.
C) uncertain.
D) objective.

51

Which choice best describes the trend indicated by the information present in the graph?

A) The size of a given algal bloom often correlates with the economic damage that the bloom causes.
B) The extent of the economic damage caused by algal blooms is unlikely to fall below $1 billion in the near future.
C) The number of algal blooms has fallen at a steady rate while the economic damage caused by these blooms has risen at a steady rate.
D) The average economic damage caused by observed algal blooms has mostly increased year-over-year.

52

In relation to the graph, the loss figure mentioned in line 73 can best be understood as

A) an optimistic projection that nonetheless is accepted as convincing.
B) an apparent yet ultimately harmless exaggeration of the actual numbers.
C) a reasonable estimate based on the data that is currently available.
D) a conjecture that calls a few measurements recorded in the chart into question.

STOP

If you finish before time is called, you may check your work on this section only.
Do not turn to any other section.

Answer Key: Test 2

Passage 1	Passage 2	Passage 3	Passage 4	Passage 5
1. D	11. A	22. D	32. D	42. D
2. C	12. A	23. A	33. A	43. A
3. A	13. C	24. B	34. A	44. A
4. B	14. B	25. A	35. C	45. B
5. C	15. C	26. B	36. B	46. B
6. C	16. B	27. C	37. D	47. D
7. D	17. A	28. B	38. C	48. C
8. A	18. D	29. C	39. C	49. C
9. D	19. D	30. A	40. C	50. D
10. B	20. B	31. D	41. B	51. D
	21. A			52. C

Question Types

Major Issue
1, 11, 32-33

Passage Details
3, 7-8, 12, 18, 25, 38, 41, 42, 46-47, 50

Command of Evidence
5-6, 9-10, 13-15, 23-24, 26-27, 35-36, 39-40, 44-45, 49

Word in Context
2, 4, 16-17, 22, 28, 34, 37, 43, 48

Graphics and Visuals
19-21, 51-52

Passage Comparison
29-31

Answer Explanations
Test 2, Pages 32-47

Passage 1, Pages 32-34

1. D is the correct answer.

In the passage, Mrs. Graham mentions that she "is not so beset with visitors but that I can readily spare a few minutes to the few that do favour me with their company" (lines 36-39). This comment reveals that she rarely receives visitors; choose D to support this content. A can be dismissed since London is mentioned as a city where Mrs. Graham's artwork is sold, yet there is no direct reference to her having previously lived there. B and C can also be eliminated since Mrs. Graham is quite polite in her welcome (lines 12-15), and there is nothing to directly indicate that she is dissatisfied with her life or longs for anything else (despite her possibly negative secrecy about her painting).

2. C is the correct answer.

In line 15, "empty" refers to the grate not containing a fire, or lacking content. Choose C to reflect this meaning. A (inappropriately implying a philosophical or intellectual connotation), B (inappropriately implying a comment on physical strength), and D (inappropriately indicating a formal cancellation or elimination) all introduce improper contexts and should thus be eliminated.

3. A is the correct answer.

In the third paragraph, the narrator observes that Mrs. Graham's painting depicts Wildfell Hall, and then subsequently notices that she has labeled the house using a different name. This fact leads him to ask the question of why she has done so. Thus, his observation in the third paragraph sets the stage for a later question; choose A to support this content. B and C can also be dismissed, since the narrator (who simply intends to visit Mrs. Graham) does not have a question in mind at the start of the passage, and since the inclusion of the painting's subject (which is simply a name) provides information but NOT imagery (which could be provided ELSEWHERE in the passage). Be careful not to choose D, because the depiction of the house in the painting does NOT necessarily confirm or establish the novel's setting (which has been mentioned EARLIER).

Answer Explanations, Test 2

4. B is the correct answer.

In line 42, "surveying" refers to how the narrator gazes appreciatively at the painting. Choose B to reflect this meaning. A (inappropriately implying inspection with the aim of finding fault), C (inappropriately implying gathering opinions from a group), and D (inappropriately implying calculating dimensions) all introduce improper contexts and should thus be eliminated.

5. C is the correct answer.

In lines 17-24, the narrator describes how Mrs. Graham continues to look at and occasionally work on her painting, "as if she found it impossible to wean her attention entirely from her occupation to fix it upon her guests" (lines 19-24). This continual attention to her work leads the narrator to wonder if he is a somewhat unwelcome visitor; choose C to support this content. A can be dismissed as illogical since Gilbert goes accompanied by Rose, and B can also be eliminated since Mrs. Graham brings her guests into a room where a fire is lit. D can be eliminated since the child's participation in the conversation would not indicate whether or not Gilbert is welcome, an issue that would be more clearly addressed by Mrs. Graham's OWN response.

6. C is the correct answer.

See the previous answer explanation for analysis of the correct line reference. A describes the narrator's surprise at encountering painting supplies, while B shows Mrs. Graham being attentive to the comfort of her guests. D shows Arthur explaining how his mother makes money from her artwork. None of these other answers explain why Gilbert would worry that he is intruding, and they should all be eliminated.

7. D is the correct answer.

One of Mrs. Graham's paintings is a "simple but striking little picture of a child brooding" (lines 75-76); she therefore DOES include human figures in her artwork, and that fact means that D is NOT a strategy that she uses to remain anonymous. A, B and C can all be dismissed since these are strategies Mrs. Graham DOES employ in her effort to disguise her identity (lines 54-61).

8. A is the correct answer.

In the passage, the narrator is impressed by the quality of the paintings that Mrs. Graham creates. From this content, it is reasonable to infer that he regards her as a skilled artist; choose A to reflect this content. Be careful not to choose C, since while Mrs. Graham does take precautions to disguise her identity, it does NOT necessarily follow that she is paranoid (and in fact she is willing to have guests without worry). B and D can be dismissed since Mrs. Graham makes an effort to be welcoming to her guests; not enough information is available to make assumptions about her emotional state beyond the few mostly pleasant interactions depicted.

9. D is the correct answer.

The narrator asks Mrs. Graham why she mislabels the painting's subject, but then notices that she seems uncomfortable being asked the question and regrets having caused her discomfort: "immediately I was sensible

Answer Explanations, Test 2

of having committed an act of impertinence in so doing; for she coloured and hesitated" (lines 49-51). Choose D to support this content. A can be dismissed since Mrs. Graham answers the question willingly and without any pressure, while B can be dismissed since Gilbert observes the paintings with pleasure but mostly offers praise EARLIER (lines 30-34). C can also be ruled out since the subject of profit only comes up when Arthur volunteers this information, so that this answer references the wrong character.

10. B is the correct answer.

See the previous answer explanation for analysis of the correct line reference. A describes how Gilbert admires the painting but does not say so out loud, while C describes the manner in which Mrs. Graham answers his question about her deceptive labeling. D describes a question that Gilbert asks as a way to move the conversation to a new topic. None of these other answers characterize how Gilbert feels after asking his question, and therefore all should be eliminated.

Passage 2, Pages 35-37

11. A is the correct answer.

The passage describes a recent requirement instituted in one specific location (D.C.) and provides evidence to argue that "From an educational standpoint, [the requirement] makes a lot of sense" (lines 16-17). This content indicates that the author is arguing in favor of upholding this requirement. Choose A to support this content. Be careful not to choose B or C, since while the author does describe some potential benefits and rebut critiques of this requirement, these aspects of the passage serve to reinforce the PRIMARY purpose, which is arguing for why the standard should be promoted. D can be eliminated since the passage mentions critiques of the new requirement and mostly presents VALID supporting data; this answer also wrongly presents the author's purpose (which involves a positive recommendation) as mainly negative.

12. A is the correct answer.

In lines 11-14, the author identifies her position in a leadership role that is related to education. This content indicates that, on account of her profession and credentials, she possesses expertise on debates related to early childhood education. Choose A to support this content. Be careful not to choose B, since the author identifies her current position but NOT the earlier education that she has received. C and D can be eliminated since she designates the organization that she works for but does NOT explain its merits, nor does she contrast her credentials with those held by opponents of the requirement (who are in fact mentioned as commentators, NOT educators).

13. C is the correct answer.

Lines 31-36 describe how young children have the potential to experience important intellectual development but require knowledgeable guidance from educators in order to be able to do so effectively. This content supports the idea that preschool teachers need to be educated about child development; choose C as appropriate. A can

Answer Explanations, Test 2

be eliminated since it makes a statement of support for the requirement but does not offer specific reasons that relate to the issue of development, while B can be eliminated since it describes the potential future impact of effective early education but does not explain how a well-educated teacher can contribute to that education. D can be ruled out since it merely states how many hours some children spend in preschool care each week without explaining the desired qualifications of early childhood teachers.

14. B is the correct answer.

In lines 21-23, the author describes how the essential foundations for key areas of knowledge begin to develop during infancy and continue to be refined during early childhood years. This content indicates that early childhood includes a continuation of the developmental progress that begins during infancy; choose B to reflect this content. A, C, and D can all be rejected since the passage does NOT discuss the motor skills, socialization, or empathy development of young children; instead, the author focuses on academic skills and problem solving as indicated by B.

15. C is the correct answer.

See the previous answer explanation for analysis of the correct line reference. A indicates a negative reaction to a desired qualification, B indicates the author's support for a requirement, and D calls attention to available information in terms of early childhood research. While all of these answers relate to the topic of early childhood, these choices call attention to debates and research but NOT to the topic of different developmental stages as required by the previous question.

16. B is the correct answer.

In line 34, "structure" refers to how skilled educators develop and design learning experiences. Choose B to reflect this meaning. A (inappropriately implying emotional nurturing), C (inappropriately implying changing or modifying), and D (inappropriately implying instruction and evaluation) all introduce improper contexts and should thus be eliminated.

17. A is the correct answer.

In line 66, "performance" refers to achievements and accomplishments that a child may demonstrate later in life. Choose A to reflect this meaning. B (inappropriately implying visibility and display), C (inappropriately implying fulfillment of tasks but NOT necessarily skill), and D (inappropriately implying creation of physical objects) all introduce improper contexts and should thus be eliminated.

18. D is the correct answer.

In lines 60-63, the author explains that "Critics rightly point out that there is a lack of conclusive evidence that teachers with college degrees improve educational outcomes for young children." Choose D to support this content. A can be eliminated since there is no discussion of whether daycare staff play educational or supervisory roles (ONLY of the credentials that should be required overall). B and C can be eliminated since the passage does NOT mention critics' belief that degrees (though objected to generally) are overly expensive or irrelevant to classroom performance as specific liabilities.

Answer Explanations, Test 2

19. D is the correct answer.

The opinion poll considered in the graphs features the same number of participants for each question, so look for similar percentages. D (38% and 37%, respectively) features two response groups that differ by only one percentage point. Choose this answer as indicating almost equal numbers and eliminate A (31% and 38%, respectively), B (51% and 39%, respectively), and C (23% and 18%, respectively) as choices that indicate significantly greater differences in participant numbers.

20. B is the correct answer.

Both Yglesias and Sasse are clearly AGAINST the measure of requiring "an associate's degree" (line 4) for lead teachers who work with very young children. Yglesias and Sasse would thus be directly opposed to the measure considered in Question 2. Choose B, and eliminate A because Question 1 indicates that there may be desired minimum education requirements OTHER than an associate's degree (a topic that is never directly mentioned in relation to Yglesias and Sasse). The reasoning that Yglesias and Sasse use in opposing the associate's degree requirement is also never discussed in the passage, so that C and D (Question 3, which deals with one possible line of reasoning in terms of effectiveness) can be eliminated as out of scope.

21. A is the correct answer.

Lines 55-59 indicate that the author would agree that advanced study is beneficial for teachers of very young children, particularly in terms of classroom performance. This information is highly relevant to Question 3, which was met with "Yes" responses from 45% of the participants; A properly reflects this level of agreement with the author's ideas. B and D wrongly indicate that the information in the graphs (which shows that the author's argument, though not universally accepted, is often met with approval) renders the author's ideas problematic. C wrongly raises the idea of support that "will grow significantly," when in fact the graphs mainly consider ideas about early childhood education in a SINGLE instance of time.

Passage 3, Pages 38-40

22. D is the correct answer.

In line 2, "chased" refers to how a researcher approached "bumble bees" with the aim of examining and studying. Choose D to reflect this meaning. A (inappropriately implying a negative outcome that eliminates energy), B (inappropriately implying guesswork or similarity), and C (inappropriately implying that the researcher competed with the bumblebees) all introduce improper contexts and should thus be eliminated.

23. A is the correct answer.

In lines 24-26, the author explains, in relation to bumble bees, that "it is important to recognize what the species boundaries are because estimates of infection prevalence might be not be done correctly due to the

Answer Explanations, Test 2

inability to tell the species apart." This information indicates that incorrect taxonomic classification (under which one species might be confused with another) can cause problems for epidemiological studies (by which the spread of disease is monitored); choose A to reflect this content. B and C can both be eliminated since the passage does NOT discuss hybridization or species decline. Be careful not to choose D, since genetic studies are discussed as a way of verifying species identification, NOT as a liability in terms of classification error.

24. B is the correct answer.

See the previous answer explanation for analysis of the correct line reference. A offers an initial description of the problem, while C describes a research goal. D focuses on a researcher's positive reaction to the research being imperfect. None of these other answers describe the connection between taxonomic classification and epidemiology, and therefore all should be eliminated.

25. A is the correct answer.

Passage 2 describes "the global decline of wild bumble bee populations due to disease, pesticides, urbanization, and agricultural intensification," implying that both disease and human activity are responsible for declining bee populations. Choose A to support this content. B and C can both be dismissed since natural predators are NOT mentioned anywhere in the passage. D can also be eliminated because it is illogical that species conservation efforts would lead to declining numbers; it is more likely that such efforts would be ineffectual at limiting losses due to OTHER factors.

26. B is the correct answer.

Lines 91-94 explain, in reference to bumble bees, that "The dependence on setal coloration patterns to delineate between closely related species has caused debate on the species status of many of these taxonomic groups." Choose B to support this content. Be careful not to choose A, since the COI gene is a source of species differentiation, NOT species confusion. C and D can both be readily eliminated since there is no mention of species hybridization and since the passage asserts that bumble bees DO differ at the genetic level.

27. C is the correct answer.

See the previous answer explanation for analysis of the correct line reference. A describes how a lack of consensus about taxonomic classification can make it harder to conserve species, while B emphasizes that bumble bees can only be effectively protected if they are differentiated from one another. D describes how genetic studies have helped to resolve some areas of confusion. None of these other answers discuss the reliance of scientists on setal coloration patterns, so they can all be eliminated.

28. B is the correct answer.

In line 92, "delineate" refers to distinguishing one distinct group of animals from another. Choose B to reflect this meaning. A (inappropriately implying mixing or combining), C (inappropriately implying the use of something as an example of a concept), and D (inappropriately implying separating two groups or imposing a boundary between them) all introduce improper contexts and should thus be eliminated.

Answer Explanations, Test 2

29. C is the correct answer.

Passage 1 provides context about a specific researcher and his area of interest, while Passage 2 offers more detailed information drawn from his published research results. Choose C to support this content. Be careful not to choose D, since the problem of taxonomic confusion is described in both passages, NOT just in Passage 1. A and B can both be eliminated since the passages support, rather than question, one another, and the focus of Passage 1 is context for a research endeavor, NOT the definition of terms as the priority.

30. A is the correct answer.

Both passages discuss the importance of accurate species designation among bumble bees and suggest that this goal can best be achieved through a combination of multiples strategies; choose A to support this content. B can be dismissed as illogical, since reliance on setal coloration is part of what has led to taxonomic confusion. C and D can also be dismissed, since threats to bees are discussed in the passage but pesticides are NOT identified as the primary threat, nor are forecasts made about long-term species survival.

31. D is the correct answer.

The author of Passage 1 refers casually to how "Jon and I agree that that's a pretty good record for fieldwork with cryptic species," a statement which suggests a friendly relationship between the two authors. Choose D to support this content. A can be eliminated, since the two authors seem to be supportive of each other's research and results. B and C can be dismissed as illogical since nothing in either passage suggests that one author is in a position of superiority or authority relative to the other author.

Passage 4, Pages 41-43

32. D is the correct answer.

The author of the passage explains that those who are aware of economic disparities "are demanding general consent as to what materials shall be privately owned and as to how materials shall be used" (lines 80-82). This content suggests that the main ethical debate revolves around resource distribution; choose D to support this information. Be careful not to choose A or B, since the author seems to accept that some materials will always be privately owned and thus does NOT debate private ownership in general or (since he acknowledges long-lasting tensions between social groups) indicate that wealth disparity can be readily addressed. C can be eliminated since the author seems to believe that the equitable distribution of wealth and resources will resolve racial hatred, which is thus a SECONDARY issue in the passage.

33. A is the correct answer.

The passage begins with a discussion of different groups and categories of people (lines 1-28), then moves on to a discussion of race and inequality in America, and then climaxes with a demand to debate questions around private ownership (lines 68-82). Choose A to reflect this content. B and C can be dismissed, since the

Answer Explanations, Test 2

author's argument does NOT engage with psychological questions or (despite acknowledgments of deep-seated difficulties) with clear counter-arguments. D can also be eliminated since the author does NOT provide a clear thesis about equitable wealth distribution or positive examples of what this practice could look like, even though economic injustice is indeed a focus of the passage.

34. A is the correct answer.

In line 21, "passed" refers to transitioning or evolving, a concept understood in terms of two "worlds" or states of society described by the author. Choose A to reflect this meaning. B (inappropriately implying conquest or victory), C (inappropriately implying failure), and D (inappropriately implying handing over an object or asset) all introduce improper contexts and should thus be eliminated.

35. C is the correct answer.

In lines 37-44, the author argues that if individuals were economically secure and well-compensated for their labor, they would not be mistrustful or hateful towards individuals of other races. This claim suggests that the author believes that racial hatred is linked to income inequality and social justice; choose C to support this content. A can be eliminated since the author does discuss racial hatred against Jewish people, but discusses OTHER groups as well, while B can be eliminated since the author uses examples of racial mistrust among groups that both have and have NOT been historically oppressed. Be careful not to choose D, since the author does eventually focus on the ownership of goods, but begins his discussion with a more general argument about racial hatred and social justice.

36. B is the correct answer.

See the previous answer explanation for analysis of the correct line reference. A describes the author's rejection of the idea that some races are inherently superior to others, while C describes a previous way of understanding why economic inequality existed. D connects ownership to inequality but does not address present problems in terms of racial hatred. None of these other answers focus on the link between racial hatred and an issue in CURRENT social justice for the author, and therefore they should all be eliminated.

37. D is the correct answer.

In line 47, "shadow" refers to the "hunger" that is a threat or danger to a large number of people. Choose D to reflect this negative meaning. A (inappropriately implying pursuing or coming after something), B (inappropriately implying a change of color), and C (inappropriately implying providing shelter or protection) all introduce improper contexts and should thus be eliminated.

38. C is the correct answer.

The author describes how earlier economic theories relied on the assumption that the wealthy were being rewarded for making good decisions and the poor were being punished for making bad ones. He responds by stating that "To this the answer is sharp: Sacrifice calls for no such reward and Ignorance deserves no such punishment" (lines 55-57). This statement shows the author's full disagreement with these economic theories;

choose C to support this content. A and B can be dismissed as illogical since the author does not agree with anything about these theories; D can also be eliminated since his rebuttal shows a strong conviction, rather than ambivalence.

39. C is the correct answer.

In lines 62-64, the author explains that "Yesterday we righted one great mistake when we realized that the ownership of the laborer did not tend to increase production." This statement suggests that he believes that slavery does not promote a thriving economy; choose C to support this content. A can be dismissed as illogical since the author notes that most civilizations have already abolished slavery, while B can be eliminated because the author does not connect the existence of slavery to racial hatred, which is a larger problem that (as the author explains earlier in the passage) PERSISTS even beyond slavery. Be careful not to choose D, since while the author does suggest that slavery is not linked to economic progress, he does NOT argue that slavery functioned as the basis for economic inequality, which in fact has persisted beyond slavery.

40. C is the correct answer.

See the previous answer explanation for analysis of the correct line reference. A points to instances of racial oppression that do NOT clearly involve slavery, while B explains the author's belief that individual choices are not the causes of economic inequality. D describes the circumstances under which private ownership of the means of production creates economic disparity. Because these answers discuss social justice issues that may be related to slavery but not slavery ITSELF, these answers should be eliminated as deviating from the exact topic required by the previous question.

41. B is the correct answer.

The author believes that when one group of individuals has total control of a resource, economic inequalities are perpetuated and worsened (lines 75-78). Choose B to support this content. A and C can be dismissed as illogical, since free trade is not discussed within the scope of the passage's consideration of OTHER economic forces, and since no connection is drawn between monopolies and slavery (even though the author sees both as manifestations of injustice). Be careful not to choose D, since monopolies are connected to race hatred indirectly (as worsening economic inequality, which subsequently encourages racial tension) but NOT directly.

Passage 5, Pages 44-47

42. D is the correct answer.

The passage mentions some types of toxins that can damage the liver or kidneys, while others primarily impact the nervous system. The stomach is not mentioned (even though nearby organs ARE); choose D to support this content. A, B, and C can all be dismissed as illogical since they refer to systems or organs that are VULNERABLE to cyanobacterial toxins according to lines 41-45.

Answer Explanations, Test 2

43. A is the correct answer.

In line 22, "explosive" refers to the quick speed of growth. Choose A to reflect this meaning. B (inappropriately referring to a tendency to catch on fire), C (inappropriately implying an ominous or crucial decision), and D (inappropriately implying volatile or irregular behavior) all introduce improper contexts and should thus be eliminated.

44. A is the correct answer.

In lines 63-64, the author states that "cyanobacteria are a natural and vital part of the food web," implying that cyanobacteria are not useless or purely harmful. This acknowledgment of the value of cyanobacteria would support a tendency to disapprove of eliminating them; choose A to support this content. B and D can be dismissed as illogical, since the author articulates the value of cyanobacteria in an ecosystem and would NOT want to see cyanobacteria eliminated. C can also be dismissed since the author makes a clear and forceful statement about the importance of cyanobacteria.

45. B is the correct answer.

See the previous answer explanation for analysis of the correct line reference. A describes the visual effect of an algae bloom and the consequences it caused, while C explains the harmful impact when an algae population experiences a dramatic surge. D explains that it can be difficult to precisely calculate the economic consequences of an algae bloom. None of the other answers show whether the author would be willing to see cyanobacteria either completely eliminated or preserved, and therefore these choices should all be eliminated.

46. B is the correct answer.

In the sixth paragraph, the author reinforces the idea that M. aeruginosa can cause harm to human health, but also notes that other bacteria species are dangerous as well in lines 24-27. Choose B to support this content. Be careful not to choose A, since the author notes that M. aeruginosa is well-known for being dangerous but is NOT necessarily the most dangerous species. C and D can both be dismissed since the author does NOT discuss which of the potential toxins produced by the bacteria is the most deadly.

47. D is the correct answer.

In the seventh paragraph, the author focuses on how dangerous toxins can be ingested, noting that "simple skin contact with them is normally not enough to cause harm to humans (as they have to be ingested)." Choose D to support this content. A and B can be eliminated, since the paragraph does NOT define any terms (despite explaining various concepts) or suggest that cyanobacteria are not harmful (since the OPPOSITE is in fact true). C can be dismissed as illogical since the information that skin contact is insufficient to cause harm diminishes rather than heightens the idea of how sensitive humans are.

Answer Explanations, Test 2

48. C is the correct answer.

In line 22, "pulls" refers to bacteria being allowed to enter a water source. Choose C to reflect this meaning. A (inappropriately referring to a tendency to remove from a water source), B (inappropriately implying a tendency to be deliberately drawn into), and D (inappropriately implying being required to enter) all introduce improper contexts and should thus be eliminated.

49. C is the correct answer.

Lines 81-83 state that researchers still do not understand why a bloom will sometimes, but not always, be triggered when specific conditions are present. This information suggests that environmental factors trigger blooms, but not in a consistent way; choose C to support this content. A describes how many species of cyanobacteria seem to be present during a bloom, while B describes the conditions that make a bloom more likely to occur. D explains that it is not known why one species will bloom rather than another. None of these other answers support the idea that environmental factors play a not yet fully understood role in algae blooms, and therefore all should be eliminated.

50. D is the correct answer.

The final paragraph refers to the role of scientific research in minimizing the frequency and scale of algae blooms; the tone, as in D, is best described as objective. Be careful not to choose B, which is too strong and too emotional in connotation for the tone used here. A and C can also be eliminated since the author is stating a possible outcome, not trying to persuade the reader, and is also not wavering between multiple possibilities.

51. D is the correct answer.

With the exception of the gray bars for 2017 and 2018 (which indicate a slight decrease), the gray bars in the graph indicate that economic damage from algal blooms has mostly increased from one year to the next. Choose D to support this reasoning. A considers a factor (bloom size) that the graph (which only concerns number of blooms and total economic damage) does not consider, while B makes a future projection that is out of scope, since the graph focuses entirely on data from the past. C is contradicted by the fact that, despite a general pattern of increase for damage and decrease for number, the number of algal blooms did rise at one point (2014-2015) and the economic damage did decrease at one point (2017-2018).

52. C is the correct answer.

The passage indicates that yearly damage from algal blooms is "close to $1 billion," a figure that the graph (with damage consistently between $750 million and $1.25 billion) clearly supports. C is thus the best choice, while A, B, and D all indicate that the estimate from the passage is called into question by the data in the graph (OR that the data in the graph are called into question by the estimate from the passage). Eliminate these choices as wrongly introducing negative relationships for statistics that are, in fact, primarily in agreement.

Answer Explanations, Test 2

NOTES

- Passage 2 on Pages 35-36, "Why your child's preschool teacher should have a college degree," is an excerpt from the article of the same name by Anne Douglass (in affiliation with the University of Massachusetts) and published by The Conversation. 2 January 2018, The Conversation. https://theconversation.com/why-your-childs-preschool-teacher-should-have-a-college-degree-88514. Accessed 28 July 2019.

- Passage 3, Reading 1 on Page 38, "Bumble and Bumble: what's black and yellow and maybe more than one species?" is adapted from the article of the same name by Caitlin MacDonough and published by the PLOS Ecology Community Blog. 31 December 2018, PLOS ONE. https://blogs.plos.org/ecology/2018/12/31/bumble-and-bumble-whats-black-and-yellow-and-maybe-more-than-one-species/. Accessed 28 July 2019.

- Passage 3, Reading 2 on Pages 38-39, "Phylogeny and population genetic analyses reveal cryptic speciation in the Bombus fervidus species complex," is adapted from the article of the same name by Jonathan B. Koch et al. and published by the PLOS ONE research journal. 21 November 2018, PLOS ONE. https://journals.plos.org/plosone/article?id=10.1371/journal.pone.0207080. Accessed 28 July 2019.

- Passage 5 on Pages 44-45, "USGS Finds 28 Types of Cyanobacteria in Florida Algal Bloom," is adapted from the article of the same name published by the United States Geological Survey. 31 May 2017, USGS. https://www.usgs.gov/news/usgs-finds-28-types-cyanobacteria-florida-algal-bloom. Accessed 28 July 2019.

About the Figures: The various visual resources that accompany the passages in this section are primarily meant to facilitate critical thinking skills and may not reflect historical data.

Test 3

Full Reading Section

2020 SAT Practice

Test 3

Reading Test

65 MINUTES, 52 QUESTIONS

Turn to Section 1 of your answer sheet to answer the questions in this section.

DIRECTIONS

Each passage or pair of passages below is followed by a number of questions. After reading each passage or pair, choose the best answer to each question based on what is stated or implied in the passage or passages and in any accompanying graphics (such as a table or graph).

Questions 1-10 are based on the following passage.

This passage is adapted from the short story "Scars" by Marsh Cassidy (copyright Marsh Cassidy, 2019).

I walked into my room in the freshman dorm, suitcases in both hands. A boy my age, black hair falling over his forehead, knelt by one of the two single beds, hands clasped and resting on the
Line
5 mattress. Eyes closed, he spoke softly, almost in a chant.
   He wore flannel slacks, a peach-colored dress shirt with a rounded collar. He didn't glance up, didn't acknowledge my presence. Suddenly, what
10 I was hearing sunk in. "Our Thomas Wolfe, who art in heaven, hallowed be thy name . . . Give us this day our daily writing."
   The Lord's Prayer! I walked to the other bed, set down my suitcases, sat on the edge of the
15 mattress.
   In a moment, he finished, rose, grinned. "There's no deity," he said. "No heaven, except what we create in our minds. Thomas Wolfe is my god." He shrugged, came toward me, held out his
20 hand. . . .

   "I'm Timothy U. Landis," he said. "Since I arrived first, I took this half of the room, this bed, this half of the dresser." He indicated the large, squat chest of drawers.
25 "Fine," I said." I have no preference."
   He smiled. "No preference? Everyone has preferences. We have to find what they are, not deny them. We have to be true to ourselves. We have to analyze."
30 I laughed, placing one of the suitcases atop a student desk by the bed. The room was airy, diaphanous curtains billowing in the breeze through the open window. I frowned at the almost dainty quality of the decor.
35 "Maybe that's why I'm here," I said. "To find out my preferences, what I want out of life. There are so many things." I pulled socks and underwear from the suitcase, shoving them into drawers.
   "Need any help?" he asked. I looked up,
40 surprised. He stood beside and slightly behind me, almost touching.

I rooted around and pulled out a couple of shirts, a pair of jeans. "You can hang these up, if you like."

45 He took them, walked to the closet. "I'm aware of my preferences," he said. "All of them. I know what I want." I watched him drape a short-sleeved shirt around a hanger, shaping it just right so there'd be no wrinkles.

50 "You do?" I asked, thinking he was kidding. How could anyone at the age of seventeen or eighteen be so certain? "That's wonderful," I said. "But if that's the case, why are you even here?"

"Scoff, if you want to," he answered, hanging
55 up the pants. "But I'm going to be a writer." He sighed. "I may not last here, I don't know. I'll see what they have to show me. If it's nothing I like, I'll go south to the country where Wolfe was reared."

60 "Thomas Wolfe," I said. I'd heard the name, known the man had been a writer, but that was it.

"That's right," he answered. "My lord and god."

"You're serious about that," I said.

65 He came back, reached for a couple of other shirts. "Of course." He returned to the closet. I shut the first suitcase, slid it under the bed, opened the other. He spoke over his shoulder. "I understand that for freshman English, each person
70 is required to do a final project. It can be a piece of fiction. I've written mine, a novella. I showed it to the head of the department. He said it was more like a creative thesis for a master's program."

I wondered what I'd gotten into, realizing the
75 first of many contradictions. I found Tim likable, yet he certainly was a little bizarre.

1

The text as a whole presents Tim as a character who

A) is serious about his devotion to writing.
B) is rude to strangers.
C) has already met the narrator before the events that the passage describes.
D) experiences pronounced social anxiety.

2

A central difference between the narrator and Tim is that

A) Tim isn't religious while the narrator is.
B) Tim has a more specific plan for his future than the narrator does.
C) Tim likes to write while the narrator does not.
D) Tim is cordial while the narrator is not.

3

As used in line 42, "rooted" most nearly means

A) agitated.
B) felt.
C) grounded.
D) embedded.

4

It can be inferred from the passage that the narrator sees the world as

A) needing to be analyzed a great deal.
B) too perilous for intense conflict to be desirable.
C) populated by bizarre people.
D) full of possibilities.

Test 3

5

Which choice provides the best evidence for the answer to the previous question?

A) Lines 27-28 ("We have . . . them")
B) Lines 31-34 ("The room . . . decor")
C) Lines 35-37 ("Maybe . . . things")
D) Lines 75-76 ("I found . . . bizarre")

6

As used in line 47, "drape" most nearly means

A) hang.
B) relax.
C) honor.
D) throw.

7

It can be inferred from lines 50-53 ("You . . . here?") that the narrator believes that the function of college is to

A) discover personal preferences, while Tim sees college as a way to study a particular author
B) discover his own inclinations, while Tim sees college as a way to hone his skills.
C) form social connections, while Tim sees college as a way to excel as an author.
D) meet new people, while Tim sees college as a waste of time.

8

The purpose of lines 68-73 ("He spoke . . . program") is to establish

A) the narrator's lack of knowledge about college.
B) Tim's knowledge of the college curriculum.
C) Tim's confidence in his writing abilities.
D) Tim's plans for graduate school.

9

Which choice provides the best evidence to support the notion that Tim does NOT see the university as a definitive authority on writing?

A) Lines 28-29 ("We have to be . . . analyze")
B) Lines 45-47 ("I'm aware . . . want")
C) Lines 56-59 ("I'll see . . . reared")
D) Lines 68-71 ("I understand . . . a novella")

10

The function of the first sentence of the final paragraph is to

A) hint that Tim is ultimately hypocritical.
B) repeat information given elsewhere in the passage.
C) foreshadow other incongruities.
D) create an ominous tone.

Questions 11-21 are based on the following passages.

Passage 1 is adapted from "Feminist Intentions," a chapter of the book *The Intelligence of Women* (1916) by W.L. George. Passage 2 is adapted from a 1918 address to the United States Senate by President Woodrow Wilson. In 1920, the 19th Amendment to the U.S. Constitution granted women the right to vote and thus resolved a debate central to these passages.

Passage 1

The Feminist propaganda—which should not be confounded with the Suffrage agitation—rests upon a revolutionary biological principle. Substantially, the Feminists argue that there are no
5 men and that there are no women; there are only sexual majorities. To put the matter less obscurely, the Feminists base themselves on Weininger's theory, according to which the male principle may be found in woman, and the female principle in
10 man. It follows that they recognize no masculine or feminine "spheres," and that they propose to identify absolutely the conditions of the sexes.

Now there are two kinds of people who labor under illusions as regards the Feminist movement,
15 its opponents and its supporters: both sides tend to limit the area of its influence; in few cases does either realize the movement as revolutionary. The methods are to have revolutionary results, are destined to be revolutionary; as a convinced
20 but cautious Feminist, I do not think it honest or advisable to conceal this fact. I have myself been charged by a very well-known English author (whose name I may not give, as the charge was contained in a private letter) with having "let the
25 cat out of the bag" in my little book, *Woman and To-morrow*. Well, I do not think it right that the cat should be kept in the bag. Feminists should not want to triumph by fraud. As promoters of a sex war, they should not hesitate to declare it, and
30 I have little sympathy with the pretenses of those who contend that one may alter everything while leaving everything unaltered.

An essential difference between "Feminism" and "Suffragism" is that the Suffrage is but part of
35 the greater propaganda; while Suffragism desires to remove an inequality, Feminism purports to alter radically the mental attitudes of men and women. The sexes are to be induced to recognize each other's status, and to bring this recognition
40 to such a point that equality will not even be challenged.

Passage 2

Are we alone to ask and take the utmost that our women can give—service and sacrifice of every kind—and still say we do not see what
45 title that gives them to stand by our sides in the guidance of the affairs of their nation and ours? We have made partners of the women in this war*; shall we admit them only to a partnership of suffering and sacrifice and toil and not to a
50 partnership of privilege and right? This war could not have been fought, either by the other nations engaged or by America, if it had not been for the services of the women—services rendered in every sphere—not merely in the fields of effort
55 in which we have been accustomed to see them work, but wherever men have worked and upon the very skirts and edges of the battle itself. We shall not only be distrusted but shall deserve to be distrusted if we do not enfranchise them
60 with the fullest possible enfranchisement, as it is now certain that the other great free nations will enfranchise them. We cannot isolate our thought or our action in such a matter from the thought of the rest of the world. We must either conform or
65 deliberately reject what they propose and resign the leadership of liberal minds to others.

The women of America are too noble and too intelligent and too devoted to be slackers whether you give or withhold this thing that is
70 mere justice; but I know the magic it will work in their thoughts and spirits if you give it to them. I propose it as I would propose to admit soldiers to the Suffrage, the men fighting in the field for our liberties and the liberties of the world, were they
75 excluded. The tasks of the women lie at the very heart of the war, and I know how much stronger that heart will beat if you do this just thing and show our women that you trust them as much as you in fact and of necessity depend upon them.

*Wilson is referring to World War I (1914-1918).

Test 3

11

As used in line 2, "agitation" most nearly means

A) irritation.
B) movement.
C) disruption.
D) antagonism.

12

According to the author of Passage 1, the opponents and supporters of Feminism both

A) fail to recognize Feminism as revolutionary.
B) want to enfranchise women to some extent.
C) fail to recognize each other's intellectual status.
D) privately reached out to the author of Passage 1.

13

According to the author of Passage 1, the relationship between Feminism and Suffragism is that

A) Suffragism aims to identify wrongdoing whereas Feminism aims to punish wrongdoers.
B) Suffragism is based on social theory whereas Feminism is based on biological principles.
C) Suffragism aims to prevent a problem whereas Feminism aims to conceal the problem.
D) Suffragism aims to right a wrong whereas Feminism aims to remove the root of a problem.

14

Which choice provides the best evidence for the answer to the previous question?

A) Lines 1-3 ("The Feminist . . . principle")
B) Lines 4-6 ("Substantially . . . majorities")
C) Lines 26-32 ("I do not . . . unaltered")
D) Lines 35-41 ("while Suffragism . . . challenged")

15

As used in line 42, "take" most nearly means

A) request.
B) steal.
C) benefit from.
D) endure.

16

In Passage 2, the discussion of male soldiers (lines 71-75) serves to

A) demonstrate that the author is not arguing for special treatment of women.
B) show an apparent biological difference between the sexes.
C) refute the claim that women are important in the war effort.
D) illustrate the cross-generational importance of the right to vote.

17

According to the author of Passage 2, the United States will benefit from enfranchising women because

A) all spheres of society will become more equal if women gain the right to vote.
B) its war effort will become more formidable if women are given more elevated social roles.
C) it will become more powerful than its allies if American women gain new political rights.
D) women will work harder for society if they are motivated by a greater sense of civic worth.

18

Which choice provides the best evidence for the answer to the previous question?

A) Lines 53-56 ("services rendered . . . them work")
B) Lines 60-62 ("it is now . . . enfranchise them")
C) Lines 67-71 ("The women . . . it to them")
D) Lines 75-79 ("The tasks . . . upon them")

19

Which choice best states the relationship between the two passages?

A) Passage 1 examines a movement while Passage 2 advocates a specific solution.
B) Passage 1 argues in support of a movement while Passage 2 argues against it.
C) Passage 1 explains the purpose of Passage 2 by introducing new historical details.
D) Passage 1 questions a figure of authority while Passage 2 appeals to a figure of authority.

20

The author of Passage 2 would most likely view lines 28-29 ("As promoters . . . declare it") of Passage 1 with

A) confusion.
B) skepticism.
C) agreement.
D) resentment.

21

Based on the passages, both authors would agree with which of the following claims?

A) The United States should follow the example of its allies in ensuring political participation.
B) Suffragism aims to remedy an evident inequality.
C) Feminists operate under fundamental illusions about their cause.
D) Women toil in every profession offered by society.

Questions 22-31 are based on the following passage.

This passage is adapted from Claire Saravia of the Goddard Space Flight Center, "NASA's Fermi Finds Possible Dark Matter Ties in Andromeda Galaxy," a NASA news release originally published* in 2017.

NASA's Fermi Gamma-ray Space Telescope has found a signal at the center of the neighboring Andromeda galaxy that could indicate the presence of the mysterious stuff known as dark [Line 5] matter. The gamma-ray signal is similar to one seen by Fermi at the center of our own Milky Way galaxy.

Gamma rays are the highest-energy form of light, produced by the universe's most energetic [10] phenomena. They're common in galaxies like the Milky Way because cosmic rays, particles moving near the speed of light, produce gamma rays when they interact with interstellar gas clouds and starlight.

[15] Surprisingly, the latest Fermi data shows that the gamma rays in Andromeda—also known as M31—are confined to the galaxy's center instead of spread throughout. To explain this unusual distribution, scientists are proposing that the [20] emission may come from several undetermined sources. One of them could be dark matter, an unknown substance that makes up most of the universe.

"We expect dark matter to accumulate in the [25] innermost regions of the Milky Way and other galaxies, which is why finding such a compact signal is very exciting," said lead scientist Pierrick Martin, an astrophysicist at the National Center for Scientific Research and the Research Institute [30] in Astrophysics and Planetology in Toulouse, France. "M31 will be a key to understanding what this means for both Andromeda and the Milky Way."

. . . Another possible source for this emission [35] could be a rich concentration of pulsars in M31's center. These spinning neutron stars weigh as much as twice the mass of the sun and are among the densest objects in the universe. One teaspoon of neutron star matter would weigh a billion tons [40] on Earth. Some pulsars emit most of their energy in gamma rays. Because M31 is 2.5 million light-years away, it's difficult to find individual pulsars. To test whether the gamma rays are coming from these objects, scientists can apply what they know [45] about pulsars from observations in the Milky Way to new X-ray and radio observations of Andromeda.

Now that Fermi has detected a similar gamma-ray signature in both M31 and the Milky Way, [50] scientists can use this information to solve mysteries within both galaxies. For example, M31 emits few gamma rays from its large disk, where most stars form, indicating fewer cosmic rays roaming there. Because cosmic rays are [55] usually thought to be related to star formation, the absence of gamma rays in the outer parts of M31 suggests either that the galaxy produces cosmic rays differently or that they can escape the galaxy more rapidly. Studying Andromeda may help [60] scientists understand the life cycle of cosmic rays and how it is connected to star formation.

"We don't fully understand the roles cosmic rays play in galaxies, or how they travel through them," said Xian Hou, an astrophysicist at Yunnan [65] Observatories, Chinese Academy of Sciences in Kunming, China, also a lead scientist in this work. "M31 lets us see how cosmic rays behave under conditions different from those in our own galaxy."

[70] The similar discovery in both the Milky Way and M31 means scientists can use the galaxies as models for each other when making difficult observations. While Fermi can make more sensitive and detailed observations of the Milky [75] Way's center, its view is partially obscured by emission from the galaxy's disk. But telescopes view Andromeda from an outside vantage point impossible to attain in the Milky Way.

"Our galaxy is so similar to Andromeda, it [80] really helps us to be able to study it, because we can learn more about our galaxy and its formation," said co-author Regina Caputo, a research scientist at NASA's Goddard Space Flight Center in Greenbelt, Maryland. "It's like [85] living in a world where there's no mirrors but you

*See Page 90 for the citation for this text.

have a twin, and you can see everything physical about the twin."

While more observations are necessary to determine the source of the gamma-ray excess, the discovery provides an exciting starting point to learn more about both galaxies, and perhaps about the still elusive nature of dark matter.

"We still have a lot to learn about the gamma-ray sky," Caputo said. "The more information we have, the more information we can put into models of our own galaxy."

22

The main point of the passage is that

A) the similar gamma ray profiles of M31 and the Milky Way may provide insights into both those galaxies and dark matter.
B) the Fermi telescope is NASA's primary method of observing distant galaxies such as M31.
C) dark matter accounts for most of the mass of the universe, but scientists presently know very little about dark matter itself.
D) cosmic rays are affiliated with star formation and are the predecessors of gamma rays.

23

As used in line 35, "rich" most nearly means

A) high.
B) prosperous.
C) valuable.
D) deep.

24

It can be inferred from the passage that scientists know the least about

A) cosmic rays.
B) gamma rays.
C) pulsars.
D) dark matter.

25

As used in line 49, "signature" most nearly means

A) self-expression.
B) pattern.
C) authority.
D) formation.

26

The author indicates that Fermi data quality

A) is dependent on X-ray and radio data.
B) is not yet high enough to produce plausible models.
C) is better for the core of the Milky Way than for the core of M31, but better for the outer regions of M31 than for the outer regions of the Milky Way.
D) is better for the outer regions of the Milky Way than for the outer regions of M31, but better for the core of M31 than for the core of the Milky Way.

27

Which choice provides the best evidence for the answer to the previous question?

A) Lines 1-7 ("NASA's Fermi . . . galaxy")
B) Lines 41-47 ("Because M31 . . . Andromeda")
C) Lines 73-78 ("While Fermi . . . Milky Way")
D) Lines 88-92 ("While more . . . dark matter")

28

According to the information presented in the passage, all of the following are sources of gamma rays EXCEPT

A) pulsars.
B) dark matter.
C) cosmic rays interacting with gas clouds and light.
D) X-rays.

29

It can be inferred from the passage that gamma rays are typically

A) formed exclusively in the Milky Way.
B) similar in nature among different galaxies.
C) destroyed by the motion of a galaxy's disk.
D) not necessarily confined to a galaxy's center.

30

Which choice provides the best evidence for the answer to the previous question?

A) Lines 10-14 ("They're common . . . starlight")
B) Lines 15-18 ("Surprisingly . . . throughout")
C) Lines 48-51 ("Now that . . . galaxies")
D) Lines 59-61 ("Studying . . . formation")

31

The author includes the information in the ninth paragraph (lines 79-87) in order to

A) add much-needed levity to a serious discussion.
B) transition from analysis of a discovery to a synopsis of applications of the discovery.
C) support the main point of the previous paragraph.
D) question an assumption made earlier in the passage.

Questions 32-41 are based on the following passage and supplementary material.

This passage is an excerpt from Margee Kerr, "Why is it fun to be frightened?" an article originally published* in The Conversation in 2018.

John Carpenter's iconic horror film *Halloween* celebrates its 40th anniversary this year. Few horror movies have achieved similar notoriety,
Line and it's credited with kicking off the steady stream
5 of slasher flicks that followed.

Audiences flocked to theaters to witness the seemingly random murder and mayhem a masked man brought to a small suburban town, reminding them that picket fences and manicured lawns
10 cannot protect us from the unjust, the unknown or the uncertainty that awaits us all in both life and death. The film offers no justice for the victims in the end, no rebalancing of good and evil.

Why, then, would anyone want to spend
15 time and money to watch such macabre scenes filled with depressing reminders of just how unfair and scary our world can be?

I've spent the past 10 years investigating just this question, finding the typical answer
20 of "Because I like it! It's fun!" incredibly unsatisfying. I've long been convinced there's more to it than the "natural high" or adrenaline rush that many describe—and, indeed, the body does kick into "go" mode when you're startled
25 or scared, amping up not only adrenaline but a multitude of chemicals that ensure that your body is fueled and ready to respond. This "fight or flight" response to threats has helped to keep humans alive for millennia.

30 That still doesn't explain why people would want to intentionally scare themselves, though. As a sociologist, I've kept asking, "But, why?" After two years collecting data in a haunted attraction with my colleague Greg Siegle, a cognitive
35 neuroscientist at the University of Pittsburgh, we've found that the gains from thrills and chills can go further than the natural high.

To capture in real time what makes fear fun, what motivates people to pay to be scared out
40 of their skin and what they experience when engaging with this material, we needed to gather data in the field. In this case, that meant setting up a mobile lab in the basement of an extreme haunted attraction outside Pittsburgh,
45 Pennsylvania.

This adults-only extreme attraction went beyond the typical startling lights and sounds and animated characters found in a family-friendly haunted house. Over the course of about
50 35 minutes, visitors experienced a series of intense scenarios where, in addition to unsettling characters and special effects, they were touched by the actors, restrained and exposed to electricity. It was not for the faint of heart.

55 For our study, we recruited 262 guests who had already purchased tickets. Before they entered the attraction, they completed a survey about their expectations and how they were feeling. We had them answer questions again about how they were
60 feeling once they had gone through the attraction. We also used mobile EEG technology to compare 100 participants' brainwave activity as they sat through 15 minutes of various cognitive and emotional tasks before and after the attraction.

65 Guests reported significantly higher mood, and felt less anxious and tired, directly after their trip through the haunted attraction. The more terrifying the better: feeling happy afterward was related to rating the experience as highly intense
70 and scary. This set of volunteers also reported feeling that they'd challenged their personal fears and learned about themselves.

Analysis of the EEG data revealed widespread decreases in brain reactivity from before to after
75 among those whose mood improved. In other words, highly intense and scary activities—at least in a controlled environment like this haunted attraction—may "shut down" the brain to an extent, and that in turn is associated with feeling
80 better. Studies of those who practice mindfulness meditation have yielded a similar observation.

---

*See Page 90 for the citation for this text.

Together, our findings suggest that going through an extreme haunted attraction provides gains similar to choosing to run a 5K race or
85 tackling a difficult climbing wall. There's a sense of uncertainty, physical exertion, a challenge to push yourself—and eventually achievement when it's over and done with.

32

The author's attitude toward the question of what makes fear fun can best be described as

A) skeptical.
B) sympathetic.
C) curious.
D) anxious.

33

Which of the following choices best supports the idea that film can prevent viewers from falling into a false sense of security?

A) Lines 2-5 ("Few horror . . . followed")
B) Lines 8-12 ("reminding . . . death")
C) Lines 36-37 ("gains from . . . natural high")
D) Line 54 ("It was . . . of heart")

34

The author includes a side comment on the fight or flight response in lines 23-29 ("and indeed . . . for millennia") in order to

A) offer a counterargument to another researcher's thesis.
B) illustrate an example from a previous study.
C) provide the biological basis for the author's own theory.
D) concede a point as true but insufficiently rigorous.

35

Which choice provides the best evidence for the answer to the previous question?

A) Lines 18-21 ("I've spent . . . unsatisfying")
B) Lines 30-31 ("The still . . . though")
C) Lines 38-42 ("To capture . . . the field")
D) Lines 65-67 ("Guests . . . attraction")

36

As used in line 36, "chills" most nearly means

A) weakness.
B) fever.
C) excitement.
D) solidity.

37

According to the information presented in the passage, being scared offers similar psychological benefits to all of the following EXCEPT

A) doing pilates.
B) climbing.
C) meditating.
D) running a race.

Test 3

Outcomes of a "Fear Event" Experiment
(75 Participants, Performed in 2015)

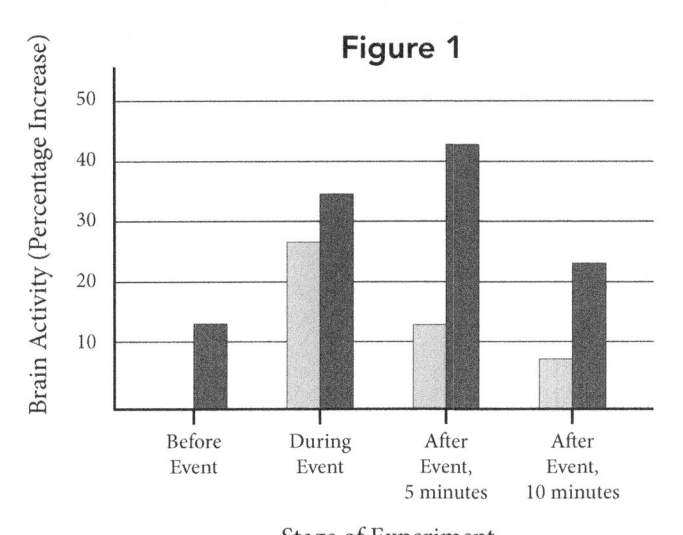

Figure 1

[Bar chart showing Brain Activity (Percentage Increase) on y-axis from 0 to 50, across Stage of Experiment on x-axis: Before Event, During Event, After Event 5 minutes, After Event 10 minutes. Control Group (light) and Mindfulness Group (dark) bars.]

Approximate values:
- Before Event: Control ~0, Mindfulness ~13
- During Event: Control ~27, Mindfulness ~35
- After Event, 5 minutes: Control ~13, Mindfulness ~43
- After Event, 10 minutes: Control ~7, Mindfulness ~23

Control Group: ☐ Mindfulness Group: ■

Figure 2

Self-Reported Reaction to the Fear Event	Yes (%)	No (%)
Felt anxious before	57	43
Felt happy during	51	49
Felt anxious after	75	25
Felt happy after	63	37

38

It can be inferred from the passage that the author and Greg Siegle asked the survey respondents about their feelings before the haunted house stage so that

A) the researchers could divide the respondents into appropriate study groups.

B) the researchers could see if anxious people are more likely to attend haunted houses.

C) the EEG machine could be calibrated.

D) the researchers could compare the respondents' pre- and post-haunted house reactions.

39

As used in line 74, "reactivity" most nearly means

A) instability.
B) sensitivity.
C) emotions.
D) alertness.

40

Together, the two figures suggest that some of the participants in the relevant experiment

A) were unaware of how the fear event influenced their brain activity.

B) felt unable to fully explain their own responses.

C) purposefully avoid experiences that cause fear.

D) see happiness and anxiety as compatible.

41

In what way are the findings in the figures and the self-reporting information in the passage in conflict?

A) The passage indicates that fear events increase brain activity.

B) The passage links fear events to survival tactics.

C) The passage indicates that fear events decrease anxiety.

D) The passage only considers long-term fears.

Questions 42-52 are based on the following passage and supplementary material.

This passage is an excerpt from Stephen Clark, "Could laser-powered superconductors spark a technological revolution?" an article that originally appeared* in The Conversation in 2016.

One of the most remarkable and unexpected discoveries of the 20th century is that some materials can become "superconductors" when cooled down to very low temperatures. This means that they can conduct electricity with no resistance and are used in applications ranging from MRI scanners and particle accelerators to the "maglev trains" that move without touching the ground.

Liquid helium or nitrogen is used to cool most materials down to low enough temperatures so that they become superconductors and then stay that way. But as this process is expensive and impractical, physicists have for decades tried to find new materials where the phenomenon exists at room temperature, which has proven difficult. An international research team that I am a part of has now come up with a new technique to induce superconductivity at high temperatures by shining lasers on the material, a technique which could pave the way for superconductors that can work at room temperature.

While this is just a first step, the returns could one day be huge. Just as the creation of semiconductors laid the foundations for the entire digital world, a room-temperature superconductor could launch a similar technological revolution. It would make electronic devices more efficient and require less power consumption, and could even herald new technologies such as ultra-fast switches that could replace transistors, currently used to flip electrical signals in computers.

Materials are often categorised by their ability to conduct electricity. Metals allow electrons to move freely and carry with them electrical charge. In insulators, such as rubber or wood, electrons are stuck so that no electrical current can flow.

Normal conductors always have some resistance because the mobile electrons within the material bounce off jiggling positive ions (atoms that have lost their mobile electrons), which slows down the current. But in 1911, Kamerlingh Onnes discovered that this resistance vanished abruptly in mercury when it was cooled close to absolute zero (or -273.15°C). A superconductor also expels magnetic fields, which are crucial to magnetic levitation (the "maglev" effect in those trains).

It took over 50 years—and a number of Nobel prizes—to explain this effect. It is caused by mobile electrons pairing up together when the temperature is cooled enough. This occurrence makes electrical resistance vanish because, unlike single electrons, these pairs tend to be deflected by ions in a way which keeps them harnessed together and allows them to continue their journey essentially unscathed.

In the 1980s, an entirely new class of superconductor was discovered in ceramic-like materials called cuprates that were capable of operating at 138K (-135.15°C). This higher temperature meant that cheap coolants like liquid nitrogen could be used to cool the substance down enough to become a superconductor, rather than using more expensive liquid helium.

Our experiment investigated a particular material built out of bucky-balls, which are large molecules composed of 60 carbon atoms arranged in a football*-like cage. When squashed together, bucky-balls form a regular solid, which is a fairly boring insulator. But if alkali atoms like potassium are added to fill up the spaces between the carbon cages, things change. Potassium atoms have a single "loose" electron far from the nucleus, which can easily transfer to the bucky-balls. There, it can hop from one bucky-ball to another—making the material metallic at room temperature. However, the most striking feature occurs when the material is cooled down. Below 20K (-253.15°C), it is naturally a superconductor.

A useful feature of molecular solids like this is that they can vibrate in a number of different ways, corresponding to the cage being stretched or compressed. In our new study, my colleagues used

---

*See Page 90 for the citation for this text.

*The author is referring to soccer, not American football.

a powerful laser that generated very short pulses
85 at a frequency resonant with one of the cage's
vibrational modes, making the bucky-balls shake
in unison. They then used another much weaker
laser pulse to probe how the material behaved.

Properties of Three Superconductors

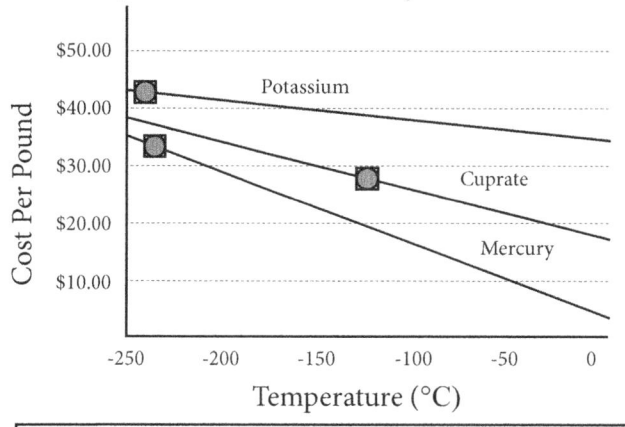

[Graph showing Cost Per Pound (y-axis, $10.00 to $50.00) vs Temperature °C (x-axis, -250 to 0) for three substances: Potassium, Cuprate, and Mercury. Data points marked for each substance indicating the highest temperature at which the substance functions as a superconductor.]

Highest temperature at which the substance functions as a superconductor: ●

42

The author hopes that his superconductor research will lead to

A) new kinds of high-speed computers.
B) the prototype for a functional maglev train.
C) superconductors that work at room temperature.
D) greater recognition for specialists engaged in superconductor research.

43

Which choice provides the best evidence for the answer to the previous question?

A) Lines 4-9 ("This means . . . ground")
B) Lines 17-22 ("An international . . . temperature")
C) Lines 28-32 ("It would . . . computers")
D) Lines 48-49 ("It took . . . this effect")

44

As used in line 23, the word "returns" functions to

A) emphasize the fact that the utility of superconductors that work at room temperature would outweigh the investment cost of creating them.
B) show how information technology will eventually regress to its previous state even if new superconductors are discovered.
C) highlight the fact that superconductors are an overlooked area of financial investment.
D) demonstrate that superconductors use much less power than their more traditional counterparts employ.

45

The author's research group used a powerful laser to

A) break the bonds holding bucky-balls together.
B) illuminate precise areas of superconductivity in bucky-balls.
C) differentiate bucky-balls that were acting as superconductors from those that were not.
D) cause nearby bucky-balls to vibrate in much the same way as one another.

46

As used in line 70, the effect of the word "boring" is to show how

A) the general public is not interested in superconductor research.
B) bucky-balls usually have no practical applications to superconductor research.
C) superconductor researchers whose ideas conflict with those of the author do not deserve attention.
D) insulators are a relatively uninteresting topic.

Test 3

47

The author mentions the fact that it took over 50 years and multiple Nobel prizes worth of research to explain the maglev effect in order to

A) suggest that the processes behind the maglev effect are very complex.

B) hint that modern superconductor research is a very slow process.

C) add an air of authority to the passage as a whole.

D) argue that further developments in this area of science are very unlikely.

48

Pre-1980 superconductors would have been less practical to use in large-scale manufacturing than current superconductors because the former superconductors

A) exude magnetic fields.

B) are too costly to cool.

C) have paired electrons.

D) have unpaired electrons.

49

Which choice provides the best evidence for the answer to the previous question?

A) Lines 45-47 ("A superconductor . . . trains)")

B) Lines 51-56 ("This . . . unscathed")

C) Lines 57-64 ("In the 1980s . . . helium")

D) Lines 72-75 ("Potassium . . . bucky-balls")

50

Which of the following, assuming equivalent performance per ounce and according to the graph, would be most cost-efficient superconductor?

A) Potassium, -250° C

B) Mercury, -250° C

C) Potassium, -100° C

D) Mercury, -100° C

51

Unlike the passage, the graph directly considers whether

A) cooling makes the same amount of a given superconductor material more expensive.

B) a given material is liquid or solid at 0° C.

C) any known materials can function as superconductors at absolute zero.

D) cuprates are more widely used than the metal-based superconductors developed earlier.

52

The author of the passage would argue that the graph provides

A) possible reasons for skepticism regarding the passage's main argument.

B) little-known information that is nonetheless of importance to researchers.

C) direct corroboration for some of the passage's own statistics.

D) compelling evidence of the need for future inquiry.

STOP

**If you finish before time is called, you may check your work on this section only.
Do not turn to any other section.**

Answer Key on the Next Page

Answer Key: Test 3

Passage 1	Passage 2	Passage 3	Passage 4	Passage 5
1. A	11. B	22. A	32. C	42. C
2. B	12. A	23. A	33. B	43. B
3. B	13. D	24. D	34. D	44. A
4. D	14. D	25. B	35. B	45. D
5. C	15. C	26. C	36. C	46. B
6. A	16. A	27. C	37. A	47. A
7. B	17. B	28. D	38. D	48. B
8. C	18. D	29. D	39. B	49. C
9. C	19. A	30. B	40. D	50. B
10. C	20. C	31. C	41. C	51. A
	21. B			52. C

Question Types

Major Issue
1-2, 12, 22, 32

Passage Details
7-8, 10, 16, 24, 28, 31, 37-38, 45, 47

Command of Evidence
4-5, 9, 13-14, 17-18, 26-27, 29-30, 33-35, 42-43, 48-49

Word in Context
3, 6, 11, 15, 23, 25, 36, 39, 44, 46

Graphics and Visuals
40-41, 50-52

Passage Comparison
19-21

Answer Explanations
Test 3, Pages 62-76

Passage 1, Pages 62-64

1. A is the correct answer.

From the moment that Timothy is introduced (while praying to a writer he idolizes) to his explanation of the project he has already completed, his passion for writing is evident in the passage. Choose A. Be careful not to choose B or D, since while Timothy displays strange behavior which leaves the narrator uncertain, Tim is NOT ever explicitly rude or anxious. C can be dismissed as illogical because the narrator's entire description of Timothy highlights the fact that Timothy is encountering his roommate for the first time.

2. B is the correct answer.

When Timothy states that he knows what he wants, the narrator responds with shock: " 'You do?' I asked, thinking he was kidding. How could anyone at the age of seventeen or eighteen be so certain?" (lines 50-52). This content shows that Timothy has a more specific vision for his future; choose B. Be careful not to choose A, since while Timothy is shown praying, he prays to a writer rather than to a deity. C can also be ruled out, since the passage makes it clear that Timothy likes to write but NOT whether the narrator does. D can be eliminated because both boys are relatively polite to one another.

3. B is the correct answer.

In line 42, "rooted" refers to the act of rummaging or digging. Choose B to reflect this meaning. A (inappropriately implying a mental state rather than a physical action), C (inappropriately referring to a state of being calm and centered), and D (inappropriately implying something being located inside of something else) all introduce improper contexts and should therefore be eliminated.

Answer Explanations, Test 3

4. D is the correct answer.

In lines 35-37, the narrator reflects on his situation: " 'Maybe that's why I'm here,' I said. 'To find out my preferences, what I want out of life. There are so many things.' " This content implies that he sees life as filled with possibility; choose D as effective. A and B both lie outside the scope of the passage and therefore should be eliminated. Be careful not to choose C; the narrator encounters one strange person in the passage, but this encounter does NOT imply that he sees the world as full of bizarre people.

5. C is the correct answer.

See the previous answer explanation for analysis of the correct line reference. A shows Timothy describing his philosophy of life, while B gives a physical description of the room and shows the narrator's reaction to it. D summarizes the narrator's impression of Timothy after a brief exchange with him. None of these other answers provide evidence as to how the narrator sees the world, and therefore they should all be eliminated.

6. A is the correct answer.

In line 47, "drape" refers to the act of arranging an item of clothing so that it hangs off of something. Choose A to reflect this meaning. B (inappropriately implying the release of tension from a body), C (inappropriately referring to showing reverence and respect), and D (inappropriately implying handling an object carelessly and launching it through the air) all introduce improper contexts and should therefore be eliminated.

7. B is the correct answer.

In lines 50-53, the narrator first reacts with surprise to Timothy's announcement that he knows what he wants, and then questions why Timothy would bother attending college if he already has established such certainty. This content, along with Timothy's response, suggests that the narrator views college as a way to learn about himself, while Timothy sees college as a way to develop skills. Choose B as appropriate. Be careful not to choose A, because while Timothy does indicate his interest in a particular author, his primary focus in college is to hone his own skills as a writer. C and D can both be eliminated since neither boy expresses much interest in meeting new people or forming social ties.

8. C is the correct answer.

Lines 68-73 depict Timothy talking about the writing project that he has already completed and record the positive response that he received from a faculty member. This content suggests that Timothy is quite confident in his writing; choose C as appropriate. A can be dismissed as illogical, because these lines reveal Timothy as very knowledgeable and well-prepared. Be careful not to choose B or D, because the lines contain a remark comparing Timothy's writing to graduate school-level work but do NOT actually imply that he plans to go to graduate school. (The lines do reflect that Timothy knows about the curriculum for his program, but their primary purpose is to convey his outlook rather than his knowledge.)

Answer Explanations, Test 3

9. C is the correct answer.

In the relevant lines, Timothy expresses some skepticism about whether he will learn anything during his time at college and outlines a back-up plan for what he will do if he feels that college is not for him. This content suggests that he does not see the university as the central authority on writing; choose C as appropriate. A and B can be dismissed since they show Timothy reflecting on how to live a meaningful life and articulating a sense of certainty about his values and goals. D summarizes how Timothy has already been proactive about meeting some of the requirements of his program. None of these other answers reflect Timothy's skepticism about the university, and therefore they should all be rejected.

10. C is the correct answer.

In the first sentence of the final paragraph, the narrator refers "the first of many contradictions," implying that his first meeting with Timothy has set a pattern for future behavior. Choose C to reflect this content. A and B can be eliminated because this information is new and because contradictions do NOT necessarily imply hypocrisy. Be careful not to choose D, since this foreshadowing does NOT necessarily imply that those contradictions will be threatening or bad.

Passage 2, Pages 65-67

11. B is the correct answer.

In line 2, "agitation" refers to activism and demands for change. Choose B to reflect this meaning. A (inappropriately implying emotions of frustration or anger), C (inappropriately referring to interfering with processes and activities), and D (inappropriately implying an emotional state) all introduce improper contexts and should therefore be eliminated.

12. A is the correct answer.

In lines 13-15, the author of Passage 1 states that "there are two kinds of people who labor under illusions as regards the Feminist movement, its opponents and its supporters"; choose A to reflect this content. B can be dismissed as illogical, since the opponents of Feminism are unlikely to want to enfranchise women, while C can be rejected because the passage does not discuss how opponents and supporters regard one another. D should be eliminated because the author references only one individual who reached out privately.

13. D is the correct answer.

In lines 35-41, the author explains that Suffragism seeks to resolve one specific inequality (denying women the right to vote), while Feminism looks more systematically at the way men and women are positioned within society. Since denying women the right to vote is rooted in a belief that they are less capable than men, Feminism can be seen as addressing the underlying cause of the problem. Choose D as the best answer. A

Answer Explanations, Test 3

and B can be eliminated since the passage does NOT discus either punishment of wrongdoers or biological and social theories of nature and nurture. Be careful not to choose C, since Feminism focuses on bringing inequalities to light, NOT on concealing them.

14. D is the correct answer.

See the previous answer explanation for analysis of the correct line reference. A describes a core belief attributed to Feminism, while B elaborates on explaining that belief. C explains the author's belief about the importance of being honest and forthright. None of these other answers identify the relationship between Feminism and Suffragism and therefore they should all be eliminated.

15. C is the correct answer.

In line 42, "take" refers to individuals who receive and benefit from the hard work of women. Choose C to reflect this meaning. A (inappropriately implying emotions of frustration or anger), B (inappropriately referring to interfering with processes and activities), and D (inappropriately implying an emotional state) all introduce improper contexts and should therefore be eliminated.

16. A is the correct answer.

In lines 70-75, the author references the way male soldiers are valorized and respected in order to show that women should be given the same respect, and that the respect being demanded for women is not unique. Choose A as the best answer. B and C can be rejected since the author suggests that men and women are more similar than different and is invested in showing that women DO contribute to the war effort. D can also be eliminated since the focus of this argument is why women should be allowed to vote, NOT the importance of enfranchisement overall as it might relate to other social groups.

17. B is the correct answer.

In lines 75-79, the author explains that women are central to the war effort, and would work even harder if they were treated equally and given the right to vote. Thus, the author links women's enfranchisement to empowering the American war effort; choose B as appropriate. A can be eliminated because the author makes a focused and specific argument about one potential positive impact of giving women the right to vote, NOT a more generalized one about increasing social equality. C can also be eliminated since America is not being contrasted with other countries in this passage. Be careful not to choose D, since the author focuses on how women gaining the vote would motivate them to work harder to support the war effort specifically in the line reference, NOT to improve society in general.

18. D is the correct answer.

See the previous answer explanation for analysis of the correct line reference. A describes how the efforts of women to contribute to the war have been wide-ranging, while B suggests that other countries are likely to soon give women the right to vote. C suggests that women will work hard regardless of circumstances, but will be specifically motivated if they have the right to vote. None of these other answers provide evidence that

Answer Explanations, Test 3

the American war effort will be strengthened by giving women the right to vote, and therefore they should all be eliminated.

19. A is the correct answer.

Passage 1 gives an overall analysis of Feminism and of how it is different from Suffragism, while Passage 2 recommends that women be given the right to vote in order to strengthen the war effort. Choose A to reflect this content. B can be eliminated since both passages generally agree on the benefit of giving women the right to vote, while C can be eliminated because Passage 1 is less historically specific than Passage 2. D can also be rejected because both passages offer ideological arguments, NOT specific responses to authority figures.

20. C is the correct answer.

In lines 28-29, the author of Passage 1 states that women who advocate for Feminism should do so freely and openly. Since the author of Passage 2 also praises women for their hard work and contributions, the reaction would most likely be agreement; choose C as appropriate. A can also be eliminated since the author of Passage 2 (who speaks positively of women's advancement) is unlikely to feel confused about why individuals would freely express their Feminist beliefs. B and D can be eliminated since the author of Passage 2 shares a general outlook with the author of Passage 1 and would be unlikely to express skepticism or disagreement.

21. B is the correct answer.

Both authors clearly advocate for women to achieve greater equality in society and see enfranchisement as one way to achieve this situation. Choose B as appropriate. Be careful not to choose A, since only Passage 2 refers to other countries in order to advocate for enfranchisement. C can be eliminated since Passage 2 does not discuss illusions which supporters of Feminism may hold. D can be eliminated since the passages refer to women's valuable contributions but do NOT insist that women contribute in every profession.

Passage 3, Pages 68-70

22. A is the correct answer.

The passage discusses how scientists have concluded that the Milky Way galaxy (home to Earth) and the M31 galaxy share important similarities; the author explains that "Now that Fermi has detected a similar gamma ray signature in both M31 and the Milky Way, scientists can use this information to solve mysteries within both galaxies" (lines 48-51). Choose A to reflect this content. Be careful not to choose C; while this answer is factually accurate, it does NOT reflect the primary purpose of the passage. B and D can both be eliminated because the passage does NOT specify whether the Fermi telescope is the main way scientists observe other galaxies or whether cosmic rays are affiliated with star formation.

Answer Explanations, Test 3

23. A is the correct answer.

In line 35, "rich" refers to the notable quantity of the pulsars found in M31's center. Choose A to reflect this meaning. B (inappropriately referring to someone who possesses significant financial assets), C (inappropriately referring to something that can be exchanged for money or other financial assets), and D (inappropriately implying a physical measurement) all introduce improper contexts and should therefore be eliminated.

24. D is the correct answer.

The passage demonstrates that scientists have knowledge about cosmic rays, gamma rays, and pulsars, since there are known relationships between the three of them. These aspects of the universe have been observed and studied in various ways. However, dark matter is referred to in terms of "the still elusive nature of dark matter" (line 92), suggesting that scientists know less about it. Choose D as the best choice. All of the other answers can be eliminated since they refer to features of the universe which scientists have some knowledge about; the relevant topics for A and B are addressed in lines 8-14, while the author discusses the relevant topic for C in lines 34-36.

25. B is the correct answer.

In line 49, "signature" refers to the way in which gamma rays are present in two different galaxies. Choose B to reflect this meaning. A (inappropriately referring to the personal expression of qualities or characteristics), C (inappropriately referring to someone's status or ability to impose his or her will), and D (inappropriately implying a physical arrangement) all introduce improper contexts and should therefore be eliminated.

26. C is the correct answer.

In lines 73-78, the author explains that "While Fermi can make more sensitive and detailed observations of the Milky Way's center, its view is partially obscured by emission from the galaxy's disk. But telescopes view Andromeda from an outside vantage point impossible to attain in the Milky Way." Choose C to reflect the abilities and limitations of the Fermi telescope in an accurate way. A and B can be eliminated because the passage indicates that Fermi uses gamma-ray signals, not x-ray and radio data, and that the telescope produces data good enough to be used for models. D mischaracterizes the strengths and limitations of the telescope, and therefore should be eliminated.

27. C is the correct answer.

See the previous answer explanation for analysis of the correct line reference. A describes a new scientific discovery and some important context for that discovery, while B describes a scientific challenge and the approach that researchers will take to overcome that challenge. D cautiously expresses optimism about future research directions. None of these other answers specify what galaxy regions Fermi is best able to achieve data about, and therefore they should all be eliminated.

Answer Explanations, Test 3

28. D is the correct answer.

The passage explains that gamma rays can be emitted in a number of ways, including by pulsars, dark matter, and cosmic rays. However, the passage does NOT mention x-rays as a potential source of gamma rays, and therefore D should be selected as the correct answer. All of the other answers are factually contradicted by the passage, and should be eliminated on the basis of lines 34-36 (A), lines 18-23 (B), and lines 10-14 (C).

29. D is the correct answer.

In lines 15-18, the author explains that scientists were surprised to find that most of the gamma rays in M31 appeared to be confined to the galaxy's center. The reaction to this observation suggests that this pattern is NOT typical; therefore, choose D to indicate that gamma rays are not most frequently confined to a galaxy's center. A and B can both be eliminated since the goal of comparing gamma rays across different galaxies indicates that gamma rays would NOT be found exclusively in the Milky Way; moreover, the excitement due to the fact that gamma rays seem to appear in similar ways in the Milky Way and in Andromeda suggests that gamma rays display different patterns in different galaxies. C can also be eliminated because galaxies possess both disks and gamma rays, indicating that the former do NOT typically destroy the latter.

30. B is the correct answer.

See the previous answer explanation for analysis of the correct line reference. A explains where gamma rays most commonly occur and why. C identifies a projected hope based on a new scientific discovery, while D identifies some outcomes which may occur as a result of further research. None of these other answers provide evidence that gamma rays are not typically found solely in a galaxy's center.

31. C is the correct answer.

Lines 79-87 feature an expert perspective which supports the idea already presented in the previous paragraph. This paragraph therefore supports the main point of the earlier content; choose C as the best answer. A and B can both be eliminated because the paragraph is factual, not playful, in tone, and reiterates the value of a discovery rather than discussing its application. D can also be eliminated since the paragraph supports, rather than undermines, information being presented elsewhere in the passage.

Passage 4, Pages 71-73

32. C is the correct answer.

The author has "spent the past 10 years" (line 18) investigating the issue of what makes fear fun and has "kept asking" (line 32) questions that anticipate the research described in the passage. This content supports C and can be used to eliminate A (since "skeptical" would indicate that the author does not believe that fear is fun, NOT that the author wants to understand this situation) and D (which is purely negative and may refer to a

Answer Explanations, Test 3

possible test subject reaction). B is a trap answer, since the author understands that people enjoy experiencing fear but neither situates herself as one of these people nor expresses the pity or concern that "sympathetic" normally suggests.

33. B is the correct answer.

In lines 8-12, the author explains that *Halloween* (setting a pattern for the horror films that followed it) was a popular film despite raising disturbing topics such as "the unjust" and "the unknown." Such themes would go AGAINST a false sense of security, so that B is an appropriate answer. A refers to the popularity of *Halloween* and the horror genre but does NOT clearly explain themes that might relate to a false sense of security. C refers to frightening experiences generally and D refers to a horror-themed attraction, so that neither answer appropriately and specifically refers to film.

34. D is the correct answer.

After explaining the "fight or flight" response in a side comment, the author explains that such a response "still doesn't explain" (line 30) why people want to scare themselves; thus, the "fight or flight" content is valid science, but does NOT fully illuminate the reaction that interests the author. Such information supports D, while answers that assume that the role of the content is purely positive (such as B and C) should be eliminated. A indicates a sense of conflict but wrongly mentions "another researcher" when in fact the source of the "fight or flight" content is never named.

35. B is the correct answer.

See the previous answer explanation for analysis of the correct line reference. A offers a commentary on the author's research BEFORE the "fight or flight" response is presented and is thus out of context. C and D present specifics from the author's research but do not directly address the "fight or flight" response, even though the research (as directly indicated ONLY by B) did account for this response as a possibility.

36. C is the correct answer.

The word "chills" refers to a reaction that is linked to "thrills" (line 36) and to "a natural high" (line 37) as similar occurrences. Thus, a context of energetic or excited response to a spectacle would be appropriate, as in C. Choose this answer and eliminate A (context of lack of ability) and B (context of illness) as introducing inappropriate negatives. D (context of physical state, NOT personal response) introduces a faulty association.

37. A is the correct answer.

Within the passage, the author directly and positively compares the experience of being scared to climbing (line 85, eliminating B), meditating (lines 80-81, eliminating C), and running a race (line 84, eliminating D). While doing pilates IS a form of exercise, the fact that the author only mentions specific forms of exercise instead of exercise GENERALLY as conferring benefits makes this answer problematic. Since doing pilates is not directly mentioned, choose A as appropriate.

Answer Explanations, Test 3

38. D is the correct answer.

The author explains in lines 55-60 that two surveys of the experiment participants were conducted in order to determine "expectations" and feelings before entering the attraction, then "how [the participants] were feeling" after. This content directly supports D, while the fact that the questions were directed to the survey respondents AFTER the respondents were chosen (not as a means of selection) can be used to eliminate A and B. While C refers to an actual feature of the experiment (line 61), the author never draws a direct link between the EEG machine (which was used to determine some responses from the test subjects) and the questions (which were used to gather FURTHER information, NOT to configure the EEG machine at an early stage).

39. B is the correct answer.

The word "reactivity" refers to a feature of the brains of test subjects, which may respond to "highly intense and scary activities" (line 76) by shutting down. Such brains may thus respond strongly or be sensitive to particular conditions. Choose B and eliminate A as a negative inappropriate to a clearly observed (and possibly stable) response mechanism. C and D raise contexts that would be more appropriate to the test subjects THEMSELVES, not to an observed biological mechanism of their brains, and should thus be eliminated.

40. D is the correct answer.

The second figure indicates that, after the experiment, majorities of the participants felt BOTH anxious (75 percent) and happy (63 percent). Thus, because such majorities indicate an overlap, the self-reporting would indicate that some of the participants regarded these reactions as compatible. Choose D and eliminate A and B, since the participants were only asked to provide responses relating to specific emotions (NOT degrees of self-awareness or self-consciousness). Because it is unclear how the participants were chosen—and because overall fear preferences (NOT specific emotional responses) are never mentioned—C is out of scope.

41. C is the correct answer.

While line 66 indicates that the participants in the experiment described in the passage felt "less anxious and tired" after a fear experience, Figure 2 indicates that the number of participants who felt anxious after a fear experience increased from 57 to 63 percent. Choose C to reflect this disparity. A is contradicted by the claim in the passage that fear shuts down the brain (lines 78-80), while B raises an idea that is not directly relevant to the graphs and that the passage DISPUTES (lines 30-31). D is contradicted by the fact that both the passage and the graphs consider only short-term fears related to individual events.

Passage 5, Pages 74-76

42. C is the correct answer.

In lines 17-22, the author references his position as a member of a research team dedicated to the issue of high-temperature superconductivity and indicates his interest in finding superconductors that "can work at room-

Answer Explanations, Test 3

temperature." This content offers direct support for C and should not be mistaken for support for A, since computer components such as superconductors (NOT entire computers) interest the author. B mis-construes the author's technical explanation of maglev trains in the first paragraph (lines 4-9) as an explicit desire to develop such trains, while D wrongly assumes that overall professional renown (NOT a specific technical breakthrough) is the author's main interest.

43. B is the correct answer.

See the previous answer explanation for analysis of the correct line reference. A establishes a connection between superconductors and maglev trains, while C references the future potential of superconductors but NOT (as required by the previous question) the author's own research. D indicates the time and effort required to explain the maglev effect but should NOT be used to wrongly assume that the author wants faster professional recognition for superconductor researchers, as stated in false answer D for the previous question.

44. A is the correct answer.

The word "returns" is used in the context of something that could follow a "first step" (line 23) in superconductor research, namely a "technological revolution" (line 27). Thus, the word "returns" indicates that present work and investment would lead to immense and justified benefits, a logic properly reflected by A. Eliminate B and C as answers that are wrongly negative about future prospects regarding superconductors and technology investments, while D refers to one possible benefit (power consumption) but does NOT capture the much more broadly positive and multi-sided nature of the scenario presented by the author.

45. D is the correct answer.

In the final paragraph of the passage, the author explains that his research team used a "powerful laser" (line 84) to make "bucky-balls shake in unison" (lines 86-87). This content directly supports D, while A wrongly indicates that the laser caused structural breakage rather than vibrations that allowed bucky-balls to remain intact. While B and C may appear to refer to the author's interest in the superconductor potential of bucky-balls (lines 65-79), this discussion occurs BEFORE the author mentions the laser (which is used only to create movement, not to highlight superconductor properties); thus, both answers refer to the wrong context.

46. B is the correct answer.

The word "boring" refers to the typical status of a bucky-ball as an "insulator" (line 70), when in fact the author is mostly interested in materials that function as superconductors. Thus, this word choice helps to make a distinction between two substances and their respective levels of interest for the author; choose B and eliminate A (reference to the public) and C (reference to other researchers) as departing from consideration of the author's own views primarily. D inappropriately neglects the author's sense of preference for superconductors (which are not referenced in this choice) and introduces faulty logic, since the author might agree that insulators would be an interesting topic OUTSIDE of the context of bucky-balls or superconductors but not within such contexts.

Answer Explanations, Test 3

47. A is the correct answer.

The author's references to the background for maglev effect research introduce a discussion of how the maglev effect itself works, with "mobile electrons pairing up together" (line 50). Thus, the maglev effect can now be explained, but only after half a century and recognized scientific effort; it is reasonable to assume that the complex or elusive nature of the process would necessitate such time and effort. Choose A and eliminate B and D (since the relevant references are to PAST, not modern or future, research). C misstates the purpose of this factual, not persuasive, information; creating an air of authority would normally require an impressive reference to the author's own background, and such references are provided elsewhere but NOT at the relevant point in the passage.

48. B is the correct answer.

In lines 57-64, the author explains that the emergence of cuprates was linked to cost savings, since cheaper coolants could be used to create functional superconductors. Thus, post-1980 superconductors both feature lower temperature requirements and more desirable price points. B is the best answer, while A, C, and D refer to features or stages of the maglev effect (explained in lines 45-56), NOT to comparative issues in terms of developing superior superconductors.

49. C is the correct answer.

See the previous answer explanation for analysis of the correct line reference. A establishes a connection between superconductors and the maglev effect, B describes how the maglev effect functions, and D indicates how bucky-balls and potassium atoms can interact. None of these choices directly consider pre- and post-1980 superconductors in a comparative manner, and thus all should be eliminated.

50. B is the correct answer.

While potassium and mercury do not function as superconductors AT ALL at -100 degrees (eliminating C and D), both substances function as superconductors at -250 degrees. At this temperature, the cost per pound of potassium is just over $40 and the cost per pound of mercury is between $30 and $40. Thus, eliminate A and choose B as indicating the most cost-efficient superconductor.

51. A is the correct answer.

Mercury, a given cuprate, and potassium all decrease in cost per pound as temperatures rise; while the passage considers coolant costs (lines 60-64), the costs of superconductor materials THEMSELVES are never mentioned. Choose A and eliminate B (since physical state is not a quality considered in the graph). C wrongly assumes that the graph (which considers -250 degrees as its lowest temperature) considers absolute zero (-273.15 degrees according to line 45). D wrongly assumes that the graph (which DOES suggest which superconductors are most cost-efficient but does not indicate popularity in any statistical way) indicates which substances have been adopted by users.

Answer Explanations, Test 3

52. C is the correct answer.

The author of the passage points out that mercury can function as a superconductor near absolute zero (lines 42-45) and that cuprates function as superconductors around -135.15 degrees Celsius (lines 57-60). The graph indicates that these substances exhibit superconductor properties at roughly these temperatures, so that C is appropriate. A wrongly indicates conflict between the graph and the passage, while B introduces a judgment ("little-known") that would wrongly critique the graph as obscure (an issue that the author never considers and that goes AGAINST the author's idea that semiconductors have practical significance). D presents a misreading of the passage, which provides historical information about semiconductor research and outlines one research project that the author has undertaken but does NOT indicate deficiencies (too strong of a negative) in knowledge or outline future projects.

NOTES

- Passage 3 on Pages 68-69, "NASA's Fermi Finds Possible Dark Matter Ties in Andromeda Galaxy," is adapted from the article of the same name by Claire Saravia and published by NASA. 6 August 2017, NASA. https://www.nasa.gov/feature/goddard/2017/nasas-fermi-finds-possible-dark-matter-ties-in-andromeda-galaxy. Accessed 28 July 2019.

- Passage 4 on Pages 71-72, "Why is it fun to be frightened?" is an excerpt from the article of the same name by Margee Kerr and published by The Conversation in association with the University of Pittsburgh. 12 October 2018, The Conversation. https://theconversation.com/why-is-it-fun-to-be-frightened-101055. Accessed 28 July 2019.

- Passage 5 on Pages 74-75, "Could laser-powered superconductors spark a technological revolution?" is an excerpt from the article of the same name by Stephen Clark and published by The Conversation in partnership with the University of Bath. 10 February 2016, The Conversation. https://theconversation.com/could-laser-powered-superconductors-spark-a-technological-revolution-54294. Accessed 28 July 2019.

About the Figures: The various visual resources that accompany the passages in this section are primarily meant to facilitate critical thinking skills and may not reflect historical data.

Test 4

Full Reading Section
2020 SAT Practice

Test 4

Reading Test

65 MINUTES, 52 QUESTIONS

Turn to Section 1 of your answer sheet to answer the questions in this section.

DIRECTIONS

Each passage or pair of passages below is followed by a number of questions. After reading each passage or pair, choose the best answer to each question based on what is stated or implied in the passage or passages and in any accompanying graphics (such as a table or graph).

Questions 1-10 are based on the following passage.

This passage is adapted from B.B. Silvers, "An Austen by Any Other Name." Though composed in 2019, this work closely approximates the style of fiction from the early 19th century and depicts characters from this time period.

Alicia Ashbrook was a lady of extraordinary assets, or so John Banfield had been informed by Richard Burke, a friend whose regrettable humor took great pleasure in practical jokes. To
Line return to John, he had assumed, forgivably, that
5 the nature of these assets lay in a comfortable monetary situation. Upon discovering that these endowments lay in the lovely form of the lady herself, John found that he could count his good
10 fortune in a manner somewhat different than he had earlier supposed.
To her credit, Alicia did not pretend to a fortune beyond her means, and openly confessed that personal charms only were to be the entirety
15 of her worldly attractions. She possessed a clever mind and affectionate heart, to a degree that, forsaking her own welfare, she urged John to discover another woman, one who could better suit his straitened circumstances and improve
20 on them. He could not, John heatedly insisted, embark on so ill-advised a project as this; his feelings for her would not allow even the mention.
Alicia arched an elegant eyebrow. "My dear John, I hope you have not referred to my
25 suggestion as 'ill-advised.' Do confirm that I was mistaken." Her tone, dulcet as usual, gave the impression of steel gauntlets gloved in velvet.
John spluttered so far as his masculinity permitted. "I—Alicia, my darling—" He had
30 meant to bewail further, very eloquently so, the cruelty of his fate, and here the object of his lamentations was interrupting at the moment he had thought of a particularly ingenious line meant to impress upon everyone the depth of his loss.
35 She regarded him serenely, waiting for him to admit to the great wrong he had done her in doubting her wisdom. Alicia was not a patient woman, as well he knew, and the slow blinks of her lovely eyes signaled the danger of a readied
40 pistol.
Admitting, "I announce to all that I was as much a fool as a man can be," he moved to the fireplace mantle, on which he leaned an elbow and

struck a dashing figure of misery.

Some weeks ago, as has been stated, Richard visited his friend John for the purpose of rousing him from a state of apathy brought on by utter helplessness. The second child of a father indulgent to his profligate oldest son, John had come back from a year abroad on the continent to find his once prosperous home run to the ground in the repayment of disreputable pursuits on the part of his elder brother.

"Good God," had been John's shocked response to the news broken to him by the anxiously hovering estate manager, Fitzwilliam. "And is there nothing to be done?"

The man had wrung his hands. "I have tried to advise your good father, sir, but—"

And so John listened with growing unease to the tale of woe unleashed upon him, the end of which told of the burden falling to him to restore the family to its former standing.

John paced the study in which they were ensconced. "I could perhaps procure an honest livelihood."

Fitzwilliam's look of absolute horror showed his feelings on the matter of a gentleman earning his keep in the world.

It was then that Richard made his entrance, lightly waving aside the footman hurrying after him. "Sir, please, Mr. Banfield said he isn't to be disturbed!"

"Yes, yes, he's quite disturbed all by himself; I can hardly cause him more harm." Richard stopped short at seeing the papers cluttered all about the room, red-inked lines across nearly all of them. "Whatever is the matter?"

John glanced at Fitzwilliam and then said, "I am distressed for money." He waited for some comment of a mildly helpful nature, but apparently none was forthcoming. "And to what do I owe the honor of your presence?" he then asked, shuffling documents in an attempt to hint that Richard was making himself a bother.

Richard beamed, planting his hands on the desk to emphasize his words. "Wonderful that you ask, my good fellow! For I encountered a lady of extraordinary assets the other night."

1

Which choice best summarizes the passage as a whole?

A) A practical joke is exposed, and the perpetrator is utterly humiliated.

B) A man who is in search of financial gain falls deeply in love.

C) Two recently-acquainted men engage in a friendly rivalry.

D) A woman outsmarts the various men trying to cajole her into marriage.

2

As used in line 8, "endowments" most nearly means

A) excesses.

B) strengths.

C) confidences.

D) funds.

3

As used in line 15, "worldly" most nearly means

A) unaffected.

B) international.

C) material.

D) knowledgeable.

4

Which choice best supports the claim that John was intentionally misled?

A) Lines 15-20 ("She possessed . . . them")

B) Lines 41-44 ("Admitting . . . misery")

C) Lines 45-48 ("Some . . . helplessness")

D) Lines 87-89 ("Wonderful . . . night")

Test 4

5

The passage suggests that John's brother had

A) wasted his family's money on expensive yet personally pleasing foreign travels.

B) unfairly confiscated John's share of the family estate.

C) repeatedly and recklessly ignored Fitzwilliam's warnings.

D) not been dissuaded by John's father from depleting the family's funds.

6

It can be reasonably inferred from the passage that prior to meeting Alicia, John's primary motivation was to

A) repair his father's reputation in the wake of his brother's disgraceful behavior.

B) achieve financial security.

C) marry as soon as possible.

D) maintain his friendship with Richard.

7

Which choice provides the best evidence for the answer to the previous question?

A) Lines 21-22 ("his feelings . . . mention")

B) Lines 29-34 ("He had . . . loss")

C) Lines 54-57 ("Good . . . done?")

D) Lines 60-63 ("And so . . . standing")

8

The author compares Alicia's tone to "steel gauntlets gloved in velvet" (line 27) primarily to suggest that Alicia is

A) disguising her true feelings.

B) tacitly furious with John.

C) graceful under pressure.

D) determined to speak her mind.

9

According to the passage, John's estate manager is taken aback to learn that

A) John's elder brother has spent the family fortune.

B) Richard has arrived unannounced.

C) Richard plans to arrange a meeting with Alicia.

D) John is considering taking a paying job.

10

The main purpose of the seventh paragraph (lines 45-53) is to

A) recount in detail how John's brother spent the family's assets.

B) explain the source of John's financial woes.

C) offer a view into the daily routines of the Banfield family.

D) provide further insight into the relationship between Richard and John.

Questions 11-21 are based on the following passage and supplementary material.

This passage is adapted from "'Covert' Neurofeedback Tunes-up the Social Brain in ASD," a 2018 news update published* by the National Institute of Mental Health.

Young people with autism spectrum disorder (ASD) thought they were just playing a picture puzzle game while undergoing functional magnetic resonance imaging (fMRI) scanning.
5 In fact, the game was rigged—by their own brain activity.

The more participants spontaneously activated social brain circuitry known to be under-connected in ASD, the more pieces of a puzzle
10 filled in to reveal the picture. Since the game was controlled by circuit activity, the participants were unknowingly tuning-up their own brains. Resting state scans following the sessions revealed increased communications between two key
15 networks of the social brain that typically don't talk with each other enough in ASD. What's more, participants' parents noted improvements in their children's social behavior linked to this boost in circuit connectivity.

20 "Rather than specifying explicit tasks, the game provided positive reinforcement for spontaneously achieved desired states of circuit activity," explained Alex Martin, Ph.D., chief of NIMH's Section on Cognitive Neuropsychology.
25 "Such implicit training resulted in significant long-term connectivity increases in the suspect circuits that were correlated with improvements in behavior. This proof-of-principle suggests that covert neurofeedback may have potential as
30 an intervention in ASD—and perhaps in other disorders of circuit under-connectivity."

However promising the findings are, the researchers note that the results of this small exploratory study would have to be confirmed in
35 larger samples, and the approach would need to be adapted to a more accessible and cost-effective form of neuroimaging before it might become a practical treatment alternative.

The NIMH researchers and others had earlier
40 linked such resting state under-connectivity in social brain circuits with symptom severity and a worsening course of symptoms in ASD. So the researchers wondered whether training to boost such connectivity might improve social behavior.

45 Conducting fMRI scans while the brain is at rest predict how well brain networks communicate with each other when performing behaviors. In this case, the networks in question are normally activated during social behaviors. However,
50 training on explicit social behavior tasks only serves to re-activate dysfunctional circuit patterns underlying the social deficits seen in the disorder.

Enter post-doctoral fellow Michal Ramot, Ph.D. She devised a training scheme based on
55 open-ended, implicit, non-social tasks. The researchers told participants in the scanner—17 young adult males with ASD and 10 without ASD—to do whatever might fill in pieces of a picture puzzle on a computer screen. Participants
60 were promised monetary rewards and bonuses for completing the puzzles.

Unbeknownst to the participants, a computer running the game was programmed to fill in pieces of the picture whenever the scanner
65 detected increased chatter between the two social brain networks that are under-communicative in ASD. The more participants spontaneously activated the targeted social brain circuitry, the more pieces of the picture appeared.

70 "Showing faces or other social stimuli would only activate networks wired in a sub-optimal way, so we found a way to bypass this," explained Ramot. "We show pictures that are completely unrelated to social behavior that we thought
75 participants would like, while still being relatively abstract—such as mechanical things or board games. Participants never really reach the 'true' strategy, because there is no explicit strategy for getting these networks to co-activate. That's why
80 the scanner is useful. When we do neurofeedback, we go directly to the networks."

Resting state scans taken immediately following each of the four training sessions revealed increased functional connectivity

---
*See Page 120 for the citation for this text.

85 between the two targeted brain regions in most participants with ASD. Participants without ASD did not show a significant change in functional connectivity between the targeted networks. Parents of participants with ASD noted
90 improvements in their children's social behavior that correlated with the increased connectivity. While falling short of an overall statistically significant change in sociability, the research demonstrated that change in the behaviorally-
95 relevant networks correlated with a change in behavior.

11

The main purpose of the second paragraph is to

A) provide a description of a medical condition.
B) describe the unexpected results of a study.
C) detail the mechanics of an exercise.
D) question the validity of a research method.

12

The author indicates that the individuals who participated in the puzzle game

A) exhibited uniform improvement across several different metrics after playing.
B) generally behaved more obediently for their parents in the aftermath of the study.
C) had previously had trouble forming social bonds with peers their own age.
D) did not consciously control the outcome of the game.

13

Which choice provides the best evidence for the answer to the previous question?

A) Lines 1-4 ("Young . . . scanning")
B) Lines 7-10 ("The more . . . picture")
C) Lines 16-19 ("What's . . . connectivity")
D) Lines 25-28 ("Such . . . behavior")

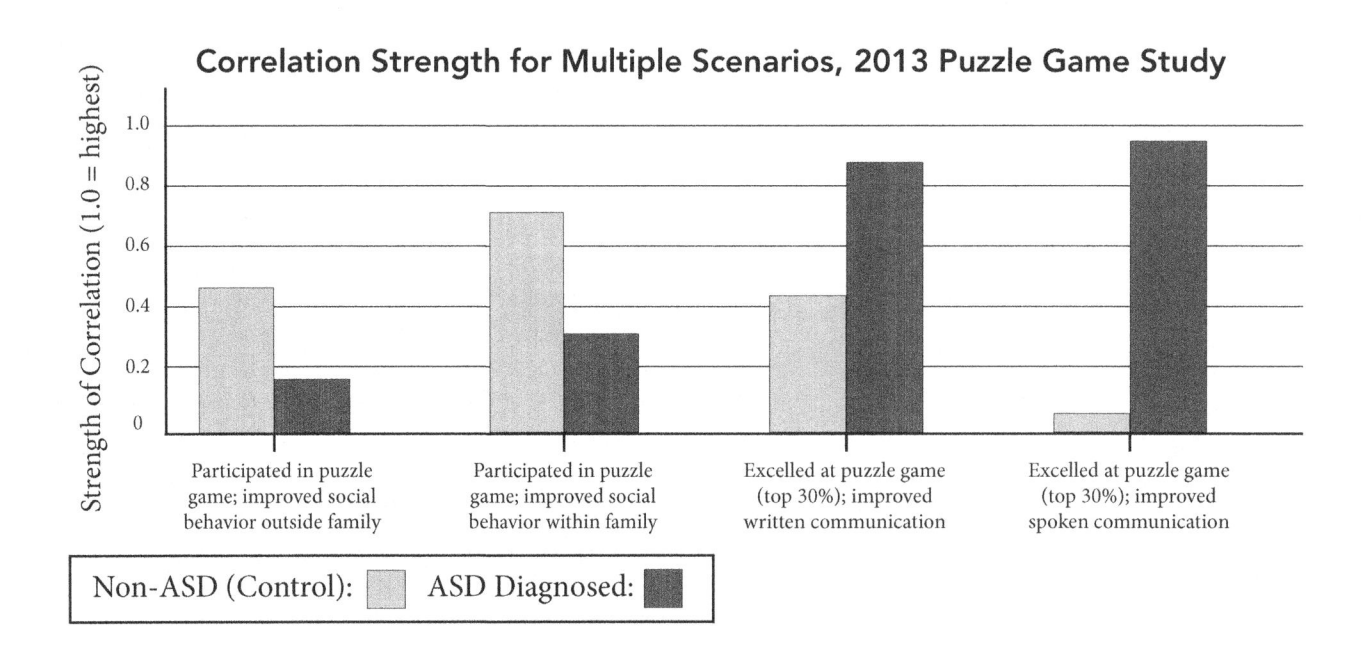

Correlation Strength for Multiple Scenarios, 2013 Puzzle Game Study

Bar chart showing Strength of Correlation (1.0 = highest) for four scenarios, comparing Non-ASD (Control) and ASD Diagnosed groups:

- Participated in puzzle game; improved social behavior outside family: Non-ASD ≈ 0.46, ASD ≈ 0.16
- Participated in puzzle game; improved social behavior within family: Non-ASD ≈ 0.71, ASD ≈ 0.31
- Excelled at puzzle game (top 30%); improved written communication: Non-ASD ≈ 0.44, ASD ≈ 0.88
- Excelled at puzzle game (top 30%); improved spoken communication: Non-ASD ≈ 0.05, ASD ≈ 0.95

14

Which choice implies that designing interventions for autism spectrum disorder can be a difficult task?

A) Lines 5-6 ("In fact . . . activity")
B) Lines 10-12 ("Since . . . brains")
C) Lines 49-52 ("However . . . disorder")
D) Lines 92-96 ("While . . . behavior")

15

As used in line 50, "explicit" most nearly means

A) egregious.
B) coarse.
C) obvious.
D) threatening.

16

The data from the NIMH study can be described as

A) somewhat inconclusive.
B) ethically obtained.
C) unequivocally promising.
D) rigorously assessed.

17

Which of the following situations is most analogous to the dynamic created by the puzzle game?

A) A teacher gives an A+ to a student chosen at random.
B) A parent buys her son a car as a reward for his high grades.
C) A company offers a bonus to employees who exercise for at least five hours per week.
D) A gardener gives extra water to flowers that display a particular shade of pink.

18

As used in line 93, "significant" most nearly means

A) measurable.
B) distinguished.
C) symbolic.
D) powerful.

19

Which of the following factors, according to the graph, exhibits the weakest correlation for the control group?

A) Participated in game, behavior within family
B) Participated in game, behavior outside family
C) Excelled at game, written communication
D) Excelled at game, spoken communication

20

The research endeavors detailed in the graph and in the passage are similar in that both projects involve

A) incentives for performing well in a puzzle game.
B) clear benchmarks that indicate high performance.
C) correlations between behavior and brain activity.
D) a non-ASD experimental group.

21

Which of the following considerations would most effectively help to place the findings recorded in the graph in the context of Alex Martin's research?

A) How early in life ASD is typically diagnosed
B) How fMRI data relates to improved behavior
C) Academic performance statistics for the control group subjects
D) Family size statistics for the ASD group subjects

Questions 22-32 are based on the following passages.

Passage 1 is an excerpt from John Woinarski and Peter Harrison, "To save Australia's mammals we need a change of heart." Passage 2 is an excerpt from William Lynn, "Australia's war on feral cats: shaky science, missing ethics." The two articles were published* by The Conversation in 2014 and 2015, respectively.

Passage 1

Cats are the greatest threat to Australia's mammals. Like many other threats, they are now a pervasive and deeply-entrenched problem, and we recognise that it will not be solved simply or quickly.

There are some measures we can implement immediately: translocating threatened species, establishing a network of cat-proof enclosures, and better management of dingoes and wild dogs (which can help control cat populations).

But we also need to look at long-term solutions. This has formidable challenges. Current trials in cat-baiting are promising, but we don't yet know if they will work on a large scale. Biological control (such as a disease) may take decades to develop, and has to overcome concerns from cat owners and risks to other Australian wildlife and cat species overseas.

Even so, controlling cats is likely to do more for the conservation of Australia's biodiversity than any other single action. But we have concluded that we will not solve the mammal extinction crisis simply by repeating the same actions over and over. The problem is far more fundamental.

Conservation is not just an environmental problem; it also charts a moral landscape. How does our society fit into this land? What do we consider important? Is it reasonable that we leave our descendants only a faint shadow of our country's extraordinary nature?

We have worked extensively in remote Australia. We have shown old Aboriginal men and women stuffed museum specimens of now-vanished mammals and been struck to our core by their responses: singing the song of that animal, stroking it, telling its story, crying at its loss. Here is an affinity to nature, a deep connection to our land, an ache of responsibility, that we settler Australians have not yet felt or learned. To become part of this country, to care for it properly, we need to grow some of that sense of belonging and affinity. Otherwise, extinctions will continue to be viewed as inconsequential.

Passage 2

In July 2015, the Australian government announced a "war on feral cats," with the intention of killing over two million felines by 2020. The threat abatement plan to enforce this policy includes a mix of shooting, trapping, and a reputedly "humane" poison.

Some conservationists in Australia are hailing this as an important step toward the rewilding of Australia's outback, or the idea of restoring the continent's biodiversity to its state prior to European contact. . . .

Traditional conservation likes to think of lethal measures such as hunting, trapping, and poisoning as unproblematic tools for achieving management goals. The legitimacy of this idea rests on the assumption that "individuals don't matter," itself a reflection that only people and/or ecosystems, not individual animals, have intrinsic moral value.

Yet there is a powerful movement of wildlife advocates and managers pushing back against this presumption. Flying under various names—like humane wildlife management and compassionate conservation—its proponents say we should consider the well-being of both ecosystems and individual animals. This is right not only because of the intrinsic value of the animals being managed, but also because many of these animals require stable social structures to thrive.

While feral cats may live solitary lives, outdoor cats in general are very social, frequently living with human beings, being cared for as community cats, and interacting with other felines in extended cat colonies. Out of respect for cats and the people who care for them, we should give preference to nonlethal alternatives in management first and foremost.

---

*See Page 120 for the citations for these texts.

To be sure, advocates for outdoor cats often have their own scientific and ethical blind spots about cats on the whole and about
85 nonlethal management strategies. There may even be times when the threat of feral cats to a vulnerable species is so great that lethal action may be justified. Nevertheless, even the most ardent supporter of rewilding should admit
90 that it is human beings who bear direct moral responsibility for the ongoing loss of biodiversity in our world. A war on cats ignores their intrinsic value, wrongly blames them for mistakes of our own making, and fails to adequately use nonlethal
95 measures to manage cats and wildlife.

As an ethicist, I care about both native wildlife and cats. It is time to stop blaming the victim, face up to our own culpability, and seek to rewild our world with an eye to the ethics of our actions.
100 There is no justification for a war on outdoor cats—feral or otherwise—based on shaky science and an absence of ethical reasoning.

22

The authors of Passage 1 concede that efforts to control feral cats

A) could be costly.
B) will have not have measurable effects in the near term.
C) should not take priority over efforts to confront larger ecological threats.
D) might cause collateral damage.

23

Which choice provides the best evidence for the answer to the previous question?

A) Lines 2-5 ("Like . . . quickly")
B) Lines 6-10 ("There . . . populations")
C) Lines 15-18 ("Biological . . . overseas")
D) Lines 21-24 ("But we . . . and over")

24

As used in line 25, "fundamental" most nearly means

A) foundational.
B) outrageous.
C) dire.
D) simplistic.

25

The author of Passage 2 suggests that conservationists who advocate aggressive population control tactics are

A) manufacturing scientific evidence to support their claims.
B) pushing a dangerous and unpopular agenda.
C) overlooking the value of particular living beings.
D) well-intentioned but ultimately self-sabotaging.

26

Which choice provides the best evidence for the answer to the previous question?

A) Lines 51-55 ("Some . . . contact")
B) Lines 59-63 ("The legitimacy . . . value")
C) Lines 88-92 ("Nevertheless . . . world")
D) Lines 100-102 ("There . . . reasoning")

27

As used in line 51, "hailing" most nearly means

A) summoning.
B) idolizing.
C) explaining.
D) celebrating.

28

As used in line 66, "presumption" most nearly means

A) entitlement.
B) belief.
C) discourtesy.
D) anticipation.

29

Both authors would agree that a portion of Australia's population of feral cats

A) should be treated no differently than any other animal population.
B) can be justifiably exterminated under certain conditions.
C) is at least partially responsible for the extinction of certain Australian mammals.
D) has indirectly harmed the Aboriginal population.

30

The author of Passage 2 would characterize the anecdote about Aboriginal Australians provided by the authors of Passage 1 in lines 32-40 ("We have . . . learned") as

A) unfairly valuing some animals over others.
B) arrogantly patronizing an oppressed people.
C) neglecting the point of an indigenous tradition.
D) overly concerned with an obscure problem.

31

How might the authors of Passage 1 respond to the argument in lines 97-99 ("It is . . . actions") in Passage 2?

A) There is scant scientific evidence that animals have any "intrinsic value."
B) Human beings should not suffer to preserve another species.
C) Regardless of who bears responsibility for Australia's ecological degradation, the most effective measure to address it is control of feral cats.
D) Certain tough moral decisions must be made to address the environmental emergency that can be linked to the presence of feral cats.

32

Which choice best summarizes the ways that the passages assess the risks created by Australia's feral cats?

A) Passage 1 indicates that feral cats pose an existential threat to Australia's mammals, while Passage 2 argues that killing animals is wrong under all scenarios.
B) Passage 1 indicates that feral cats have negative effects beyond ecological damage, while Passage 2 argues that a "war on feral cats" is ethically suspect.
C) Passage 1 indicates that feral cats can be completely eliminated, while Passage 2 argues that such a scheme would be impractical.
D) Passage 1 indicates that feral cats disrupt Australia's ecological balance, while Passage 2 argues that wiping them out would result in an extensive public backlash.

Questions 33-42 are based on the following passage.

This passage is adapted from John Quincy Adams, the 1821 Speech on Independence Day delivered to the United States House of Representatives.

   Long before the Declaration of Independence, the great mass of the people of America and of the people of Britain had become total strangers to each other. The people of America were known to the people of Britain only by the transactions of trade; by shipments of lumber and flax-seed, indigo and tobacco. They were known to the government only by half a dozen colonial agents, humble, and often spurned suitors at the feet of power, and by royal governors, minions of patronage, sent from the footstool of a throne beyond the seas, to rule a people of whom they knew nothing; as if an inhabitant of the moon should descend to give laws to the dwellers upon earth. Here and there, a man of letters and a statesman, conversant with all history, knew something of the colonies, as he knew something of Cochin China and Japan. Yet even the prime minister of England, urging upon his omnipotent parliament laws for grinding the colonies to submission, could talk, without amazing or diverting his hearers, of the island of Virginia: even Edmund Burke, a man of more ethereal mind, apologizing to the people of Bristol, for the offence of sympathizing with the distresses of our country, ravaged by the fire and sword of Britons, asked indulgence for his feelings on the score of general humanity, and expressly declared that the Americans were a nation utter strangers to him, and among whom he was not sure of having a single acquaintance. The sympathies therefore most essential to the communion of country were, between the British and American people, extinct. Those most indispensable to the just relation between sovereign and subject had never existed and could not exist between the British government and the American people. The connexion was unnatural, and it was in the moral order no less than in the positive decrees of Providence, that it should be dissolved.

   Yet, fellow-citizens, these are not the causes of the separation assigned in the paper which I am about to read. The connexion between different portions of the same people and between a people and their government is a connexion of duties as well as of rights. In the long conflict of twelve years which had preceded and led to the Declaration of Independence, our fathers had been not less faithful to their duties, than tenacious of their rights. Their resistance had not been rebellion. It was not a restive and ungovernable spirit of ambition, bursting from the bonds of colonial subjection; it was the deep and wounded sense of successive wrongs, upon which complaint had been only answered by aggravation, and petition repelled with contumely, which had driven them to their last stand upon the adamantine rock of human rights.

   It was then fifteen months after the blood of Lexington and Bunker's hill, after Charlestown and Falmouth, fired by British hands, were but heaps of ashes, after the ear of the adder had been turned to two successive supplications to the throne; after two successive appeals to the people of Britain, as friends, countrymen, and brethren, to which no responsive voice of sympathetic tenderness had been returned,

   "Nought but the noise of drums and timbrels loud, Their children's cries unheard that passed through fire To the grim idol."*

   Then it was that the thirteen United Colonies of North America, by their delegates in Congress assembled, exercising the first act of sovereignty by a right ever inherent in the people, but never to be resorted to, save at the awful crisis when civil society is solved into its first elements, declared themselves free and independent states.

*A quotation from the epic poem *Paradise Lost*.

Test 4

33

The main purpose of the passage is to

A) repair a damaged relationship.
B) offer a detailed account of an event.
C) provide justification for a course of action.
D) criticize a former rival.

34

The author's tone can best be described as

A) world-weary.
B) questioning.
C) cynical.
D) self-assured.

35

According to Adams, the authors of the Declaration of Independence can best be characterized as

A) idealistic rebels furthering a righteous cause.
B) loyal subjects who had been treated unfairly.
C) skilled strategists whose violence was justified
D) wealthy landowners who were excessively burdened.

36

Which choice provides the best evidence for the answer to the previous question?

A) Lines 4-6 ("The people . . . trade")
B) Lines 7-13 ("They . . . nothing")
C) Lines 31-34 ("The sympathies . . . extinct")
D) Lines 53-58 ("it was . . . rights")

37

In describing the history of the colonies that eventually became the United States, Adams sets forward the idea that

A) monarchy is an inherently unjust system of government.
B) rebellion against a ruling authority should avoided except in extreme circumstances.
C) reconciliation between world powers that were once at war is desirable.
D) the United States should maintain powerful armed forces in order to prevent civil unrest.

38

Which choice provides the best evidence for the answer to the previous question?

A) Lines 15-18 ("Here . . . Japan")
B) Lines 41-43 ("Yet . . . read)
C) Lines 59-64 ("It was . . . throne")
D) Lines 71-77 ("Then . . . states")

39

As used in line 19, "omnipotent" most nearly means

A) accommodating.
B) forceful.
C) uncontrolled.
D) respected.

40

The author employs the phrase "the island of Virginia" (line 22) primarily to

A) demonstrate that the colonies were completely cut off from the outside world.
B) show that the British held a low opinion of the American colonists.
C) suggest that British leaders lacked a grasp of fundamental colonial issues.
D) indicate that the prime minister was in disagreement with parliament.

41

As used in line 50, "tenacious of" most nearly means

A) protective of.
B) rebellious for.
C) understanding of.
D) stubborn towards.

42

The main purpose of the description of the events referenced in lines 59-67 is to

A) demonstrate that the colonists had exhausted all of their options when they ultimately declared independence.
B) accuse the British of excessive violence during the war for independence.
C) appeal to the British people in a spirit of friendship despite past conflicts.
D) explain the monarch's role in the conflict between Britain and the colonies.

Questions 43-52 are based on the following passage and supplementary material.

This passage is adapted from Tina Garrett, "Sharing Is Caring: Varied Diets in Dinosaurs Promoted Coexistence," an article originally published* in 2014 by EveryONE, the community blog of the research journal PLOS ONE.

Everyone loves a good dinosaur discovery. Though they're few and far between, sometimes we get lucky, finding feather imprints, mohawks, or birthing sites that reinvigorate public interest
5 and provide bursts of insight about how these animals ruled the Earth before our arrival.
　Dinosaurs must have been doing something right because they coexisted for millions of years, much longer than we humans have even been
10 on the planet. In an article recently published in PLOS ONE, University of Calgary researchers studied markings on dinosaur teeth to determine how a diverse group of megaherbivores—plant-eating species whose adults weighed in at over
15 1,000 kg—was able to coexist in Canada for at least 1.5 million years. The authors' findings suggest that these dinosaurs managed to last so long by eating things that the others didn't, thereby reducing competition for food and
20 promoting a more harmonious (if dinosaur life could be considered so) coexistence.
　The authors of this study started by taking a look at general tooth shape and any markings visible to the naked eye before moving onto
25 examine the microscopic markings on teeth. The presence of certain small shapes or marks on teeth may indicate what type of food an individual ate during its lifetime, and can be analyzed using a technique called microwear analysis. As you
30 might guess, foods with different textures or hardness leave different markings on our teeth. For instance, pits in the teeth suggest consumption of hard foods like nuts, while scratches are linked to the ingestion of tough leaves or meat. A
35 combination of both reflects a varied diet.

*See Page 120 for the citation for this text.

The researchers analyzed a group of 76 fossils from 16 species in three ancestral groups, focusing on teeth still connected to skulls to provide more accurate species identification. These three groups lived together during the Cretaceous period in the Dinosaur Park Formation of Alberta, Canada, which at that point was on an island continent called Laramidia.

Ankylosauria were a group of armored, stocky dinosaurs. One subgroup, the ankylosaurids, had small, cusp-like teeth good for eating fruits and softer plant tissues, while another, the nodosaurids, had blade-like teeth useful for tougher and more fibrous plant tissues. Microwear analysis showed no significant difference between these two subgroups, meaning that, despite differences in general tooth shape, results indicate that their diets did not differ significantly. The evidence of both pits and scratches on their teeth suggests that both ate a variety of fruits and softer foliage.

Hadrosauridae—identifiable by their duckbill-shaped face—had similar microwear to the Ankylosauria, suggesting that they also had a generalized diet, though their broad teeth, likely used for crushing food, may have made it easier for them to consume all parts of targeted plants, including stems and seeds, than would the cusp or blade-like teeth found in the Ankylosauria.

Ceratopsidae, a family of thick-skulled, horned dinosaurs, including the well-known Triceratops, had teeth that functioned as shears, suggesting that they consumed particularly tough plants. Microwear analysis supports this idea, indicating more scratches than pits, and showing that these dinosaurs may have subsisted on mainly rough foliage, like twigs and leaves.

The evidence provided by microwear analysis, incorporated with other known facts about these species—such as height, skull shape, and jaw mechanics—helps paint a broader picture of the dinosaur food scene in Laramidia and supports previous research suggesting that the varied diets allowed these large species to coexist for more than 1.5 million years. Maybe we can take some cues from them to make sure we are at least as successful. Fingers crossed no meteors come along to ruin our chances.

43

The tone of this passage can best be described as

A) opinionated and elevated.
B) skeptical and analytical.
C) conversational and informative.
D) abstract and nostalgic.

44

According to the passage, microwear analysis supports the hypothesis that megaherbivores coexisted peacefully as a result of

A) the unique vegetation native to Laramidia.
B) the diverse designs of their teeth.
C) an inherent aversion to physical violence
D) different food preferences for dinosaur groups.

45

Which choice provides the best evidence for the answer to the previous question?

A) Lines 16-21 ("The authors' . . . coexistence")
B) Lines 25-29 ("The presence . . . analysis")
C) Lines 32-34 ("For instance . . . meat")
D) Lines 39-43 ("These . . . Laramidia)

46

It can be inferred from the passage that if the researchers were to find a set of teeth several inches away from a skull, they would

A) run microwear analysis on the teeth in order to classify the skull as a particular species.
B) not immediately assume that the two items belonged to the same species.
C) excavate the surrounding area to find any other potential samples.
D) document their discoveries in an academic study even while voicing possible reservations.

47

What does the passage imply about using microwear analysis to draw conclusions about the past?

A) It can, with a high degree of accuracy, provide the age of a fossilized tooth.
B) Its conclusions are habitually considered in light of other archaeological observations.
C) In some cases, it is deeply unreliable.
D) It is used specifically to gauge the dietary habits of megaherbivores during the Cretaceous period.

48

Which choice provides the best evidence for the answer to the previous question?

A) Lines 10-16 ("In an article . . . years")
B) Lines 45-49 ("One subgroup . . . tissues")
C) Lines 49-53 ("Microwear . . . significantly")
D) Lines 73-80 ("The evidence . . . years")

49

It can be inferred from the passage that microwear analysis conducted on the teeth of a primarily carnivorous dinosaur would most likely contain

A) more scratches than pits.
B) more pits than scratches.
C) an approximate balance of pits and scratches.
D) very few pits or scratches.

50

As used in line 78, "varied" most nearly means

A) balanced.
B) distinct.
C) changing.
D) random.

Test 4

Microwear Analysis of Dinosaur Teeth (Fossilized)

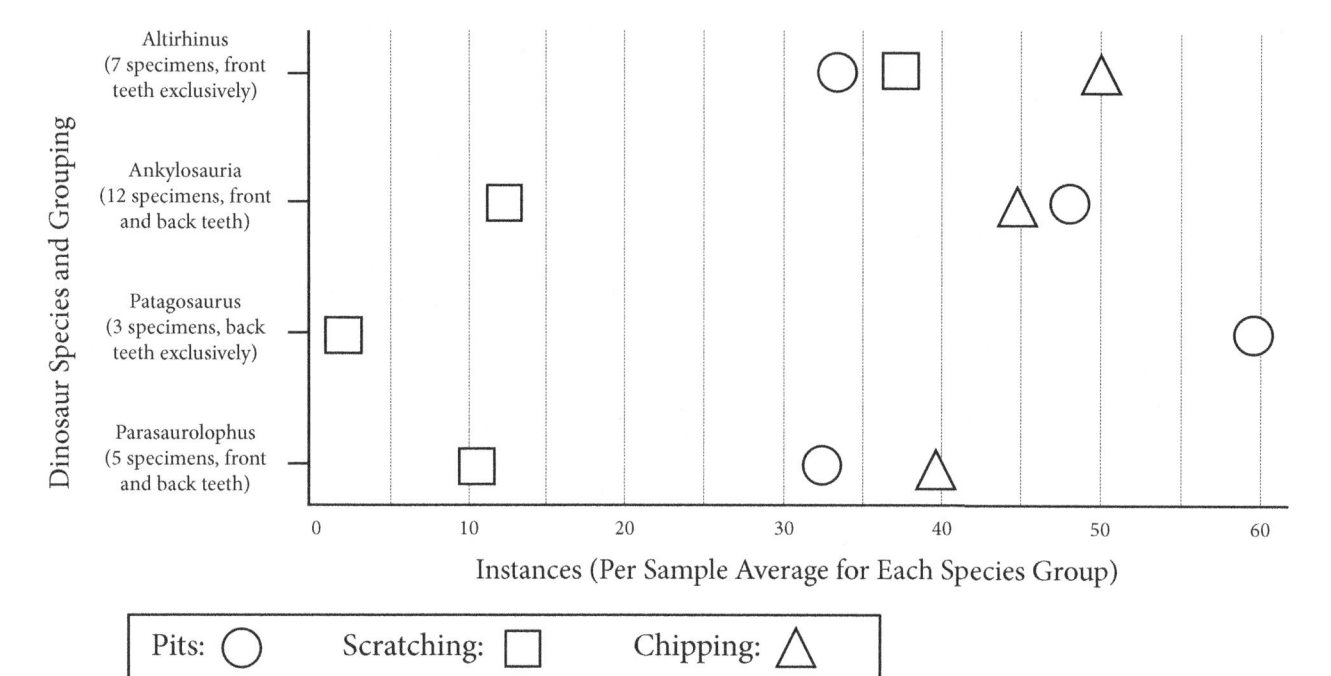

Dinosaur Species and Grouping	Instances (Per Sample Average for Each Species Group)
Altirhinus (7 specimens, front teeth exclusively)	Pits ~33, Scratching ~37, Chipping ~50
Ankylosauria (12 specimens, front and back teeth)	Scratching ~12, Chipping ~45, Pits ~48
Patagosaurus (3 specimens, back teeth exclusively)	Scratching ~2, Pits ~60
Parasaurolophus (5 specimens, front and back teeth)	Scratching ~10, Pits ~33, Chipping ~40

Pits: ○   Scratching: □   Chipping: △

51

A student claims that chipping is characteristic of carnivorous dinosaurs only. Which information, in relation to the passage and the graph, best disproves the student's claim?

A) Parasaurolophus was primarily a herbivore but would consume small animals when appropriate plant sustenance was unavailable.

B) Pantagosaurs fed largely on tough plants that much smaller dinosaurs could not easily digest.

C) Altirhinus was carnivorous yet was itself hunted by larger meat-eating dinosaurs.

D) Anyklosaurs were known to feed exclusively on plant matter but consumed both tough and soft vegetation.

52

On the basis of the passage, which dinosaur species considered in the graph most likely had a varied diet?

A) Altirhinus
B) Ankylosauria
C) Pantagosaurus
D) Parasaurolophus

STOP

If you finish before time is called, you may check your work on this section only.
Do not turn to any other section.

Answer Key on the Next Page

Answer Key: Test 4

Passage 1	Passage 2	Passage 3	Passage 4	Passage 5
1. B	11. C	22. D	33. C	43. C
2. B	12. D	23. C	34. D	44. D
3. C	13. B	24. A	35. B	45. A
4. D	14. C	25. C	36. D	46. B
5. D	15. C	26. B	37. B	47. B
6. B	16. A	27. D	38. D	48. D
7. D	17. D	28. B	39. B	49. A
8. A	18. A	29. B	40. C	50. B
9. D	19. D	30. A	41. A	51. D
10. B	20. D	31. C	42. A	52. A
	21. B	32. B		

Question Types

Major Issue
1, 33-34, 43

Passage Details
5, 8-10, 11, 16-17, 40, 42, 46, 49

Command of Evidence
4, 6-7, 12-14, 22-23, 25-26, 35-38, 44-45, 47-48

Word in Context
2-3, 15, 18, 24, 27-28, 39, 41, 50

Graphics and Visuals
19-21, 51-52

Passage Comparison
29-32

Answer Explanations
Test 4, Pages 92-106

Passage 1, Pages 92-94

1. B is the correct answer.

In the passage, John Banfield is informed by Richard Burke of a "lady of extraordinary assets" and incorrectly assumes that the assets are monetary (lines 1-7). When John meets Alicia, he discovers that she is not wealthy (lines 12-15). However, John falls in love with Alicia, attracted to her beauty and other characteristics (lines 15-22). John is then taken aback when Alicia firmly tells him to move on (lines 23-25). Together, such pieces of evidence support B, while A is incorrect because John does not feel humiliated, but rather defeated. C is incorrect because no rivalry exists between Richard and John (who are instead friends). D is incorrect because Richard (despite mentioning Alicia to John) does not interact with Alicia himself.

2. B is the correct answer.

In lines 8-9, the narrator states that Alicia's "endowments lay in the lovely form of the lady herself," leading John to conclude in lines 10-11 that the endowments, which are not financial, were "somewhat different than he had earlier supposed." In this context, the term relates to something potent or admirable (whether in terms of money or appearance), so that B is appropriate. Choices A (negative) and C (social interaction) are incorrect because they raise improper contexts for discussing naturally positive attributes, while D goes AGAINST the passage's central idea that Alicia is not in fact wealthy.

3. C is the correct answer.

In lines 12-15, the narrator states that "Alicia did not pretend to a fortune beyond her means" and that "personal charms only were to be the entirety of her worldly attractions." Then, the narrator states in lines 17-19 that Alicia "urged John to discover another woman, one who could better suit his straitened circumstances." In this context, the circumstances refer to John's dire financial situation, and "fortune" refers to material possessions. C is thus appropriate. A (sense of calm), B (travel or connections), and D (learning or information) appear to raise positives but are NOT directly relevant to a discussion of finances as required by the passage.

Answer Explanations, Test 4

4. D is the correct answer.

In lines 87-89, Richard excitedly shares that he "encountered a lady of extraordinary assets the other night," following John's admission in line 80 that he is "distressed for money." Richard was clear in his intention to trick John (lines 1-4), as Alicia's assets were personal characteristics that could not be used to cover his debts, as D appropriately indicates. A wrongly refers to Alicia's positive attributes, while B wrongly refers to John's response to Alicia; neither choice refers to Richard or his apparent trickery. C is incorrect because it refers to the beginning of Richard and John's interaction, NOT to an outcome relating to one character being misled.

5. D is the correct answer.

After the narrator states that John's brother was involved "in the repayment of disreputable pursuits" (line 52), Fitzwilliam tells John that he "tried to advise your good father" (lines 58-59), suggesting that John's father was notified. D is thus appropriate, while A is incorrect because John had returned from foreign travel, NOT his brother. B is incorrect because there is no mention of stealing from John (despite the brother's OTHER problematic behavior), while C is incorrect because (even though a warning against bad behavior would be reasonable) Fitzwilliam did not directly state that he warned John's brother. If anything, lines 58-59 indicate that Fitzwilliam had attempted to warn John's father instead.

6. B is the correct answer.

In lines 60-63, John feels "the burden falling on him to restore the family to its former standing" after learning of his brother's depletion of the family funds. Thus, he sought a financial solution to the issue. Moreover, the author provides several hints that display John's true intention for meeting Alicia. It is stated in line 2 that John "had been informed" of Alicia's "assets," which were expected to "lay in a comfortable monetary situation" (line 7). Since these phrases were written in the past tense, preceding John's meeting with Alicia, it can be reasonably inferred that John was primarily motived for financial reasons; B is thus the best answer. A (family reputation) and C (marriage) refer to themes that are indeed present in the passage but that are not EXPLICITLY linked to John's set of goals (which mostly involves finances). D similarly calls attention to an actual feature of the passage (continuing a friendship with Richard) that, while important as a theme, is not explicitly designated as a primary goal.

7. D is the correct answer.

See the previous answer explanation for analysis of the correct line reference. A indicates the intensity of John's feelings for Alicia, B indicates that John finds himself in an intense predicament, and C indicates that John is displeased with his family's situation. Though these answers call attention to themes such as finances and marriage, they do not outline specific goals and should all be eliminated as irrelevant to the previous question.

8. A is the correct answer.

The term "steel gauntlets gloved in velvet" refers to a type of concealment, since the steel is covered in velvet as a form of disguise. Alicia was stern in her suggestion to John, although her fair voice "gave the impression" of disguise (lines 26-27), so that A is appropriate. Other answers overstate the sense of conflict present in the passage: B is incorrect because Alicia was not furious with John, and C is incorrect because Alicia did not feel pressure. D is incorrect because it directly CONTRADICTS the idea that Alicia is concealing the force of her emotions.

9. D is the correct answer.

In lines 65-66, John states that he "could perhaps procure an honest livelihood." In response, Fitzwilliam has a "look of absolute horror" (line 67), so that D properly captures Fitzwilliam's disconcerted reaction to John's desire to earn a living. A is incorrect because Fitzwilliam was troubled to share the news with John but NOT surprised or necessarily offended. B is incorrect because this answer confuses Fitzwilliam's reaction to Richard with the strongly negative reaction of a footman (lines 71-74), when in fact Fitzwilliam is mostly put off by John's prospects. C is incorrect because, although Fitzwilliam was present during the invitation to meet Alicia, Fitzwilliam did not react to this news in a significantly surprised or negative manner.

10. B is the correct answer.

In the seventh paragraph, the narrator provides a backstory leading to an explanation of John's financial situation. The narrator states that John's brother was involved "in the repayment of disreputable pursuits," while John was abroad (line 52). Thus, the paragraph highlights how the situation was suddenly presented to John, who was away while the issue arose, so that B is appropriate. A is incorrect because details aren't provided as how the family assets were spent (only that they WERE spent in a problematic way). C is incorrect because everyday family information is omitted (beyond the discussion of the poor finances), while D is incorrect because the paragraph doesn't concern Richard (who enters the scene later on).

Passage 2, Pages 95-97

11. C is the correct answer.

In the second paragraph, the author explains how participants in an experiment completed a puzzle to reveal a picture, mentions the "Resting state scans" (lines 12-13) that yielded information, and notes "improvements" (line 17) that resulted. This content justifies C, since the paragraph is dedicated to a process and its outcomes. A mistakes a detail ("medical condition") for the ENTIRE focus of the paragraph, which examines procedures rather than providing a definition alone. B (surprise) and D (questioning) go against this mostly neutral and informative paragraph, which does not challenge ideas or raise clear grounds for skepticism.

12. D is the correct answer.

In lines 7-10, the author indicates that the puzzle game results were "spontaneously" activated; this content is explained by the earlier statement that the game was "rigged" (line 5) so that spontaneous, but not intentional or conscious, actions yielded results. D reflects this information. While the study did result in overall behavioral improvements (lines 16-19), A (uniform) overstates the degree of improvement and B (obedience) is overly

Answer Explanations, Test 4

specific in explaining the type of improvement. C wrongly criticizes the individuals involved in the study, who did exhibit improvements but were NOT characterized as troubled before the study took place.

13. B is the correct answer.

See the previous answer explanation for analysis of the correct line reference. A indicates an assumption made by the participants but does NOT (in the manner of B) indicate that such an assumption about the game's function might not be fully reliable. C and D both note positive outcomes but are neither broad enough to justify the idea of uniformity in A in the previous question nor precise enough to justify the discussion of obedience in B in the previous question.

14. C is the correct answer.

In lines 49-52, the author indicates that "training on explicit social behavior tasks," a possible intervention, is a problematic approach that (according to the subsequent discussion) required a corrective in Ramot's research. Choose C and eliminate A and B, both of which note the design of an ASD intervention game but do NOT clearly signal challenges. D notes that not all goals of an inquiry were achieved but that the findings were nonetheless significant; this predominantly positive choice notes problems in outcomes, NOT design.

15. C is the correct answer.

The word "explicit" refers to tasks that are problematic for use in addressing ASD and that are contrasted with the maneuvers of a more "implicit" (line 55) or indirect approach. These tasks are thus evident or unconcealed when presented to the participants. Choose C and eliminate A (indicating that something is extremely bad), B (indicating lack of refinement), and D (indicating fear or danger) as inappropriately negative.

16. A is the correct answer.

In explaining the results of the NIMH study, the author notes that the findings fall "short of an overall statistically significant change in sociability" (lines 92-93). If the findings have not resolved a key statistical issue related to a desired outcome (sociability), then such findings are inconclusive at least in this respect. Choose A and eliminate B (ethics) as an answer that raises a topic (morality or medical standards) that the passage does not explicitly consider or analyze in explaining how statistics were obtained. C and D are both overly positive and are thus inappropriate for findings that were not entirely definitive.

17. D is the correct answer.

The passage explains that the individuals who participated in the puzzle game achieved desired results WITHOUT themselves being conscious of how the results were achieved, since their standards and those of the game did not align (lines 1-10 and 62-67). D presents a scenario that involves rewards that are earned WITHOUT consciousness (the unconscious flowers) of the standards for the rewards. In contrast, A, B, and C all present human subjects who, in each situation, would or could naturally be conscious that their positive activities would align with rewards; these answers should thus be eliminated.

Answer Explanations, Test 4

18. A is the correct answer.

The word "significant" is used in the context of statistics and refers to a quantity that is seen as "falling short" (line 92) of a specific level or measurement. A is thus appropriate, while B and D are wrongly positive for a measure that would in fact fall short. C (indicating one item or thing that opens different, often creative interpretations) is inappropriate for a context of quantities and measurements.

19. D is the correct answer.

For the control group (light bar), A represents a correlation of just over 0.4, B represents a correlation of roughly 0.7, C represents a correlation of just over 0.4, and D represents a correlation of under 0.1. Because higher numbers indicate stronger correlations, D indicates the weakest correlation.

20. D is the correct answer.

While the research described in the passage considered test subjects without ASD (lines 56-58), the graph directly records the reactions of a non-ASD control group. This information supports D as the best answer. A and C consider factors that are considered ONLY in the passage, while B mis-construes the graph's different correlation strengths as benchmarks for performance; while results varied, there is no DEFINED standard or correlation number that would distinguish "low performance" and "high performance."

21. B is the correct answer.

Because the NIMH research involved fMRI scans alongside behavioral considerations (lines 45-47), the graph (which considers behavior only) could be placed in the context of this research with the introduction of fMRI data. Choose B as appropriate. A, C, and D all introduce factors about the backgrounds of ASD subjects, but the passage does not explicitly consider these factors in the manner that it considers behavioral improvement. Thus, eliminate these choices as irrelevant to both the passage AND the graph.

Passage 3, Pages 98-100

22. D is the correct answer.

In lines 15-18, the authors of Passage 1 indicate several liabilities that are linked to control of cat populations, including concerns from cat owners and threats to animals that are not direct control targets. This information supports D as appropriate. A raises a liability (cost) that may or may not link to collateral damage but that, in any case, the passage does not directly consider. B is directly contradicted by lines 6-7, while C is contradicted by the fact that the authors of the passage see controlling cat populations as an urgent threat that should ITSELF be a priority.

Answer Explanations, Test 4

23. C is the correct answer.

See the previous answer explanation for analysis of the correct line reference. A calls attention to the severity of the problem posed by cats but does NOT call attention to population control measures. B calls attention to population control measures but does not align with an answer to the previous question (and in fact CONTRADICTS answer B in the previous question). D indicates the need for new solutions but does not, in a specific manner that might involve concessions, indicate what those solutions are.

24. A is the correct answer.

The word "fundamental" refers to a problem that may be difficult to solve through repeating past measures and that is "moral" (line 27) and social in its implications. The problem is thus far-reaching and highly important, so that A is an appropriate choice. B and C both criticize a problem that the author points out mainly for its significance and importance, while D is contradicted by the passage's discussion of the difficulty of solving a deep-rooted moral and social problem.

25. C is the correct answer.

In lines 59-63, the author critically references the assumption that "individuals don't matter," which in the context of the passage is tied to advocates of "Traditional conservation" (line 56). C properly supports this content, while A (falsehood) and B (unpopularity) are indeed negative but address factors that the author of the passage (in criticizing the ethical problems of harming individual beings) never raises. D raises a strong positive ("well-intentioned") when in fact the author is strongly critical of the proposed conservation methods.

26. B is the correct answer.

See the previous answer explanation for analysis of the correct line reference. A raises positive conservation outcomes welcomed by a group that does NOT include the author, C calls attention to the question of human responsibility in terms of rewilding, and D calls attention to the absence of ethical reasoning in eliminating cats. While D does seem relevant to the previous question, the specific REASON that eliminating cats is unethical (individuality) is only effectively established in B.

27. D is the correct answer.

The word "hailing" refers to the manner in which conservationists regard "an important step" (line 52), so that these conservationists would see the step in a strongly positive manner. D captures this context of reception and approval. A wrongly indicates physical movement or greeting, B is too extreme (indicating not just acceptance but excessive respect), and C captures a theme of analysis but NOT a strong positive tone.

28. B is the correct answer.

The word "presumption" refers to a belief (outlined in lines 56-63) that individual organisms can be eliminated for larger goals; in context, the author disapproves of this idea and notes that others are "pushing back" (line

Answer Explanations, Test 4

65). This context of viewpoints supports B as appropriate. A (indicating a formal privilege), C (indicating manners and misbehavior), and D (indicating something that may happen, NOT an idea that is present and somewhat prevalent) all introduce faulty contexts and should thus be eliminated.

29. B is the correct answer.

While Passage 1 as a whole offers arguments in support of the elimination of feral cats, Passage 2 contains some content (lines 85-88) that indicates that feral cats can be lethally eliminated under some circumstances. This information supports B, while A is contradicted by the fact that the authors of Passage 1 see the cat population as a unique threat (lines 1-5) that requires special treatment. C (extinction of other species) and D (Aboriginal population) call attention to issues that are ONLY addressed in Passage 1 and should thus be eliminated.

30. A is the correct answer.

The relevant anecdote calls attention to the value of animals that are extinct, yet the author of Passage 2 takes the position that individual life has value (lines 88-102) and that ecosystem-wide concerns should not obscure this ethical position. This content supports A, while B and C assume that the author of Passage 2 (who discusses animal populations but NOT the Aboriginal population) would take a strong position on Aboriginal culture or practices. D is incorrect because the problem raised by the anecdote, namely species dynamics in Australia, is a problem that deeply interests the author of Passage 2 and that would not be seen as receiving undue attention.

31. C is the correct answer.

While the relevant statement from Passage 2 indicates that extreme measures to control feral cats are undesirable, the authors of Passage 1 see feral cats as the source of a supremely dangerous ecological problem (lines 1-5) and support urgent control measures. C properly reflects such an attitude, while A and D raise moral and ethical considerations that are important to the author of Passage 2 but that the authors of Passage 1 (who are more interested in practical control measures and outcomes) do not consider. B misreads the idea (present in the discussion of the Aboriginal population in Passage 1) that humans HAVE suffered as a recommendation regarding FUTURE human suffering and should thus be eliminated as out of scope.

32. B is the correct answer.

In Passage 1, the authors call attention both to the ecological damage caused by feral cats and to the emotional suffering that related species extinctions have caused in the Aboriginal community; in Passage 2, the author opposes mass elimination of animals on ethical grounds but DOES concede that some animals can be eliminated under special circumstances (lines 85-88). This content supports B and can be used to eliminate A, which wrongly indicates that the author of Passage 2 is against killing animals in ALL circumstances. C misstates the goal of the authors of Passage 1 (population control of feral cats for positive ecological outcomes, NOT extinction of feral cats), while D misconstrues a point in Passage 2 (that feral cats can coexist well with humans) as the overly extreme point that there would be a decisive public reaction to the elimination of feral cats.

Answer Explanations, Test 4

Passage 4, Pages 101-103

33. C is the correct answer.

In the passage, Adams outlines "the causes of the separation" (lines 41-42) between the Colonies and Britain, indicating that the relationship was already distant and problematic, and lists some of the violent events that preceded the "first act of sovereignty" (line 73) by the Colonies themselves. Such content indicates that the rebellion was justified and supports C, while the fact that Adams's writing is historical (NOT meant to impact present international relations) can be used to eliminate A and D. While Adams does list specific events, he is interested in explaining how MULTIPLE events justified the rebellion, so that B is too narrow in scope.

34. D is the correct answer.

In the passage, Adams assertively presents his reading of the poor relationship between the Colonies and Britain (lines 1-40) and also offers strong opinions about the general nature of government (lines 43-46). He is thus strongly advocating a specific set of positions, so that D is appropriate. A, B, and C all indicate that Adams has negative sentiments not towards the problems faced by the Colonists but towards his OWN task (which he in fact addresses with assurance and conviction) and should thus be eliminated.

35. B is the correct answer.

In lines 53-58, Adams (continuing a discussion of the authors of the Declaration of Independence that was begun in line 46) mentions that the authors of the Declaration of Independence suffered successive wrongs and were driven to extreme measures after attempts to address their grievances. This content supports B but should NOT be taken as justification for A, since the Colonists are described as attempting to improve upon a situation, not as idealistically pure or as automatically rebellious. C (warriors) and D (landowners) assign roles that Adams himself never cites and should be eliminated as going against the explicit evidence of the passage.

36. D is the correct answer.

See the previous answer explanation for analysis of the correct line reference. A and B explain the distant relationship between America and Britain, while C similarly explains the absence of sympathy or loyalty between the Colonists and the British. These answers do not clearly refer to the authors of the Declaration of Independence (and could easily refer to EARLIER colonists, since the Declaration of Independence is initially mentioned in line 48) and should thus be eliminated as unrelated to the exact topic of the previous question.

37. B is the correct answer.

In lines 71-77, Adams explains that the creation of the United States as an independent country involved an action "never to be resorted to" except in an "awful crisis." This content supports the idea that the Colonies took special or extreme measures, as indicated in B. Choose this answer and eliminate A, since Adams criticizes the actions of the British monarchy but does not argue, more broadly, that monarchies are inherently unjust. C and D indicate future courses of action tend and are thus inappropriate to Adams's mostly historical analysis.

Answer Explanations, Test 4

38. D is the correct answer.

See the previous answer explanation for analysis of the correct line reference. A indicates that the British were generally unfamiliar with conditions in the Colonies, B indicates a shift in Adams's discussion of tensions between Britain and the Colonies, and C indicates that the Colonists delayed declaring independence even beyond the initial hostilities. Though relevant to the topic of revolutionary struggle, none of these answers align with answers to the previous question; in particular, C should not be misconstrued as evidence for answer B in the previous question, since Adams outlines a historical delay but does not provide a GUIDELINE for when to take action in the manner of D.

39. B is the correct answer.

The word "omnipotent" refers to a parliament capable of ensuring the "submission" (line 21) of the Colonies; such a governing body would have the ability to exert power or to force the Colonies to obey. B is an appropriate choice, while A and D wrongly introduce positives to describe a body that Adams sees as domineering and overbearing. C (context of inability to be governed or maintained) is an inappropriate description for a governing body that, though perhaps destructive, is most likely orderly in its operations.

40. C is the correct answer.

The phrase "the island of Virgina" occurs in a discussion of how little the British prime minister knew of the Colonies and is an example of an expression that SHOULD be capable of "amazing or diverting" (lines 21-22) those who hear it. This phrase thus signals a lapse in awareness; choose C and eliminate A as criticizing the Colonies themselves, NOT the British. Despite introducing negatives, B (disrespect) and D (conflict within Britain itself) do not directly relate to the theme of limited knowledge that is Adams's true focus.

41. A is the correct answer.

The phrase "tenacious of" refers to how Americans responded to their rights; the Colonists were both "faithful to their duties" (line 49) and determined to respond to their rights in a similarly energetic and defensive manner. A is thus appropriate, while B and D are CONTRADICTED by the later content (lines 51-53) that explains that the Colonists had tried to negotiate with Britain and were not in fact rebellious radicals. C (indicating comprehension, not action or advocacy) raises a faulty context.

42. A is the correct answer.

The relevant paragraph outlines various instances of violence and explains the "supplications" and "appeals" attempted by the Colonists in order to avoid conflict with the British; Adams notes in the content that follows (lines 68-77) that only after these attempts did the Colonists declare independence. A properly reflects the idea that the Colonists tried to avoid conflict through various means, while B mistakes a detail (instances of violence) for the full content of the paragraph. C neglects the fact that Adams is portraying the past actions of the British in a negative manner, while D places too much focus on the British monarch and thus mistakes a single detail of the paragraph for the full content of the paragraph.

Answer Explanations, Test 4

Passage 5, Pages 103-106

43. C is the correct answer.

While the author provides information about recent findings related to dinosaurs throughout the passage, she does so while employing informal or conversational phrases such as "Everyone loves" (line 1), "doing something right" (lines 7-8), and "Fingers crossed" (line 82). This content supports C and can be used to eliminate A, since "elevated" would indicate highly technical and perhaps inaccessible word choice. B introduces an inappropriate negative ("skeptical" or involving doubt, when the author mostly presents and analyzes valid information), while D introduces an inappropriately personal implication ("nostalgic" or longing for the past) for a passage that does not deal with the author's background.

44. D is the correct answer.

In lines 16-21, the author refers back to megaherbivores ("these dinosaurs") and explains that their diverse feeding habits were useful in "reducing competition." This content directly supports D and should not be mistaken as justification for A, since the choices of the dinosaurs (NOT the unique properties of the vegetation) enabled harmony. B mistakes a factor considered as part of an inquiry (dinosaur teeth) as the ultimate explanation for a sense of harmony that was explained by dietary preferences, not anatomy; C offers a characterization of herbivores as averse to violence that may or may NOT be supported by historical evidence and that is in any case not of direct interest to the author of the passage.

45. A is the correct answer.

See the previous answer explanation for analysis of the correct line reference. B indicates how the dietary preferences of dinosaurs were examined by researchers, C indicates how various tooth markings link to dietary preferences, and D indicates that dinosaur groups lived together. While B and C do not raise the theme of peaceful coexistence as required by the previous question, D does not clearly indicate WHY dinosaur species peacefully coexisted and thus does not provide the required details.

46. B is the correct answer.

The author indicates that the researchers chose to focus on "teeth still connected to skulls" (line 38) in order to ensure accuracy; the implication is that teeth disconnected from skulls in fossil groupings would be harder to trace to the correct skulls and the appropriate species. B correctly reflects the idea that separated skulls and teeth may not automatically connect despite their proximity. A wrongly indicates that the researchers described in the passage were interested in skulls themselves (NOT teeth). C describes a stage that would precede the assessment of teeth and D describes a later stage that would occur after examination; instead, the researchers would react to separate skulls and teeth WHILE conducting their fieldwork.

Answer Explanations, Test 4

47. B is the correct answer.

In lines 73-80, the author indicates that findings premised on microwear analysis are useful but must be incorporated "with other known facts." This content supports B, since the other "facts" would naturally be relevant to the study of dinosaurs if (in the context of the passage) they relate to microwear findings. A misstates the purpose of microwear analysis (determining dietary preferences, NOT age), C is wrongly critical of a technique that the author mostly finds useful, and D wrongly indicates that the SINGLE application of microwear analysis examined in the passage is the only significant use for this technique.

48. D is the correct answer.

See the previous answer explanation for analysis of the correct line reference. A explains that microwear analysis was used to determine how specific dinosaurs coexisted, B notes the different tooth structures of two dinosaur groupings, and C indicates that (according to microwear analysis) dinosaurs with different tooth shapes could have had similar diets. While A (coexistence) and C (tooth shapes) directly mention microwear analysis, these answers raise topics that are not clearly addressed in answers to the previous question.

49. A is the correct answer.

The author of the passage explains that "scratches are linked to the ingestion of tough leaves or meat" (lines 33-34); thus, the author indicates that a carnivorous dinosaur would have teeth with many scratches and relatively few pits (linked to hard non-meat foods in lines 32-33). A is appropriate, while the same line references contradict B and C. The absence of microwear traces might yield inconclusive information about a dinosaur's diet (or could indicate that the dinosaur was not eating anything), so that D does not clearly indicate a dietary preference of any kind.

50. B is the correct answer.

The word "varied" refers to the diets of different dinosaur species that were able to successfully "coexist" (line 79); in the context of the passage, the species survived alongside one another by drawing on different food sources. B properly indicates that the food sources were not identical, while A calls attention to a theme that would describe the harmonious or balanced ecosystem but NOT necessarily the food sources themselves. C and D wrongly indicate that the food sources were unpredictable or unstable, when in fact the dietary preferences of dinosaurs have been reliably identified by scientists.

51. D is the correct answer.

In lines 44-56, the author indicates that ankylosaurs were plant-eating dinosaurs, while the graph indicates that ankylosaurs exhibited significant instances of chipping for the 12 specimens under study. This content would, in the manner of D, effectively DISPROVE the idea that only carnivorous dinosaurs exhibited chipping. A and C simply support the idea that a carnivorous dinosaur would exhibit chipping, while B indicates that a dinosaur that would not eat meat would not (on the basis of the graph) exhibit chipping and thus does not disprove the student's assumed connection between chipping and carnivorous habits.

Answer Explanations, Test 4

52. A is the correct answer.

In lines 32-35, the author of the passage indicates that a combination of pits and scratches would suggest a varied diet. Of the dinosaurs considered in the graph, altirhinus exhibits roughly the same number of pits and scratches. A is the best choice, while B, C, and D all refer to dinosaurs that exhibited relatively large numbers of pits and relatively small numbers of scratches, a combination that would NOT indicate a varied diet.

NOTES

- Passage 2 on Pages 95-96, " 'Covert' Neurofeedback Tunes-up the Social Brain in ASD," is adapted from the article of the same name published by the National Institute of Mental Health. 17 July 2018, NIMH. https://www.nimh.nih.gov/news/science-news/2018/covert-neurofeedback-tunes-up-the-social-brain-in-asd.shtml. Accessed 28 July 2019.

- Passage 3, Reading 1 on Page 98, "To save Australia's mammals we need a change of heart," is an excerpt from the article of the same name by John Woinarski and Peter Harrison and published by The Conversation in partnership with Charles Darwin University and Southern Cross University. 11 June 2014, The Conversation. https://theconversation.com/to-save-australias-mammals-we-need-a-change-of-heart-27423. Accessed 28 July 2019.

- Passage 3, Reading 2 on Pages 98-99, "Australia's war on feral cats: shaky science, missing ethics," is an excerpt from the article of the same name by William Lynn and published by The Conversation. 7 October 2015, The Conversation. https://theconversation.com/australias-war-on-feral-cats-shaky-science-missing-ethics-47444. Accessed 28 July 2019.

- Passage 5 on Pages 103-104, "Sharing is Caring: Varied Diets in Dinosaurs Promoted Coexistence," is adapted from the article of the same name by Tina Garrett and published by EveryONE, the PLOS ONE community blog. 11 August 2014, PLOS ONE. https://blogs.plos.org/everyone/2014/08/11/sharing-caring-varied-diets-dinosaurs-promoted-coexistence-2/. Accessed 28 July 2019.

About the Figures: The various visual resources that accompany the passages in this section are primarily meant to facilitate critical thinking skills and may not reflect historical data.

Test 5
Full Reading Section
2020 SAT Practice

Test 5

Reading Test

65 MINUTES, 52 QUESTIONS

Turn to Section 1 of your answer sheet to answer the questions in this section.

DIRECTIONS

Each passage or pair of passages below is followed by a number of questions. After reading each passage or pair, choose the best answer to each question based on what is stated or implied in the passage or passages and in any accompanying graphics (such as a table or graph).

Questions 1-10 are based on the following passage.

This passage is adapted from the 1879 short story "Miss Sydney's Flowers" by Sarah Orne Jewett.

However sensible it may have been considered by other people, it certainly was a disagreeable piece of news to Miss Sydney, that the city
Line authorities had decided to open a new street from
5 St. Mary Street to Jefferson. It seemed a most unwarrantable thing to her that they had a right to buy her property against her will. It was so provoking, that, after so much annoyance from the noise of St. Mary Street during the last dozen
10 years, she must submit to having another public thoroughfare at the side of her house also. If it had only been at the other side, she would not have minded it particularly, for she rarely sat in her drawing-room, which was at the left of the
15 hall. On the right was the library, stately, dismal, and apt to be musty in damp weather; and it would take many bright people, and a blazing wood-fire, and a great deal of sunshine, to make it pleasant. Behind this was the dining-room,
20 which was really bright and sunny, and which opened by wide glass doors into a conservatory. The rattle and clatter of St. Mary Street was not at all troublesome here; and by little and little Miss Sydney had gathered her favorite possessions
25 from other parts of the house, and taken one end of it for her sitting-room. The most comfortable chairs had found their way here, and a luxurious great sofa which had once been in the library, as well as the bookcase which held her favorite
30 books.

The house had been built by Miss Sydney's grandfather, and in his day it had seemed nearly out of the city: now there was only one other house left near it; for one by one the quiet,
35 aristocratic old street had seen its residences give place to shops and warehouses, and Miss Sydney herself had scornfully refused many offers of many thousand dollars for her home. It was so changed! It made her so sad to think of the dear
40 old times, and to see the houses torn down, or the small-paned windows and old-fashioned front-doors replaced with French plate-glass to display better the wares which were to take the places of the quaint furniture and well-known faces of her
45 friends! But Miss Sydney was an old woman, and her friends had diminished sadly. "It seems to me

that my invitations are all for funerals in these days," said she to her venerable maid Hannah, who had helped her dress for her parties fifty years
50 before. She had given up society little by little. Her friends had died, or she had allowed herself to drift away from them, while the acquaintances from whom she might have filled their places were only acquaintances still. . . .
55 If calling were not a regulation of society, if one only went to see the persons one really cared for, I am afraid Miss Sydney would soon have been quite forgotten. Her character would puzzle many people. She put no visible hindrance in
60 your way; for I do not think she was consciously reserved and cold. She was thoroughly well-bred, rich, and in her way charitable; that is, she gave liberally to public subscriptions which came under her notice, and to church contributions.
65 But she got on, somehow, without having friends; and, though the loss of one had always been a real grief, she learned without much trouble the way of living the lonely, comfortable, but very selfish life, and the way of being the woman I
70 have tried to describe. There were occasional days when she was tired of herself, and life seemed an empty, formal, heartless discipline. Her wisest acquaintances pitied her loneliness; and busy, unselfish people wondered how she could be deaf
75 to the teachings of her good clergyman, and blind to all the chances of usefulness and happiness which the world afforded her; and others still envied her, and wondered to whom she meant to leave all her money.

1

Over the course of the passage, the main focus of the narrative shifts from

A) the enjoyment that a central character feels towards spaces inside her home to reservations that the character has about her relationship with others.

B) the sentimental value that a central character attaches to her home to her abiding ambivalence about the importance of spending time with others.

C) the frustration that a central character feels towards perceived government overreach to concern over the character's social life.

D) the interests that a central character harbors in terms of maintaining her household to irritation concerning outside opinions.

2

The description in the first paragraph (lines 1-30) indicates that Miss Sydney is most displeased by

A) the racket from the nearby thoroughfare.
B) the presence of her neighbors.
C) the government buying property against her will.
D) laws that support confiscation of land.

3

Which choice provides the best evidence for the answer to the previous question?

A) Lines 3-5 ("the city . . . Jefferson")
B) Lines 7-11 ("It was . . . also")
C) Lines 13-16 ("for she . . . weather")
D) Lines 16-19 ("and it . . . pleasant")

Test 5

4

Which choice supports the idea that Miss Sydney acts to avoid outside noise disturbances?

A) Lines 19-21 ("Behind . . . conservatory")
B) Lines 22-26 ("The rattle . . . sitting-room")
C) Lines 31-33 ("The house . . . city")
D) Lines 45-50 ("But Miss Sydney . . . before")

5

The main purpose of the second paragraph (lines 31-54) is to

A) show how Miss Sydney embraced loneliness.
B) provide a meticulous timeline for an aging character.
C) prove Miss Sydney's disdain for noise.
D) describe changes in a particular locality.

6

The term "aristocratic" (line 35) most directly suggests that

A) a particular neighborhood was affluent.
B) members of a governing family lived in the area.
C) prospering warehouses had replaced antiquated homes.
D) urban spread resulted in a demographic change.

7

The author includes the descriptions of the windows, the front doors, and the plate glass (lines 41-43) primarily to

A) mention architectural quirks of a neighborhood.
B) highlight examples of former, squandered wealth.
C) acknowledge Miss Sydney's desire to socialize.
D) show a transition in Miss Sydney's neighborhood.

8

According to the passage, the narrator's decision to mention that the central character's friends had died serves the purpose of

A) amplifying the poor mental and financial state that Miss Sydney had been enduring.
B) reinforcing the narrative that Miss Sydney was living a lonely existence with little to be positive about.
C) supplying background information to show why Miss Sydney did not want the thoroughfare to be built.
D) adding an evocation of another burden to the list of misfortunes that Miss Sydney had dealt with throughout her life.

9

The author of the passage uses the quote in lines 46-48 primarily as a

A) sentimental reminder to describe a character's dismal social life.
B) nostalgic interlude that evokes a character's past.
C) reflection on a character's younger years.
D) flashback to show how neighborhood demographics had changed.

10

As used in line 63, "liberally" most nearly means

A) waywardly.
B) generously.
C) happily.
D) moderately.

Questions 11-20 are based on the following passages.

Passage 1 is adapted from William Wilberforce, the "Abolition Speech" (1789). Passage 2 is adapted from George Wilson Bridges, "A Voice from Jamaica in Reply to William Wilberforce" (1823). Both passages address the possibility of abolishing slavery within the British Empire, a policy that was approved in 1833.

Passage 1

When I consider the magnitude of the subject which I am to bring before the House—a subject, in which the interests, not of this country, nor of Europe alone, but of the whole world, and of posterity, are involved: and when I think, at the same time, on the weakness of the advocate who has undertaken this great cause—when these reflections press upon my mind, it is impossible for me not to feel both terrified and concerned at my own inadequacy to such a task. But when I reflect, however, on the encouragement which I have had, through the whole course of a long and laborious examination of this question, and how much candour I have experienced, and how conviction has increased within my own mind, in proportion as I have advanced in my labours—when I reflect, especially, that however averse any gentleman may now be, yet we shall all be of one opinion in the end—when I turn myself to these thoughts, I take courage—I determine to forget all my other fears, and I march forward with a firmer step in the full assurance that my cause will bear me out, and that I shall be able to justify upon the clearest principles, every resolution in my hand, the avowed end of which is the total abolition of the slave trade. I wish exceedingly, in the outset, to guard both myself and the House from entering into the subject with any sort of passion. It is not their passions I shall appeal to—I ask only for their cool and impartial reason; and I wish not to take them by surprise, but to deliberate, point by point, upon every part of this question. I mean not to accuse any one, but to take the shame upon myself, in common, indeed, with the whole parliament of Great Britain, for having suffered this horrid trade to be carried on under their authority....

Having now disposed of the first part of this subject, I must speak of the transit of the slaves in the West Indies. This I confess, in my own opinion, is the most wretched part of the whole subject. So much misery condensed in so little room, is more than the human imagination had ever before conceived. I will not accuse the Liverpool merchants: I will allow them, nay, I will believe them to be men of humanity; and I will therefore believe, if it were not for the enormous magnitude and extent of the evil which distracts their attention from individual cases, and makes them think generally, and therefore less feelingly on the subject, they would never have persisted in the trade.

Passage 2

Sir, I write only as the feeble advocate of a Church Establishment, whose domestic as well as foreign institutions you appear to take every opportunity of impugning—I reply only as the impartial spectator, the friend of truth and justice, who, equally anxious as yourself to hasten the period when emancipation may be safely made subservient to the moral happiness of our fellow creatures here, would nevertheless not see that object pursued by unworthy means, nor gained in a field of blood.

The total extinction of the British slave trade is sufficient of itself to render to you, the father of that benevolent measure, all the honor which the relieved sufferings of humanity can bestow on one individual; that need is as great as it falls to the lot of the age of man. Its desired consequence, the abolition of slavery itself... must be left for the accomplishment of another generation, to prove the philanthropy of a succeeding age. Anxious, ambitiously solicitous, as you may naturally be, to monopolize both these philanthropic objects, to attach them to your name, to descend to the grave with the accumulated honours of your completed views, such a consummation cannot, in the nature of things, be comprehended within the narrow compass of one man's life.

11

As used in line 6, "advocate" most nearly means

A) activist.
B) optimist.
C) legislator.
D) judge.

12

Which choice supports the idea that William Wilberforce believes that those who support the slave trade might be persuaded to oppose it?

A) Lines 10-16 ("But when . . . labours")
B) Lines 23-28 ("I shall . . . passion")
C) Lines 32-35 ("I mean . . . Great Britain")
D) Lines 46-52 ("and I will . . . trade")

13

In Passage 1, the term "task" (line 10) most likely refers to

A) the abolition of the slave trade.
B) Wilberforce's composition of the speech itself.
C) examination of differing sides in the slavery debate.
D) consideration of the economic repercussions of slavery.

14

Why did the author of Passage 2 state that he was an "advocate of a Church Establishment" (lines 53-54)?

A) To establish his expert knowledge of the slave trade
B) To indicate his position of morality and responsibility
C) To provide details on the doctrines of the Church
D) To unveil a novel approach in the struggle against the slave trade

15

According to the author of Passage 2, to successfully abolish slavery, legal measures to this effect must be passed

A) following a bloody war.
B) after careful deliberation by intellectuals.
C) within a court of justice.
D) at a later time.

16

Which choice provides the best evidence for the answer to the previous question?

A) Lines 56-61 ("I reply . . . here")
B) Lines 64-68 ("The total . . . individual")
C) Lines 69-72 ("Its desired . . . age")
D) Lines 72-77 ("Anxious . . . views")

17

It can be inferred that the author of Passage 2 believes that William Wilberforce

A) only cares about his reputation as a reformer.

B) is flawed in his determination to pursue the abolition of slavery.

C) has a deep misunderstanding of customs in the British Colonies.

D) would change his stance on slavery if he were a member of the Church establishment.

18

Which choice best describes the overall relationship between Passage 1 and Passage 2?

A) Passage 2 purposefully misrepresents the reasoning present in Passage 1.

B) Passage 2 directly challenges the feasibility of extending a humanitarian project set forth in Passage 1.

C) Passage 2 sympathetically and for the most part predictably expands on the perspective that guides Passage 1.

D) Passage 2 voices mild misgivings while reiterating most of the ideas espoused in Passage 1.

19

The authors of both passages would most likely agree with which of the following statements concerning the British slave trade?

A) The British slave trade is ironically beneficial to the economic life of a local elite.

B) The British slave trade should be abolished as the first step in a broader international initiative.

C) The British slave trade should have been abolished in an earlier century.

D) The British slave trade has a vicious effect on human society.

20

Which of the following is a writing technique that is employed by both the author of Passage 1 and the author of Passage 2 in presenting their arguments?

A) Oblique yet self-aggrandizing descriptions of the reputational harm that may befall the author and his allies

B) Cautionary phrases about the consequences of undue optimism in matters of social and political debate

C) Allusions to sufferings that the author has personally witnessed yet declines to explain in full detail

D) Self-deprecating references that position the author in relation to the ideology and issues that concern him

Questions 21-30 are based on the following passage.

This passage is adapted from "Better medicine through machine learning: What's real, and what's artificial?" Published in 2018, the article appeared* in its final form as an editorial in PLOS Medicine.

Artificial Intelligence (AI) as a field emerged in the 1960s when practitioners across the engineering and cognitive sciences began to study how to develop computational technologies that, [Line 5] like people, can perform tasks such as sensing, learning, reasoning, and taking action. Early AI systems relied heavily on expert-derived rules for replicating how people would approach these tasks. Machine Learning (ML), a subfield of AI, [10] emerged as research began to leverage numerical techniques integrating principles from computing, optimization, and statistics to automatically "learn" programs for performing these tasks by processing data—hence the recent interest in "big [15] data."

While progress in AI has been uneven, significant advances in the present decade have led to a proliferation of technologies that substantially impact our everyday lives: computer [20] vision and planning are driving the gaming and transportation industries; speech processing is making conversational applications practical on our phones; and natural language processing, knowledge representation, and reasoning have [25] enabled a machine to beat the Jeopardy and Go champions and are bringing new power to Web searches.

Simultaneously, however, advertising hyperbole has led to skepticism and [30] misunderstanding of what is and is not possible with ML. Here, we aim to provide an accessible, scientifically and technologically accurate portrayal of the current state of ML (often referred to as AI in the medical literature) in health and [35] medicine, and its potential, using examples of recent research—some from PLOS Medicine's November 2018 Special Issue on Machine Learning in Health and Biomedicine, for which we served as Guest Editors. We have selected [40] studies that illustrate different ways in which ML may be used and their potential for near-term translational impact.

Of the myriad opportunities for use of ML in clinical practice, medical imaging workflows [45] are most likely to be impacted in the near term. ML-driven algorithms that automatically process 2 or 3 dimensional image scans to identify clinical signs (e.g., tumors or lesions) or determine likely diagnoses have been published and some are [50] progressing through regulatory steps toward the market. Many of these use Deep Learning, a form of ML based on layered representations of variables, referred to as neural networks. To understand how Deep Learning methods leverage [55] image data to perform recognition tasks, imagine you are entering a dark room and looking for the light switch. From past experience, you have learned to associate light switches with predictable locations within the configuration of a room. [60] Many computer vision-based image processing algorithms, including Deep Learning, mimic this behavior to identify factors that are associated with the recognition task at hand. Deep Learning is especially powerful in its ability to interpret [65] images due to the complexity of the factors it can consider.

The power of Deep Learning has been most evident within ophthalmology. Recently, Olaf Ronneberger and colleagues applied a two- [70] step process using deep learning to a clinically heterogeneous set of three-dimensional optical coherence tomography (CT) scans from patients referred to a major UK eye hospital. They demonstrated performance in making a referral [75] recommendation that reaches or exceeds that of experts on a range of sight-threatening retinal diseases after training on only 14,884 scans. In another effort, IDx, a health care automation company, has developed Deep Learning-based [80] software to be used by health providers who treat patients with diabetes to scan images for signs of diabetic retinopathy. Their cloud-based, autonomous detection software has received regulatory approval by the US Food and Drug [85] Administration (FDA). With the volume and

---

*See Page 152 for the citation for this text.

complexity of diagnostic imaging increasing faster than the availability of human expertise to interpret it (especially in low resource settings), screening for referable or detecting treatable
90 disease in patients who would not otherwise receive eye exams may save both vision and money.

21

The main purpose of the entire passage is to

A) explain how Artificial Intelligence increases efficiency in medical workplaces.

B) take a position on using Deep Learning to lower medical expenses.

C) report on Machine Learning's capabilities in modernizing outdated medical procedures.

D) investigate the impact of Artificial Intelligence on medical advertising costs.

22

How do the words "develop," "replicating," and "integrating" in the first paragraph (lines 1-15) help to establish the tone of the paragraph?

A) They create an authoritative tone that signals that the authors are experts on the topics of Machine Learning and Artificial Intelligence.

B) They create an optimistic tone that signals that the authors are confident that the progress made through computational technologies since the 1960s will continue.

C) They create an informative tone that signals the authors' intention to describe the advances in Artificial Intelligence systems leading to the advent of "big data."

D) They create a critical tone that signals that the authors are undecided about the potential of using research methods to further develop Artificial Intelligence.

23

The central idea of the authors' discussion of "progress in AI" (line 16) is that

A) Artificial Intelligence is becoming applicable to everyday pursuits.

B) speech processing is now more practical than most observers assume.

C) Machine Learning can efficiently outpace human knowledge.

D) the video game industry automatically benefits from advances in Artificial Intelligence.

24

Which choice provides the best evidence for the answer to the previous question?

A) Lines 9-15 ("Machine . . . data")

B) Lines 17-19 ("significant . . . lives")

C) Lines 23-26 ("and natural . . . champions")

D) Lines 28-31 ("Simultaneously . . . ML")

25

The author refers to Jeopardy and Go (line 25) primarily to

A) provide examples of Artificial Intelligence success in current game formats.

B) suggest that machines should replace humans in well-known game formats.

C) illustrate how Artificial Intelligence can increase the difficulty levels of popular game formats.

D) underscore the simultaneous evolution of Artificial Intelligence and various game formats.

Test 5

26

As used in line 29, "hyperbole" most nearly means

A) advancement.
B) exaggeration.
C) oddity.
D) glorification.

27

The third paragraph (lines 28-42) is primarily concerned with establishing a contrast between

A) expectations for Machine Learning and scientifically proven use.
B) the respective virtues of Machine Learning as used in advertising and in science.
C) Artificial Intelligence as used in healthcare and in biomedicine.
D) the media portrayal of Machine Learning and relevant practical applications in medicine.

28

It can be reasonably inferred that "power" (line 67) was a term generally intended to

A) elevate the status of Machine Learning in medical workplaces.
B) pinpoint the impact of Deep Learning in ophthalmology.
C) praise Artificial Intelligence applications in medical science.
D) identify Deep Learning as a productive tool in workflow management.

29

One of the author's important points about the benefits of the technologies addressed in the passage is that

A) Artificial Intelligence is saving patients money on formerly expensive procedures.
B) Deep Learning efficiently addresses differing patient conditions in the field of ophthalmology.
C) Deep Learning is outpacing human expertise.
D) health care automation is superior to manual administration of therapeutic measures.

30

Which choice provides the best evidence for the answer to the previous question?

A) Lines 53-57 ("To understand . . . switch")
B) Lines 63-66 ("Deep Learning . . . consider")
C) Lines 67-73 ("The power . . . hospital")
D) Lines 82-85 ("Their cloud-based . . . FDA")

Questions 31-41 are based on the following passage and supplementary material.

This passage is an excerpt from Lawrence J. Saha, "Dictatorship 101: killing the internet plays into the hands of revolutionaries," an article originally published* by The Conversation in 2011.

    In the euphoria following the downfall of the Mubarak regime in Egypt, Wael Ghonim, the so-called "hero" of the revolution, proclaimed:
Line "technology played a great role here. You know, it
5 helped keeping people informed, it helped making all of us collaborate."
    He said the Egyptian government was "stupid" to close down the internet because that showed the world that Mubarak was afraid. The
10 revolutionaries even had back-up plans in the event of a government closure of internet access. But according to Yale scholar Navid Hassanpour, the apparent positive role the internet played in the revolution has been misrepresented. Yes,
15 shutting down the internet backfired for the Mubarak regime, but not in the way Ghonim and many others assumed.
    According to Hassanpour, it was only after access to the internet was removed that
20 the revolution began to take off. In a widely circulated American Political Science Association conference paper, he argues that shutting down the internet did make things difficult for sustaining a centralised revolutionary movement in Egypt. But,
25 he adds, the shutdown actually encouraged the development of smaller revolutionary uprisings at local levels where the face-to-face interaction between activists was more intense and the mobilisation of inactive lukewarm dissidents was
30 easier. In other words, closing down the internet made the revolution more diffuse and more difficult for the authorities to contain.
    Hassanpour uses what he calls "dynamic threshold models" and social network theory,
35 which are very complex and based on some mind-bending equations. He shows that the higher levels of communication and connectivity made possible by the internet and social media actually limit revolutions by centralising them.
40   Technology works for those who are highly connected in the centre, but it does not work well for those on the fringes. When social media is the primary mode of communication, a significant number of potentially active demonstrators
45 become observers rather than participants. So what does the electronic media, which inhibits rather than contributes to revolutionary activism, actually do? Noam Cohen, writing in the *New York Times*, put it this way:

50   "The mass media, including interactive social-networking tools, make you passive, can sap your initiative, leave you content to watch the spectacle of life from your couch or smartphone."

    So, intense exposure to the electronic media
55 can make a person a couch revolutionary. Why take to the streets when one can be a participant by watching events on Facebook or other sites on the internet? The real implication of Hassanpour's paper for regimes trying to suppress revolutionary
60 uprisings (President Assad, are you listening?) is to leave the internet up and running: in the long-term, the uprisings will be more centralised and by extension more containable.
    There are many reasons why leaving the
65 internet "open" can work to the advantage of the authorities, not the revolutionaries. This may surprise British Prime Minister David Cameron, who recently threatened to shut down social media services in the face of the UK riots.
70   As has already happened in some countries, such as Iran, the government can use the internet to monitor dissident activity and even identify some of the leaders. But more than that, the government in power can also use the internet
75 to send out false information and manipulate the knowledge circulating among the general population. This kind of action (and struggles over knowledge and information) is not unique to the modern electronic age. It has been going on since
80 the main sources of revolutionary knowledge dissemination were the newspaper and pamphlets.

---

*See Page 152 for the citation for this text.

Test 5

There is evidence that prior to the internet being shut down in Egypt, revolutionary activists were aware that their electronic communication
85 and movements were being monitored. In late 2010, during the early days of protest planning, members of the Revolutionary Youth Council took precautionary measures so that their meetings and other forms of communication, which they
90 believed were under surveillance, could not be detected by authorities.

Regarding cell-phones, one female member said:

"We also took the batteries out, because the
95 police have the ability to listen in even when phones are off."

31

One of the author's central ideas in the passage is that

A) "couch" revolutionaries can be encouraged to participate in social movements through the proper use of social media outlets.

B) modern communication media can be potent tools for both regimes and insurgents.

C) the spread of revolutionary activity is only made possible by shutting down Internet services.

D) the Internet allows political participation for those who are prohibited from protesting in public.

32

Over the course the passage, the main focus of the author's discussion shifts from

A) creating a theory of government involvement in the Internet to promoting a freer society through the application of diminished government regulation.

B) encouraging the shutdown of the Internet for political protest to discouraging Internet use during times of political upheaval.

C) providing reasons as to how shutting down the Internet contributes to political revolution to revealing how a government can utilize the Internet to misinform constituents.

D) excusing government interference on social media networks to defending broad-based freedom of speech and dialogue on websites.

33

Which choice provides a secondary perspective on how social media is counterproductive to the purpose of political protest?

A) Lines 18-20 ("According... off")
B) Lines 50-53 ("The mass ... smartphone")
C) Lines 55-58 ("Why take ... internet")
D) Lines 64-66 ("There ... revolutionaries")

34

What does Hassanpour's paper cite as a disadvantage for governments in shutting down the Internet?

A) An increase in dissident activism

B) Limited mass communication

C) Inability to inform the population of important policy changes

D) Lack of justification for political rule

35

Which choice provides the best evidence for the answer to the previous question?

A) Lines 20-24 ("In a widely . . . Egypt")

B) Lines 28-32 ("the mobilisation . . . contain")

C) Lines 33-36 ("Hassanpour . . . equations")

D) Lines 61-63 ("in the long-term . . . containable")

36

As used in line 31, "diffuse" most nearly means

A) confused.

B) versatile.

C) spread out.

D) undefined.

37

The term "couch revolutionary" (line 55) most likely refers to someone who is actively

A) supporting a protest on social media but not on the ground.

B) promoting a protest through outreach but not in a digital format.

C) involved in politics but not habitually connected to the Internet.

D) monitoring politics on television but not participating in person.

38

The main purpose of the paragraph that references "some countries, such as Iran" (lines 70-81) is to

A) defend the use of social media as a form of protest.

B) elaborate on the importance of social media in politics.

C) describe how social media is effective in regime change.

D) prove that Internet shutdown disrupts public opposition.

39

For which of the following countries considered in the table would democratic institutions have the strongest association with the prevalence of Internet usage?

A) Canada

B) United States

C) Lebanon

D) Saudi Arabia

Test 5

2018 Statistics, Selected Countries[†]

Country	Democracy Index Rating	Internet Users in Population
United States	7.96	87%
Canada	9.15	91%
United Kingdom	8.53	95%
Germany	8.68	90%
France	7.80	82%

Country	Democracy Index Rating	Internet Users in Population
Egypt*	3.36	47%
Syria*	1.43	27%
Lebanon*	4.63	82%
Libya*	2.19	21%
Saudi Arabia	1.93	93%

- Democracy Index: administered by the Economic Intelligence Unit, with scores ranging from 10 (full democracy) to 0 (authoritarian regime)
- Internet Access*: a projection based on 2011-2016 figures provided for those countries that have not reported widely-available 2018 statistics

[†]Citation for this table available on Page 152

40

The information in the tables suggests that relatively authoritarian governments

A) see Internet access as a threat to stability.
B) could become more democratic over time.
C) may not fit a single pattern of nationwide Internet usage.
D) view democratic nations as direct competitors in technology investment and enterprise.

41

The author of the passage would regard the information contained in the tables as

A) premised on faulty reasoning, but apparently useful in motivating new sociopolitical research.
B) broadly illuminating, but unlikely to be accepted by some of the more dogmatic political groups mentioned in the passage.
C) potentially valid, but incapable of capturing the nuances of how Egypt's government and civilians have deployed Internet resources.
D) methodologically sound, but troubling in its implication that democratic nations have little interest in expanding Internet usership.

Questions 42-52 are based on the following passage and supplementary material.

This passage is adapted from "Bioengineered sunscreen blocks skin penetration and toxicity," a 2016 news release* from the National Institute of Biomedical Imaging and Bioengineering.

Line
    A research team including NIBIB-funded scientists has developed a nanotechnology-based sunscreen that provides excellent protection from ultraviolet (UV) damage while eliminating
5 a number of harmful effects of currently used sunscreens. The team encapsulated the UV-blocking compounds in bio-adhesive nanoparticles, which adhere to the skin well, but do not penetrate beyond the skin's surface.
10 These properties resulted in highly effective UV protection in a mouse model, without the adverse effects observed with commercial sunscreens, including penetration into the bloodstream and generation of reactive oxygen species, which can
15 damage DNA and lead to cancer.
    Commercial sunscreens use compounds that effectively filter out damaging UV light. However, there is concern that these agents have a variety of harmful effects due to penetration past the surface
20 skin. For example, these products have been found in human breast tissue and urine and are known to disrupt the normal function of some hormones. Also, the exposure of the UV filters to light can produce toxic reactive oxygen species that are
25 destructive to cells and tissues and can cause tumors through DNA damage.
    "This work applies a novel bioengineering idea to a little known but significant health problem, adds Jessica Tucker, Ph.D., Director of the NIBIB
30 Program in Delivery Systems and Devices for Drugs and Biologics. "While we are all familiar with the benefits of sunscreen, the potential toxicities from sunscreen due to penetration into the body and creation of DNA-damaging agents
35 are not well known. Bioengineering sunscreen to inhibit penetration and keep any DNA-damaging compounds isolated in the nanoparticle and away from the skin is a great example of how a sophisticated technology can be used to solve
40 a problem affecting the health of millions of people."
    Bioengineers and dermatologists at Yale University in New Haven, Connecticut combined their expertise in nanoparticle-based drug delivery
45 and the molecular and cellular characteristics of the skin to address these potential health hazards of current commercial sunscreens. The results of their collaboration were reported in the September issue of *Nature Materials*.
50   The group encapsulated a commonly used sunscreen, padimate O (PO), inside a nanoparticle (a very small molecule often used to transport drugs and other agents into the body). PO is related to the better-known sunscreen PABA.
55   The bioadhesive nanoparticle containing the sunscreen PO was tested on pigs for penetration into the skin. A control group of pigs received the PO alone, not encapsulated in a nanoparticle. The PO penetrated beyond the surface layers of skin
60 where it could potentially enter the bloodstream through blood vessels that are in the deeper skin layers. However, the PO inside the nanoparticle remained on the surface of the skin and did not penetrate into deeper layers.
65   Because the bioadhesive nanoparticles, or BNPs are larger than skin pores it was somewhat expected that they could not enter the body by that route. However, skin is full of hair follicles that are larger than BNPs and so could be a way for
70 migration into the body. Surprisingly, BNPs did not pass through the hair follicle openings either. Tests indicated that the adhesive properties of the BNPs caused them to stick to the skin surface, unable to move through the hair follicles.
75   Further testing showed that the BNPs were water resistant and remained on the skin for a day or more, yet were easily removed by towel wiping. They also disappeared in several days through natural exfoliation of the surface skin.

---

*See Page 152 for the citation for this text.

Test 5

42

The main purpose of the entire passage is to

A) explain how BNPs will eliminate known health risks linked to sunscreen.

B) promote BNP engineering as a potential cure for skin cancer.

C) report on the benefits of BNP-modified substances for skin health.

D) discuss the drawbacks of commercial sunscreen products as proven through scientific testing.

43

In assessing the sunscreen products that are currently available, the author indicates that

A) the reactions of human and non-human test subjects to standard sunscreen compositions are almost indistinguishable.

B) UV light exposure is one of the few problems that a low-quality sunscreen can effectively address.

C) filtering out UV light does preclude the possibility of adverse effects.

D) frequency of sunscreen use correlates with increased cancer incidence.

44

Which choice provides the best evidence for the answer to the previous question?

A) Lines 10-12 ("These . . . sunscreens")

B) Lines 16-17 ("Commercial . . . UV light")

C) Lines 17-20 ("However. . . skin")

D) Lines 50-53 ("The group . . . body")

45

How do the words "developed," "encapsulated," and "resulted" in the first paragraph (lines 1-15) help to establish the tone of the paragraph?

A) They create a critical tone that challenges the central hypothesis of the current sunscreen market.

B) They create a skeptical tone that makes clear the author's perspective on current sunscreen products and the potential to remove any chance of getting cancer.

C) They create a direct tone that establishes a scientific application before the author provides details of how discoveries could improve sunscreen products.

D) They create an authoritative tone that presents the author as an expert capable of providing an argument against proponents of current sunscreen products.

46

The second paragraph (lines 16-26) is primarily concerned with establishing a contrast between

A) scientific and public consensus on commercial sunscreen risks.

B) previous and current perspectives on sunscreen application.

C) sunscreen compounds encapsulated in nanoparticles and devised without such nanoparticles.

D) the benefits and the health risks of commercial sunscreen.

47

It can be reasonably inferred that "novel" (line 27) was a term generally intended to

A) identify UV exposure as a leading cause of skin cancer.

B) champion the discovery of health risks in current sunscreen products.

C) assess scientific research in the field of nanotechnology.

D) encourage use of sunscreen containing bioadhesive nanoparticles.

48

Which choice describes the function of the references to the Yale University researchers in relation to the rest of the passage?

A) To introduce expertise outside of the NIBIB in order to present a series of experimental procedures

B) To provide a second opinion to elaborate on potentially divisive research findings

C) To make a counterargument that paradoxically adds validity to the NIBIB outcomes

D) To show how scientists from Yale selectively appropriated past data in order to promote an alternative explanation

BNP Trials for Engineered Padimate O (2017)

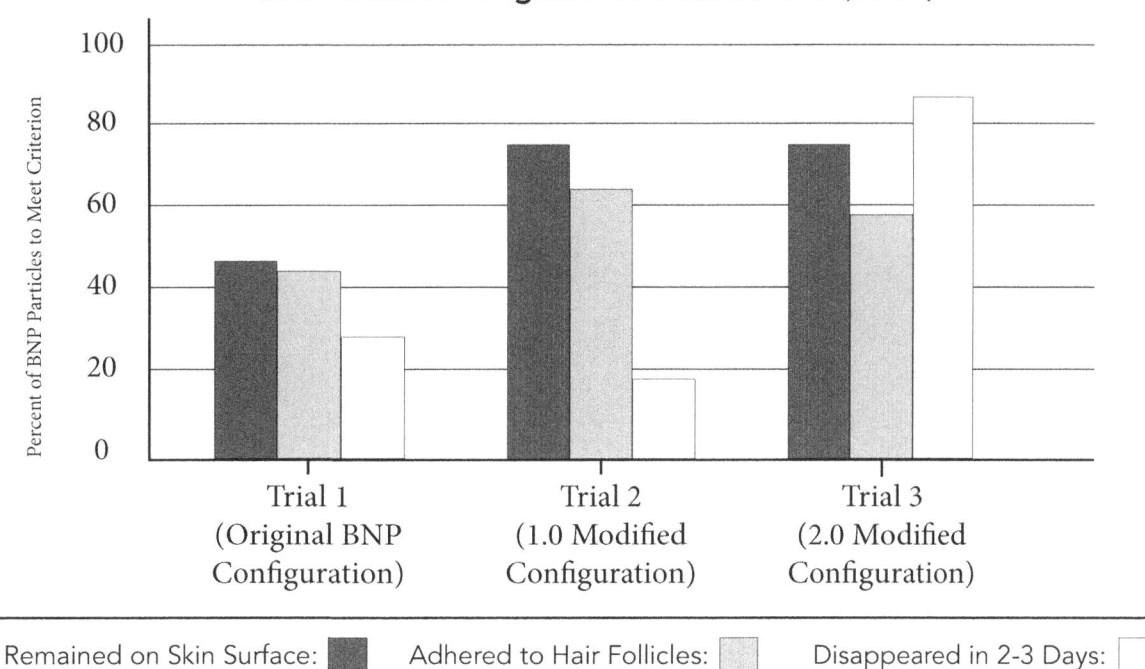

Trial	Remained on Skin Surface	Adhered to Hair Follicles	Disappeared in 2-3 Days
Trial 1 (Original BNP Configuration)	46	44	28
Trial 2 (1.0 Modified Configuration)	75	64	18
Trial 3 (2.0 Modified Configuration)	75	58	87

(Percent of BNP Particles to Meet Criterion)

49

Which choice provides the best evidence for the answer to the previous question?

A) Lines 55-57 ("The bioadhesive . . . skin")
B) Lines 65-68 ("Because . . . route")
C) Lines 70-74 ("Surprisingly . . . follicles")
D) Lines 78-79 ("They also . . . skin")

50

As used in line 79, "exfoliation" most nearly means

A) banishment.
B) flaking.
C) acquisition.
D) extraction.

51

The results recorded in the graph were classified as representing a successful outcome by the researchers involved. From this information, it can be inferred that the researchers aimed to create

A) a version of padimate O that would not adhere to hair follicles.
B) three distinct versions of padimate O that would all deflect similar quantities of UV radiation.
C) long-lasting and short-lasting versions of padimate O that are comparable in other respects.
D) a "definitive" version of padimate O that would be superior to other versions for all three criteria.

52

Unlike the research described in the passage, the research considered in the graph involved

A) a nearly perfect success rate for one of the desired experimental outcomes.
B) a control group for the purpose of assessing padimate O that has not undergone BNP configuration.
C) monitoring of blood vessels to gauge particle movement.
D) multiple BNP configurations for padimate O.

STOP

If you finish before time is called, you may check your work on this section only.
Do not turn to any other section.

Answer Key on the Next Page

Answer Key: Test 5

Passage 1	Passage 2	Passage 3	Passage 4	Passage 5
1. C	11. A	21. A	31. B	42. A
2. A	12. D	22. C	32. C	43. C
3. B	13. A	23. A	33. B	44. C
4. B	14. B	24. B	34. A	45. C
5. D	15. D	25. A	35. B	46. D
6. A	16. C	26. B	36. C	47. B
7. D	17. B	27. D	37. A	48. A
8. B	18. B	28. B	38. B	49. A
9. A	19. D	29. B	39. A	50. B
10. B	20. D	30. C	40. C	51. C
			41. C	52. D

Question Types

Major Issue
1, 17, 21, 31-32, 42

Passage Details
5, 7-9, 14, 25, 27-28, 38, 46-47

Command of Evidence
2-4, 12, 15-16, 23-24, 29-30, 33-35, 43-44, 48-49

Word in Context
6, 10, 11, 13, 22, 26, 36-37, 45, 50

Graphics and Visuals
39-41, 51-52

Passage Comparison
18-20

Answer Explanations
Test 5, Pages 122-138

Passage 1, Pages 122-124

1. C is the correct answer.

While the passage opens by registering Miss Sydney's dissatisfaction with the plan of the "city authorities" (lines 3-4) to alter the area near her home, the passage transitions to consider the state of Miss Sydney's contact with the world, which is characterized by the disappearance of her friends and by her sense of "empty, formal, heartless discipline (line 72). This content supports C, while A and B neglect the predominantly negative reactions that Miss Sydney (despite having favorite rooms and possessions) has to her living situation. D attributes the wrong negative to Miss Sydney later in the passage; she has accepted her state of isolation and does not pursue change in a manner that would indicate frustration.

2. A is the correct answer.

In lines 7-11, the author indicates that Miss Sydney finds the local government's plan to create a new "public thoroughfare" extremely provoking, in part because the street "noise" that she must endure is already a considerable source of displeasure. A is thus appropriate, while "neighbors" are not a source of inconvenience and are, instead, mostly a negative reminder of the disappearance of Miss Sydney's old way of life. Eliminate B for this reason, and eliminate C and D as answers that seem to indicate the cause of a problem (government) but not the reason (noise) that most directly explains Miss Sydney's displeasure.

3. B is the correct answer.

See the previous answer explanation for analysis of the correct line reference. A describes measures taken by the city to open a new street, C provides a description of Miss Sydney's habits, and D indicates that one of her chosen settings (a house library) is not entirely pleasant. Note that A does not indicate the direct source of displeasure (the noise) in the manner of B, and that C and D (despite a few mildly negative notes) do not align with any topics presented in the previous question.

Answer Explanations, Test 5

4. B is the correct answer.

In lines 22-26, the narrator explains that Miss Sydney has re-arranged her possessions so that she mostly uses portions of her living space not exposed to "the rattle and clatter" of a specific street; B is thus an effective choice. A and C describe the layout of Miss Sydney's house but NOT any actions that she has taken (as required by the prompt), while D presents some negatives regarding Miss Sydney's lifestyle but does not raise the crucial topic of noise.

5. D is the correct answer.

The paragraph begins with an explanation of the state of the neighborhood when Miss Sydney's current house had first been built (lines 31-33), then continues with a discussion of various changes such as new neighborhood features, the disappearance of Miss Sydney's friends, and Miss Sydney's life as an "old woman" (line 45). This focus on alterations over time in the neighborhood supports D as appropriate. A wrongly indicates that Miss Sydney had a positive (rather than simply resigned or unhappily accepting) response to loneliness. B both neglects the neighborhood as a topic and wrongly indicates that a rigorous or meticulous timeline (as opposed to various impressions that indicate a contrast) is present, while C refers to a topic that is established in the PREVIOUS paragraphs.

6. A is the correct answer.

The word "aristocratic" refers to the "old street" (line 35) that Miss Sydney reflects upon; in context, the street had been the site of her comfortable home, which she had refused to sell even for "many thousand dollars" (line 38). This content supports the idea of comfort, wealth, or affluence; choose A and eliminate B (government) as raising a topic mostly appropriate to the discussion of city authorities in the PREVIOUS paragraph. C and D similarly misdirect the reference; the word "aristocratic" should explain the former condition of the street, not the condition of the warehouses or demographic changes that re-shaped the once-aristocratic area.

7. D is the correct answer.

The author's descriptions occur in the context of Miss Sydney's reflections on "the dear old times" (lines 39-40) and the various features that are named help to explain how one group of trappings was "replaced" (line 42) with another. Thus, the descriptions call attention to the idea of change in a specific area; choose D as appropriate. A (oddities) and B (squandered) both serve to criticize the neighborhood when in fact the author is mainly interested in contrasting two states; C refers to a later topic (social life) and WRONGLY indicates that the mostly isolated Miss Sydney wants to go out in society in an active manner.

8. B is the correct answer.

In lines 65-70, the narrator links Miss Sydney's condition of not "having friends" to her generally isolated and unappealing social lifestyle; B properly reflects this strongly negative content. A rightly calls attention to emotional or psychological distress but WRONGLY indicates that Miss Sydney (who is rich and charitable according to line 62) has financial problems. C relates to a topic that is mainly considered in the opening paragraph, BEFORE Miss Sydney's absent and deceased friends become of interest, while D wrongly indicates that the loss of friends is a problem that is relevant to Miss Sydney's entire life, not simply her lonely old age.

9. A is the correct answer.

The relevant quotation indicates that Miss Sydney is mainly invited to funerals, not to social events, in her present old age; A properly reflects the strong negative emotions that her loss of friends inspires. B and C wrongly assume that the focus of the quotation is on the distant past (NOT the unappealing present), while D focuses on a topic (the neighborhood) dealt with elsewhere in the passage but not explicitly raised in the quotation itself.

10. B is the correct answer.

The word "liberally" refers to the activity of Miss Sydney, who is "charitable" (line 62), in giving to the social causes that come to her attention. B properly introduces a strong positive related to giving, while A (indicating stubbornness or disobedience) wrongly introduces a negative. C (pleasure or joy) and D (caution or reserve) introduce possible positives but are not directly relevant to the context of financial giving to causes.

Passage 2, Pages 125-127

11. A is the correct answer.

The word "advocate" refers to someone who, in terms of addressing the problems of the slave trade, has "undertaken this great cause" (line 7); thus, an advocate would be someone who is here energetic or active in pursuing political goals. A is thus appropriate, while B (context of hope) raises a strong positive when in fact Wilberforce calls attention to conflict and challenges. C and D call attention to specific administrative or governmental roles that do NOT automatically fit the simpler and perhaps unofficial act of working for a cause.

12. D is the correct answer.

In lines 46-52, Wilberforce indicates that the fact that some merchants think "generally" on the slave trade, rather than considering the subject "feelingly," explains their support. Thus, a change of mentality or perspective that eliminates abstractions and distractions would, as Wilberforce suggests, result in a change of position on the slave trade. D is an appropriate choice. A and B describe Wilberforce's OWN persistence and his determination to discuss the issue in a reasonable way, while C indicates that Wilberforce will not level accusations but does NOT raise the required topic of change of opinion.

13. A is the correct answer.

The "task" referenced by Wilberforce is not only a topic central to his efforts but also a topic which makes him aware of "inadequacy" (line 10); later content indicates that Wilberforce wants to eliminate the "horrid

Answer Explanations, Test 5

trade" (line 36) of human slaves but that he envisions a national effort that extends well beyond himself. This content supports A, while B and C raise issues that would logically be connected to Wilberforce's task but are NOT his primary challenges or "tasks," since (despite his self-conscious and fair-minded tone) he has already decided on his approach and is mostly interested in practical political change. D raises a topic that again deals with debate, NOT with bringing about political change, and that is less important to Wilberforce than the moral implications of slavery are.

14. B is the correct answer.

In line 57, Bridges continues to explain his role as a Church advocate by noting that he is "the friend of truth and justice," so that the references to his role are meant to indicate his positive values and virtues. B is thus an appropriate choice. A and D are problematic because the details of the slave trade are the topic of the NEXT paragraph of the passage, while Bridges here is explaining his own character overall. C wrongly indicates a focus on the Church itself in detail, NOT on the specific role that Bridges plays as a virtuous leader.

15. D is the correct answer.

In lines 69-72, Bridges indicates that the elimination of slavery as a whole must be left to "another generation." This indication that slavery will not be abolished in the author's own time supports D, while A, B, and C all indicate specific methods that are not mentioned as workable solutions and that, by saying that slavery will be abolished only later, Bridges declines to predict. Be especially careful of B and C, since the general fact that Bridges is a reasonable and measured author does NOT directly or logically offer support for any highly specific policy recommendation.

16. C is the correct answer.

See the previous answer explanation for analysis of the correct line reference. A indicates that the author objects to violent means in fighting slavery (and thus contradicts false answer A in the previous question). B indicates that Bridges respects Wilberforce's efforts to combat slavery but does NOT raise the topic of specific measures to end slavery entirely, while D indicates that Bridges is aware of Wilberforce's enthusiasm in the cause against slavery but does NOT call attention to the limitations of such enthusiasm as C does.

17. B is the correct answer.

In Passage 2, the author directly addresses Wilberforce and explains that, while ending the slave trade is a remarkable goal, the larger goal of ending slavery itself is beyond the scope of Wilberforce's generation (lines 69-72). This content supports B; although Bridges DOES cite Wilberforce's reputation (lines 64-69), this positive content should not be mistaken for the negative statement about Wilberforce's motives that occurs in A. The Church and areas abroad are also mentioned (lines 53-56), but only to point out that Wilberforce's criticisms of these institutions are perhaps too harsh, NOT that he is fundamentally flawed in his ideas about slavery or society; such content renders C and D problematic.

Answer Explanations, Test 5

18. B is the correct answer.

While the author of Passage 1 harshly criticizes the slave trade (lines 33-37), the author of Passage 2 indicates that such criticisms are valid but that slavery as a whole cannot be eliminated within the lifetime of the author of Passage 1 (lines 69-72). This sense of overall moral agreement but, for Passage 2, strong objections in terms of practicality supports B and can be used to eliminate both C and D, which assume more thoroughly positive relationships. A is incorrect because, even though Bridges objects to some ideas set forward by Wilberforce, he both offers praise (rather than conscious distortion) and raises a FURTHER issue (slavery as a whole) that extends the discussion beyond the consideration of the slave trade that dominates Passage 1.

19. D is the correct answer.

While Wilberforce in Passage 1 characterizes the slave trade as linked to "evil" (line 48), Bridges in Passage 2 indicates that the extinction of the slave trade would relieve the "sufferings of humanity" (line 67) for those connected to such a trade. This content supports D and can be used to eliminate A, since the authors are mostly concerned with moral righteousness, NOT economic outcomes. B points to a possible positive outcome that, though likely to relieve suffering, is NOT explicitly raised by either passage and is thus not within the bounds of the discussion. C focuses on the past, rather than on the present injustices faced by slaves or the future possibility of eliminating the slave trade, and thus misrepresents the true topics of the passages.

20. D is the correct answer.

While Wilberforce describes his own "weakness" (line 6) as an advocate for his cause, Bridges refers to himself as a "feeble advocate" (line 53) who takes a strong interest in both the affairs of the Church and the fight against slavery. This content supports D and should NOT be taken as support for A, since each author describes only himself (NOT his allies) in a somewhat negative manner. B may seem to be supported by the reservations about quickly abolishing slavery as a whole that occur in Passage 2 but is contradicted by the assertive stance against the slave trade present in Passage 1. C misconstrues the topic of suffering (which is indeed linked to the discussion of slavery) to focus on firsthand observations of suffering (when in fact it is not clear whether either author has personally or directly witnessed the sufferings of slaves or has simply heard about such injustices from a distance).

Passage 3, Pages 128-130

21. A is the correct answer.

After explaining modern advancements in AI and in the related field of ML, the author goes on to describe the "myriad opportunities" (line 43) for ML usage in medicine and indicates that such applications would "save both vision and money" (lines 91-92). This content supports A, while B and D focus ONLY on the financial side of the author's discussion and neglect the topics of personal wellness and scientific advancement. C wrongly indicates that ML is instrumental mainly in addressing problematic methods (not in providing supplemental improvements to largely effective medical procedures as described by the author).

Answer Explanations, Test 5

22. C is the correct answer.

The cited words refer to actions taken by "practitioners" (line 2) and other specialists in formulating AI and ML techniques, so that these words help the authors to provide an overview of changes in an area of science that, as described in the passage, is advancing and useful. C is thus appropriate, while A wrongly focuses on the authors' OWN credentials (which are never mentioned) instead of on background information for AI and ML. B introduces a sense of prediction, when in fact the authors are mostly recording past events, while D introduces a predominant and incorrect overall negative tone.

23. A is the correct answer.

In lines 17-19, the authors call attention to "significant advances" in AI that are applicable to everyday life; this content directly supports A. While B and D call attention to possible everyday uses, these answers are too narrow in scope (since the question calls for a "central idea" that would relate to the authors' broadly positive position, NOT for extremely precise examples). C calls attention to the usefulness of Machine Learning but indicates that this technology will overpower humans (an idea that the authors call into question in lines 28-31) rather than be of use to humans (an idea that the authors support).

24. B is the correct answer.

See the previous answer explanation for analysis of the correct line reference. A explains the development of Machine Learning but provides mostly historical information, NOT a general stance or central idea as required by the previous question. C calls attention to a few specific applications of AI but, similarly, does not offer an overall statement that captures the authors' positive position on such technology, while D calls attention to the idea that the reality of ML is misunderstood and actually suggests that false answer C in the previous question is highly problematic.

25. A is the correct answer.

The authors explain that AI advances have "enabled a machine" (line 25) to beat human Jeopardy and Go champions; thus, machines can excel in competitive tasks and can outperform human "champions" (line 26). This content supports A, while B and C wrongly indicate that AI has altered game formats in some manner, NOT simply that AI programs can excel in CURRENT gaming formats. D wrongly indicates that AI (which has indeed evolved according to lines 1-27) has evolved alongside gaming formats (which, though a platform for exceptional AI performance, are never described as having THEMSELVES changed over time).

26. B is the correct answer.

The word "hyperbole" should refer to an advertising practice that results in "skepticism and misunderstanding" (lines 29-30), so that a negative results linked to distortion or overstatement result. B is thus an appropriate choice, while A and D wrongly introduce positive connotations. C indicates that the advertising practices are unusual or outside ordinary practice, a faulty meaning since the authors indicate that advertising "hyperbole" has had a strong and widespread effect.

Answer Explanations, Test 5

27. D is the correct answer.

While the authors begin the third paragraph with a critical reference to "advertising hyperbole" (lines 28-29), the authors then go on to present their own "accurate portrayal" (lines 32-33) of present ML and AI capabilities. D is thus an acceptable choice, while A and C refer to the scientific capabilities of AI and ML but do NOT introduce contrasts (since the authors document these abilities in detail rather than, in the relevant paragraph, pointing out flaws in expectations or problems in specific fields). B wrongly neglects the fact that the authors speak NEGATIVELY of advertising depictions of ML and is for this reason problematic.

28. B is the correct answer.

In line 67, the word "power" refers to a property of deep learning that has been "most evident" (lines 67-68) in one particular medical field, ophthalmology. The authors are thus using the word "power" to positively call attention to an area of technology application, so that B is appropriate. While A, C, and D all reference branches of AI in a positive manner, these answers do NOT call attention to the specific field of ophthalmology that is of interest to the authors and thus do not capture the precise reference linked to the word "power."

29. B is the correct answer.

In lines 67-73, the authors explain that Deep Learning was successfully applied to "heterogeneous" (or markedly different) scans in ophthalmology; B is directly supported by this information. A focuses on an issue that is raised mainly in the final lines of the passage (and does so in a manner that is out of scope, since the initial expense of the procedures that are now subject to savings is NOT considered). C and D both mischaracterize the usefulness of Deep Learning; such technology is a tool that is useful to researchers, NOT a method that makes the researchers themselves obsolete.

30. C is the correct answer.

See the previous answer explanation for analysis of the correct line reference. A broadly indicates that Deep Learning is useful but does NOT suggest a specific medical application as required by the previous question. B indicates that Deep Learning considers complex images, a beneficial usage that nonetheless does not align with any answer to the previous question, while D indicates that a method that uses Deep Learning has been granted approval but NOT (as the previous question requires) what exactly the benefits of this method are.

Passage 4, Pages 131-134

31. B is the correct answer.

In the passage, the author explains that Internet access can "work to the advantage of the authorities" (lines 65-66) in oppressive countries, but later goes on to explain that "electronic communication" (line 84) was of use to activists in Egypt. This content supports B, while the passage contradicts A because the author actually

Answer Explanations, Test 5

argues that open Internet access can persuade "couch" revolutionaries to remain relatively uninvolved. C wrongly distorts the author's idea that open Internet access can dampen dissident activity and presents the more extreme statement that Internet access is incompatible with revolutionary activity; D goes against the author's idea that the possibility of political protest among those who might normally be uninvolved is often weakened, NOT strengthened, by Internet access.

32. C is the correct answer.

The author begins the passage by explaining that revolutionary activity in Egypt "began to take off" (line 20) after Internet access was restricted, but then explains that governments can use Internet resources to monitor and misinform dissidents (lines 70-77). This content supports C, while A wrongly calls attention to theoretical considerations and recommendations when in fact the author is mostly interested in demonstrated historical results. B presents a series of recommendations and indicates that protesters should welcome Internet shutdowns (NOT that such shutdowns have positive incidental effects); D wrongly takes a positive or "excusing" tone towards governments that target dissidents and that the author depicts as authoritarian or at least as not clearly desirable.

33. B is the correct answer.

In lines 50-53, the author quotes Noam Cohen, a writer who believes that mass media can make people "passive" when faced with current events. This outside perspective related to a mentality that works against social protest fits the required topic; B is thus appropriate. A provides a secondary perspective but describes an increase in already enthusiastic activism (NOT a threat to activism). C presents a response that could involve the author's OWN ideas about activism (NOT a secondary perspective), while D continues the author's own analysis instead of providing a secondary response.

34. A is the correct answer.

In lines 28-32, the author (describing Hassanpour's ideas) explains that limiting Internet access in Egypt made revolutionary activity "more diffuse and more difficult for the authorities to contain." This content directly supports A, while B avoids the focus on political repercussions that is a priority of the passage. C and D assume a breakdown in communication between the government and the population, when in fact (according to lines 70-77) even a government that has limited Internet access can provide its people with information WHILE silencing dissidents and manipulating the information that the population receives.

35. B is the correct answer.

See the previous answer explanation for analysis of the correct line reference. A calls attention to the fact that dissidents in Egypt did face difficulties in communicating after the authorities limited Internet access but should NOT be mistaken as evidence that revolutionary activity decreased. C explains how Hassanpour conducted his analysis but does NOT cite any clear historical disadvantages, while D explains that limiting Internet access can contain an uprising but provides the author's perspective, NOT Hassanpour's.

Answer Explanations, Test 5

36. C is the correct answer.

The word "diffuse" refers to revolutionary activity that was "difficult for the authorities to contain" (line 32); activity that, though intense, is scattered or spread out across a country would be naturally difficult to localize and control. C is appropriate, while A and D would both wrongly indicate that the revolutionary activity was flawed (NOT that the authorities were challenged to contain it). B, "versatile," normally indicates a variety of skills or aptitudes in one person and is thus inappropriate to the context of containing a social movement.

37. A is the correct answer.

The author explains that a "couch revolutionary" is someone notable mainly for "watching events" (line 57) rather than physically taking part in protest movements; A fits this context while B directly contradicts the author's ideas. Since the Internet (in the context of the passage) is the primary medium that "couch revolutionaries" use to observe events, C is contradicted by the author's depiction and D focuses on a medium that the author does not analyze in significant detail.

38. B is the correct answer.

The relevant paragraph calls attention to how, "As has already happened in some countries," a government can use the Internet to monitor dissidents and spread unreliable news. Thus, the author expands the discussion of the political uses of social media to consider both dissident uses and authoritarian strategies; B is an appropriate choice. A focuses on dissidents, NOT on the authorities who are the main subjects of the paragraph, while C indicates that technology can undermine (NOT assist) authorities. D returns to a topic (Internet shutdown) considered at length EARLIER in the passage but largely abandoned here in favor of a consideration of how authorities use the Internet.

39. A is the correct answer.

Of the countries named, Canada has a high Democracy Index rating out of 10 and a high percentage of Internet users in its population. A is an effective choice; B indicates a country, the United States, that in comparison to Canada exhibits a marginally lower Internet user percentage and a significantly lower Democracy Index rating (so that the correlation is not as strong). Both C and D indicate countries with high percentages of Internet users and low Democracy Index ratings, so that democracy is NOT associated with Internet usage for these countries.

40. C is the correct answer.

The table indicates that some relatively authoritarian nations (such as Saudi Arabia) have high Internet usage percentages, while others (such as Syria) have low Internet usage percentages. Thus, these countries do not fit a single trend or pattern for Internet usage. C is appropriate, while the prevalence of Internet usage in some authoritarian nations directly contradicts A. The table only considers a SINGLE year (making B, which relates to change over time, out of scope) and does not consider either public opinion or broad economic factors (making D, which assumes specific references to these issues, out of scope).

Answer Explanations, Test 5

41. C is the correct answer.

While the tables do provide information on a country (Egypt) considered at length in the passage, these resources do not explain EXACTLY how dissidents and authorities used Internet resources (even though Internet usage is broadly considered by percentage of users in the population). C properly indicates that the tables neglect factors that would interest the author despite the relevance of a country being considered. A wrongly indicates that the author would reject the findings entirely (when in fact the author would agree that Egypt is a relatively authoritarian government with a significant percentage of Internet users). B analyzes the motives of political groups (who would reject ideologies or policies but NOT necessarily broad national statistics, on the basis of the passage), while D analyzes the possible future of democratic nations (which are not considered at length in the passage's analysis of more authoritarian governments).

Passage 5, Pages 135-138

42. A is the correct answer.

As indicated in the first paragraph, the passage is devoted to a discussion of an engineered sunscreen that eliminates "a number of harmful effects" (line 5) associated with existing sunscreens; the author then proceeds to explain how BNP modifications were useful in creating such a sunscreen. A is thus the best answer, while B and C mistake the idea that the new sunscreen would AVOID harmful effects for the idea that the scientists described in the passage were seeking curative measures for various problems. D focuses on existing commercial sunscreen products, not on the new BNP-based sunscreen that was developed by the researchers, and thus does not fit the author's focus on experimentation and development.

43. C is the correct answer.

In lines 17-20, the author indicates that "penetration past the surface of the skin" is linked to the negative effects of existing sunscreens; it is entirely possible that such sunscreens (as indicated earlier in the passage) filter out UV light while causing damage due to such penetration. C is thus the best answer, while A mistakes the fact that the new BNP sunscreen developed by the researchers was tested on non-human animals for the much broader idea that humans and other animals respond to sunscreen in COMPLETELY identical ways. B and D indicate that existing sunscreens are fundamentally problematic in major ways, NOT that the BNP-modified sunscreen (as the passage actually argues) addresses a few key deficiencies of otherwise effective products.

44. C is the correct answer.

See the previous answer explanation for analysis of the correct line reference. A indicates that an experiment involving mice resulted in an improved sunscreen, B explains a benefit of existing sunscreens, and D explains an experimental procedure but does NOT reference current sunscreens. While B does fit the topic required by the previous question, this choice does not raise any negative possibilities that would effectively align with an answer to the previous question itself.

Answer Explanations, Test 5

45. C is the correct answer.

The relevant words either refer to the activities undertaken by "scientists" (line 2) or explain the outcomes of such activities; thus, the words provide direct information about a research inquiry that, in the context of the passage, involves sunscreen product improvement. C is thus appropriate, while A and B wrongly apply negatives to research that the author sees as useful in protecting the health of sunscreen users. D refers to the author's own background, NOT to the background or endeavors of the researchers, and thus raises a topic that is not directly addressed in the course of the passage.

46. D is the correct answer.

In the relevant paragraph, the author explains that commercial sunscreens "effectively" (line 17) prevent some health liabilities but do not address other "harmful effects" (line 19). D properly raises both positive and negative tones regarding commercial sunscreens, while A and B refer to broad-based opinions other than those presented by the author (the only authority whose perspective is here presented) and are thus beyond the scope of the paragraph. C raises a topic ("nanoparticles") that is only addressed LATER in the passage.

47. B is the correct answer.

The word "novel" refers to an idea in bioengineering in the context of addressing a "significant health problem" (line 28); thus, the word itself refers to research (here, involving the composition of specific sunscreens) that is meaningful and useful. B is thus an appropriate answer. A best refers to earlier content (lines 16-20) and C and D are more relevant to the LATER discussion of nanoparticles, which are not yet identified as the exact means of addressing the health risk that is the immediate focus of the word "novel."

48. A is the correct answer.

In lines 58-62, the author explains a stage of the experiment performed by the Yale University researchers, directly referencing such researchers as members of "the group" and outlining their methods. It is not clear that the Yale researchers are working entirely alongside the NIBIB experts, yet the methods used are evident; A is thus an acceptable answer. B, C, and D all assume strong disagreement between the Yale and NIBIB experts, when in fact (as indicated in lines 27-31) the NIBIB researchers generally greeted the Yale results with approval.

49. A is the correct answer.

See the previous answer explanation for analysis of the correct line reference. B and C refer to the Yale experiment but primarily present outcomes, NOT the underlying procedures that would explain these outcomes. D records an experimental result without referencing procedures in a manner that would support correct answer A in the previous question.

Answer Explanations, Test 5

50. B is the correct answer.

The word "exfoliation" refers to a skin-related process that would naturally and automatically cause particles to disappear; B, "flaking," would be appropriate. A (indicating rejection of a person, not a particle), C (a positive that indicates the exact opposite of the context), and D (indicating highly conscious or methodical action, not a natural response) all introduce faulty contexts and should thus be eliminated.

51. C is the correct answer.

In the chart, Trial 2 and Trial 3 present versions of padimate O that last for different time periods but have similar adhesive properties; one successful result, as indicated by these trials, would be the modification of one property (duration) while others remain constant. C reflects this information, while A is contradicted by the fact that NO version of padimate O avoided adhesion to hair follicles by 100%. B is out of scope because UV radiation is NOT directly considered in the graph (despite the discussion of this factor in the passage), while D is contradicted by the fact that the Trial 2 version was superior in avoiding adhesion to hair follicles while the Trial 3 version was superior in all other respects.

52. D is the correct answer.

While the researchers described in the passage developed only one padimate O variation (lines 50-57) despite running multiple tests, the graph considers three distinct variations for padimate O. This information supports D, while the passage indicates that the use of nanoparticle engineering reliably kept padimate O from penetrating the skin of test subjects; thus, A describes a SIMILARITY, not a difference between the graph (which records nearly-perfect outcomes for substance disappearance) and the passage. While the graph considers BNP modifications only (eliminating B, which assumes the presence of a non-BNP control group), both the graph and the passage (line 61) consider blood vessel movement (eliminating C, which describes a similarity instead of a difference).

NOTES

- Passage 3 on Pages 128-129, "Better medicine through machine learning: What's real, and what's artificial?" is adapted from the article of the same by Suchi Saria et al. and published by PLOS Medicine. 31 December 2018, PLOS ONE Journal (PLOS Med). https://journals.plos.org/plosmedicine/article?id=10.1371/journal.pmed.1002721. Accessed 28 July 2019.

- Passage 4 on Pages 131-132, "Dictatorship 101: killing the internet plays into the hands of revolutionaries," is an excerpt from the article of the same name by Lawrence J. Saha and published by The Conversation in affiliation with Australian National University. 8 September 2011, The Conversation. https://theconversation.com/dictatorship-101-killing-the-internet-plays-into-the-hands-of-revolutionaries-3254. Accessed 28 July 2019.

- Passage 5 on Page 135, "Bioengineered sunscreen blocks skin penetration and toxicity," is adapted from the article of the same name published by the National Institute of Biomedical Imaging and Bioengineering. 14 December 2015, NIBIB. https://www.nibib.nih.gov/news-events/newsroom/bioengineered-sunscreen-blocks-skin-penetration-and-toxicity. Accessed 28 July 2019.

About the Figures: The various visual resources that accompany the passages in this section are primarily meant to facilitate critical thinking skills and may not reflect historical data. Information on the Democracy Index Ratings used in the table on Page 134 can be found at https://www.eiu.com/topic/democracy-index.

Test 6

Full Reading Section

2020 SAT Practice

Test 6

Reading Test

65 MINUTES, 52 QUESTIONS

Turn to Section 1 of your answer sheet to answer the questions in this section.

DIRECTIONS

Each passage or pair of passages below is followed by a number of questions. After reading each passage or pair, choose the best answer to each question based on what is stated or implied in the passage or passages and in any accompanying graphics (such as a table or graph).

Questions 1-10 are based on the following passage.

This passage is adapted from "The Last Lesson" (1873) by Alphonse Daudet. The narrative addresses the consequences of the defeat of the French forces in the Franco-Prussian War (1870-1871). Originally written in French, the story was published in the translation that appears here by Francis J. Reynolds in the volume *International Short Stories* (1920).

    I started for school very late that morning and was in great dread of a scolding, especially because M. Hamel had said that he would
Line question us on participles, and I did not know the
5 first word about them. For a moment I thought of running away and spending the day out of doors. It was so warm, so bright! The birds were chirping at the edge of the woods, and in the open field in back of the saw-mill the Prussian soldiers were
10 drilling. It was all much more tempting than the rule for participles, but I had the strength to resist, and hurried off to school.
    When I passed the town hall there was a crowd in front of the bulletin-board. For the last two
15 years all our bad news had come from there—the battles we lost to the Germans, the draft, the orders of the commanding officer—and I thought to myself, without stopping:
    "What can be the matter now?"
20   Then, as I hurried by as fast as I could go, the blacksmith, Wachter, who was there, with his apprentice, reading the bulletin, called after me:
    "Don't go so fast, bub; you'll get to your school in plenty of time!"
25   I thought he was making fun of me, and reached M. Hamel's little garden all out of breath.
    Usually, when school began, there was a great bustle which could be heard out in the street, the opening and closing of desks, lessons repeated in
30 unison, very loud, with our hands over our ears to understand better, and the teacher's great ruler rapping on the table. But now it was all so still! I had counted on the commotion to get to my desk without being seen, but, of course, that day
35 everything had to be as quiet as Sunday morning. Through the window I saw my classmates, already in their places, and M. Hamel walking up and down with his terrible iron ruler under his arm. I had to open the door and go in before
40 everybody. You can imagine how I blushed and how frightened I was.

But nothing happened, M. Hamel saw me and said very kindly:

"Go to your place quickly, little Franz. We
45 were beginning without you."

I jumped over the bench and sat down at my desk. Not till then, when I had got a little over my fright, did I see that our teacher had on his beautiful green coat, his frilled shirt, and the little
50 black silk cap, all embroidered, that he never wore except on inspection and prize days. Besides, the whole school seemed so strange and solemn. But the thing that surprised me most was to see, on the back benches that were always empty, the village
55 people sitting quietly like ourselves: old Hauser, with his three-cornered hat, the former mayor, the former postmaster, and several others besides. Everybody looked sad, and Hauser had brought an old primer, thumbed at the edges, and he held it
60 open on his knees, with his great spectacles lying across the pages.

While I was wondering about it all, M. Hamel mounted his chair and, in the same grave and gentle tone which he had used to me, said:
65 "My children, this is the last lesson I shall give you. The order has come from Berlin to teach only German in the schools of Alsace and Lorraine. The new master comes to-morrow. This is your last French lesson. I want you to be very
70 attentive."

. . . Poor man! It was in honor of this last lesson that he had put on his fine Sunday-clothes, and now I understood why the old men of the village were sitting there in the back of the room.
75 It was because they were sorry, in the face of military defeat, that they had not gone to school more. It was their way of thanking our master for his forty years of faithful service and of showing their respect for the country that was theirs no
80 more.

1

Over the course of the passage, the narrator's primary focus shifts from

A) Franz's fear of being scolded to his sad realization about the outcome of the war.

B) the liberty embodied by Franz's beautiful, picturesque surroundings to the confinement of the classroom.

C) the sight of the Prussian soldiers to the sight of the old men sitting in the classroom.

D) M. Hamel's cruel attitude as a teacher to the appealing traits of old Hauser.

2

As used in line 28, "bustle" most nearly means

A) recklessness.

B) excitement.

C) commotion.

D) outcry.

3

In the context of the passage as a whole, the second paragraph functions as

A) a tangent.

B) a premonition.

C) a speculation.

D) an excuse.

Test 6

4

Which choice provides the best evidence for the answer to the previous question?

A) Lines 25-26 ("I thought . . . breath")
B) Lines 33-35 ("I had . . . morning")
C) Lines 65-66 ("My . . . you")
D) Lines 75-77 ("It was . . . more")

5

As used in line 52, "strange" most nearly means

A) implausible.
B) unusual.
C) alienated.
D) ridiculous.

6

The primary impression created by the description of M. Hamel in lines 37-39 is that this teacher

A) is quite strict.
B) is frequently self-righteous.
C) is not physically fit.
D) is inordinately cruel.

7

In explaining the situation in the schoolroom, the narrator indicates that

A) everybody in the area wanted to congregate at the school.
B) the people sitting at the back of the classroom had been very patient.
C) M. Hamel had reached customary retirement age.
D) French would not be taught in the regional schools anymore.

8

The main purpose of the final paragraph is to

A) convey an overall sense of loss and imminent change.
B) catalogue the distinctive clothing and demeanor of M. Hamel.
C) emphasize the importance of education in guiding the citizenry.
D) portray M. Hamel as a stern and unwavering teacher.

9

Which statement best characterizes the attitude of the adults in the schoolroom towards M. Hamel?

A) They were indifferent to him despite his merits.
B) They were judgmental of M. Hamel's idiosyncratic teaching style.
C) They were gratified that he was retiring and saw his actions as subtly rebellious.
D) They appreciated his contributions even when faced with misfortune.

10

Which choice provides the best evidence for the answer to the previous question?

A) Lines 51-52 ("Besides . . . solemn")
B) Line 58 ("Everybody . . . sad")
C) Lines 62-64 ("While . . . said")
D) Lines 77-78 ("It was . . . service")

Questions 11-20 are based on the following passage and supplementary material.

This passage is adapted from Liam Zachary, "It's time for universities to rethink what counts as field school," an article that first appeared* in the PLOS Early Career Researcher community blog.

Field school season is approaching for anthropology and earth science undergraduate students, and while some students have already enrolled in an exciting field school program, many are still scrambling to find a spot, and even more students are priced out of the experience altogether.

Field schools in archaeology, geology, palaeontology, and other fields of anthropology and earth science were initially envisioned to complement classroom and lab-based undergraduate science instruction, but today field school is a luxury for students. As the cost of undergraduate education continues to rise, especially in the United States, it has become more difficult for some students to justify attending field school instead of taking a summer job or paid internship. Universities need to do more to support student field training, which has tremendous benefits for the professional and academic development of students. Many undergraduate students share my experience of first connecting with a subject of passion while working in the field, which can shape the trajectory for future research careers.

My own first experience with archaeological field work was during an internship at the University of California, Santa Cruz (UCSC) campus during my senior year in 2013. We excavated a portion of the Cowell Limeworks on weekends for 10 weeks. The limeworks was in use during the 19th and early 20th century. . . . My professors reiterated that field school is the most important experience for an archaeology undergraduate student, but the coursework at universities does not reflect this sentiment. In field schools, students receive practical training in their discipline, and also meet students from other universities who are also passionate about the subject. Field schools enable students to develop practical skills, such as archaeological excavation or geologic survey, which cannot be learned in the classroom. Finally, field schools connect undergraduate students with early career scientists and senior faculty for mentorship. I would suggest that students looking for a traditional academic field school experience visit the Institute for Field Research (IFR). IFR also offers two types of field school scholarships, one that is merit based and one that is based on financial need.

Field schools have many benefits, but are also prohibitively expensive. University field schools can cost more than US$3000, which equates to more than a semester of tuition at some state colleges in the United States.

The public university system was designed to make education affordable and accessible to all students. I am troubled that field schools are not integrated in the public higher education system, when so many professionals identify fieldwork training as critical to success. Many students receive significant financial aid to attend university, but Federal Student Aid (FAFSA) will not fund summer field schools. The lack of financial aid means that the field school system is only accessible to students who can afford to pay the fees out-of-pocket, limiting the experience to students who can afford the fees. Consequently, students from low-income backgrounds are less likely to pursue an education in science disciplines where field training is crucial. Until universities make field schools part of the curriculum in anthropology and earth sciences, many bright students will be discouraged from pursuing this discipline.

Fortunately, there are affordable alternatives to university-organized field schools, but they are not well publicized to students.

Passport in Time (PIT) is a volunteer archaeology and historic preservation program of the United States Forest Service. Volunteers work with Forest Service archaeologists and historians on projects in National Forests nationwide. PIT projects are free for volunteers and housing

*See Page 182 for the citation for this text.

85 (usually camping) is provided. Today, there are two exciting PIT projects with openings for students, the Hudson-Meng Bison Bone Bed Interpretation Project and a dinosaur fossil project in South Dakota. . . .
90   Though PIT offers great programs for students, there are not enough projects to shore up the need for additional financial support for students to attend field schools. Therefore, it is imperative that universities make field schools more
95 affordable and accessible by incorporating them into the curriculum.

11

The main purpose of the passage is to

A) encourage college students to attend field schools regardless of cost considerations.
B) emphasize the problems connected to attending field schools.
C) discourage students from pursuing summer jobs or paid internships relevant to field-work.
D) give a solutions-oriented overview of the pros and cons of attending field schools.

12

One claim about the current education system as it is depicted in the passage is that

A) students who are well off are more likely to take up careers in science.
B) students should find paid internships in order to be able to afford field schools.
C) students need not worry about the long-term costs of field schools because such programs are integrated into public education systems.
D) students should avoid pursuing a science career track if they come from low-income families.

13

Which choice provides the best evidence for the answer to the previous question?

A) Lines 21-24 ("Many . . . field")
B) Lines 43-45 ("Finally . . . mentorship")
C) Lines 69-71 ("students . . . crucial")
D) Lines 81-83 ("Volunteers . . . nationwide")

14

As used in line 36, "sentiment" most nearly means

A) opinion.
B) emotion.
C) shrewdness.
D) evidence.

15

The primary purpose of the statement in lines 76-78 ("Fortunately . . . students") is to

A) depict students' disinterest in field schools as inseparable from the high cost of such institutions.
B) give an overview of the intellectual benefits of field schools.
C) show that field schools can in fact be affordable.
D) emphasize that many students are unaware of options that approximate field-work experience.

Undergraduate Field School Cost and Enrollment

- Cost: Solid Line
- Enrollment: Dashed Line

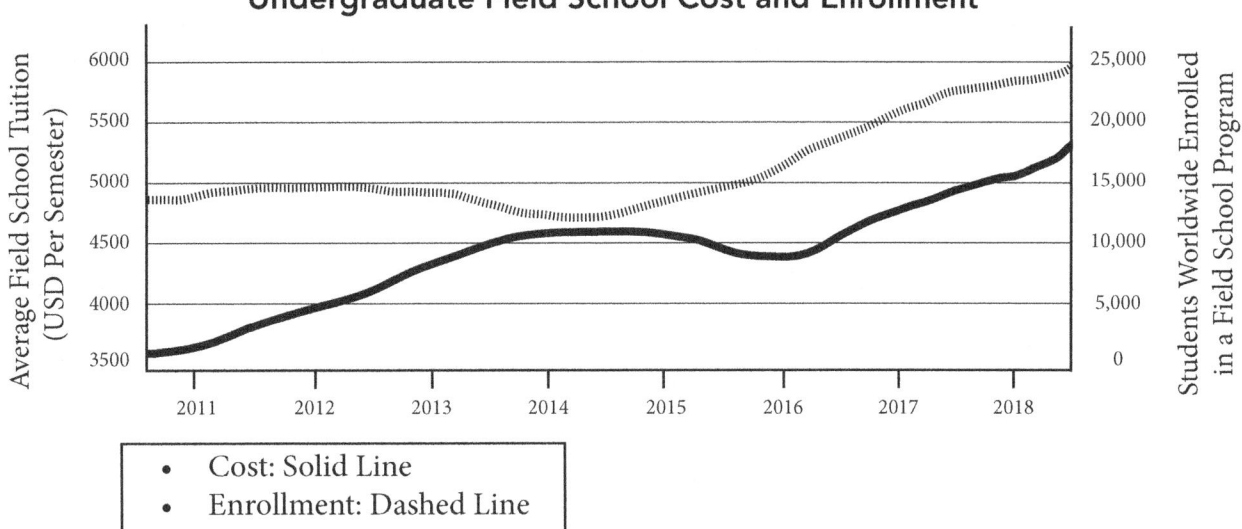

16

The passage indicates that an apparent problem with attending field schools is that

A) there are numerous choices and students have difficulty determining the best field school curriculum.

B) discrimination based on income is prevalent because field schools are quite costly.

C) there are no alternatives to field schools that would enable students to gain experience involving travel and collaboration.

D) the importance of attending field schools is not recognized among students despite the advocacy of professors.

17

Which choice provides the most direct and effective support for a point made by the author in lines 8-13 ("Field schools . . . students")?

A) Lines 33-36 ("My professors . . . sentiment")
B) Lines 45-50 ("I would . . . financial need")
C) Lines 51-55 ("Field schools . . . United States")
D) Lines 71-75 ("Until universities . . . discipline")

18

As used in line 91, "shore up" most nearly means

A) overpower.
B) support.
C) diminish.
D) discard.

19

According to the graph, between 2013 and 2014

A) average field school tuition decreased while total enrollment increased.
B) average field school tuition increased while total enrollment decreased.
C) average field school tuition began an irreversible upward trend.
D) field school enrollment began an irreversible upward trend.

20

Which of the following pieces of information would both explain the data provided in the graph and CONTRADICT the author's ideas as set forward in the passage?

A) Recent increases in household net worth have enabled larger numbers of affluent students to pursue field school despite rising tuition costs.
B) Grants that cover cost of living but do not decrease tuition have recently drawn larger numbers of low-income students to field school programs.
C) Deficiencies in accurately publicizing field school expenditures have repeatedly led low-income students to enroll in field school without making cost-efficient decisions.
D) Rising field school costs can be traced to the growing number of locations and specialized projects available to interested students.

Questions 21-30 are based on the following passage.

This passage is an excerpt from Heidi Silver, "Let them eat more fat? Researcher argues that a balance of types of fat is the key," published* in 2019 by The Conversation.

In the mid-1980s, advice to consume a low-fat diet became a strategy for weight control. Evidence from the landmark Framingham Heart
Line Study uncovered that obesity increased risk for
5 heart disease, and national data showed that the entire population was getting heavier.

Americans responded with a substantial reduction in the percentage of calories consumed as fat. But humans have a biological preference
10 for the taste of fat. And with fat off the table, millions increased their consumption of dietary carbohydrates to compensate for the loss in flavor and appeal of foods. As a result, there has been a substantial increase in the waistlines of
15 Americans.

Given the mixed scientific evidence on fat, and the diverse roles of dietary fatty acids in health and disease, about four years ago I designed a diet that is moderately high in fat, but the types of
20 fat are proportionally balanced: that is, one-third of total fat comes from saturated fats; one-third comes from monounsaturated fats; and one-third comes from polyunsaturated fats.

Based on this balanced moderately-high fat
25 diet approach, my research team developed a 14-day cycle of menus comprised of three meals and two snacks per day that increases intake of foods high in the 18-carbon monounsaturated fat, oleic acid, and the 18-carbon and longer chain
30 polyunsaturated fats (more commonly known as omega-3 and omega-6 fatty acids). To do this, we replaced high simple carbohydrate snacks with nuts, we replaced croutons in salads with avocado slices, and we used salad dressings high
35 in safflower oil, canola oil, and olive oil.

We have been studying the effects of this balanced moderately high fat diet in adults who

*See Page 182 for the citation for this text.

are overweight or obese. In a study with 144 women over a period lasting 16 weeks, we found
40 that study participants had significant reductions in abdominal fat and waist circumference; a 6 percent improvement in blood pressure; reduced blood levels of markers of inflammation; and overall a 6 percent reduction in their five- and ten-
45 year cardiovascular risk.

Study participants reported that they found our diet to be highly palatable, satisfying and economically feasible to adhere to. The firm adherence to our balanced moderately high
50 fat diet in the four-month study was reflected by significant changes in participants' plasma fatty acid profiles (the array of saturated and unsaturated fats in the blood) that reflected the fatty acid composition of the diet menus.

55 In a follow-up study using more in-depth analysis of the lipid response to the balanced moderately high fat diet, we found a difference in response between Caucasian females and African-American females. While the Caucasian females
60 had improvements in serum triglyceride and LDL-cholesterol levels, African-American females had the most significant improvement in HDL-cholesterol levels. These data support the concept that not all people respond to a dietary approach in
65 the same way and there is no one optimal diet for all people.

In another follow-up study of the response to a higher fat diet, we also found that people with a specific genotype had a stronger response, and
70 that response differed by sex, particularly with regard to improvements in HDL-cholesterol being stronger in females versus males.

Thus, I believe that the choice of an effective dietary approach must be determined based on
75 an individual's goals and an individual's clinical and metabolic response to the interaction between genes and environment.

There are limited studies on the strategy of balancing the type of dietary fat. While current
80 scientific consensus is that extremes of dietary fat intake, too high or too low, are unhealthy, I believe that a paradigm shift focusing on the types of dietary fats consumed may offer the opportunity to modify our cardiometabolic risk
85 factors without requiring major changes in the amount of fat or calories that we consume.

21

According to the information in the first paragraph,

A) a national weight problem was widely addressed through reduction of dietary fat intake.

B) the Framingham Heart Study was comprised only of people who had heart diseases.

C) diets containing exorbitant fat levels inevitably lead to cardiovascular problems.

D) heart disease can be considered a nationwide modern epidemic.

22

As used in line 9, "biological" most nearly means

A) molecular.

B) animalistic.

C) inherent.

D) visceral.

23

The main purpose of the author's analysis of the "Study participants" described in lines 46-48 is to

A) illustrate different types of diets.

B) reveal the widespread benefits of a healthy diet.

C) demonstrate that a healthy diet can be simultaneously pleasing and cost-efficient.

D) depict the major problems that people face when they begin new dietary regimens.

Test 6

24

In the course of its analysis of health recommendations, the passage indicates that

A) all of the acids under investigation carry health liabilities.
B) there are different types of fatty acids.
C) a healthy diet must be low-fat.
D) fatty acids are bad for the heart.

25

Which choice provides the best evidence for the answer to the previous question?

A) Lines 24-31 ("Based on . . . acids")
B) Lines 48-52 ("The firm . . . profiles")
C) Lines 67-69 ("In another . . . response")
D) Lines 79-81 ("While current . . . unhealthy")

26

As used in line 63, "concept" most nearly means

A) image.
B) performance.
C) scheme.
D) notion.

27

The passage's in-depth analysis of the lipid response demonstrates that

A) low-fat diets are not good for people's well-being.
B) no single diet would benefit all people equally.
C) the Caucasian females registered improvements in HDL cholesterol levels.
D) the African-American females registered minor improvements in HDL cholesterol levels.

28

Which choice provides the best evidence for the answer to the previous question?

A) Lines 46-48 ("Study . . . adhere to")
B) Lines 59-63 ("While . . . levels")
C) Lines 63-66 ("These . . . people")
D) Lines 78-79 ("There . . . fat")

29

The final paragraph serves mainly to

A) advise people to take up exercise and cut down on calorie intake.
B) underscore the fact that people must dramatically reduce the number of consumed calories.
C) reiterate facts pertaining to the importance of low-fat diets.
D) indicate that by combining different dietary fats people can improve their quality of life.

30

According to the passage, one of the conclusions that can be drawn from the author's study is that

A) every individual has unique responses to particular diets.
B) African-American women typically have high HDL cholesterol levels.
C) there are numerous and sometimes unexpected benefits of low-fat diets.
D) the results of the study itself were not affected by the race and the gender of the participants.

Questions 31-41 are based on the following passages.

Passage 1 is adapted from Susan Fenimore Cooper, "Female Suffrage," an extended letter that appeared in Harper's New Weekly Magazine in 1870. Passage 2 is adapted from a speech delivered by Clara Barton and dated to 1898.

Passage 1

We are told that women are to be elevated by the suffrage—and that by hanging on to the election tickets in the hands of their wives, the men are to be elevated with them. What, therefore, is the ground women now occupy, and from whence they are to soar upward on the paper wings of the ballot? The principal facts connected with that position are self-evident; there is nothing vague or uncertain here; we have but to look about us and the question is answered. We already know, for instance, from daily observation and actual experience, that, as a general rule, the kindness and consideration of American men have been great, both in public and in private life. We know that in American society women have been respected, they have been favored, they have been protected, they have been beloved. There has been a readiness to listen to their requests, to redress grievances, to make changes whenever these have become necessary or advisable. . . .

Whenever women make ill-judged, unnatural, extravagant demands, they must prepare to lose ground. Yes, even where the particular points in dispute are conceded to their reiterated importunity, they must still eventually lower their general standing and consideration by every false step. There are occasions where victory is more really perilous than a timely defeat; a temporary triumph may lead to ground which the victors can not permanently hold to their own true and lasting advantage. On the other hand, every just and judicious demand women may now make with the certainty of successful results. This is, indeed, the great fact which especially contributes to render the birthright of American women a favorable one. If the men of the country are already disposed to redress existing grievances, where women are concerned, as we know them to be, and if they are also ready, as we know them to be, to forward all needful future development of true womanly action, what more, pray, can we reasonably ask of them? Where lies this dim necessity of thrusting upon women the burdens of the suffrage? And why should the entire nation be thrown into the perilous convulsions of a revolution more truly formidable than any yet attempted on earth? Bear in mind that this is a revolution which, if successful in all its aims, can scarcely fail to sunder the family roof-tree, and to uproot the family hearth-stone.

Passage 2

I believe I must have been born believing in the full right of woman to all the privileges and positions which nature and justice accord to her in common with other human beings. Perfectly equal rights—human rights. There was never any question in my mind in regard to this. I did not purchase my freedom with a price; I was born free; and when, as a younger woman, I heard the subject discussed, it seemed simply ridiculous that any sensible, sane person should question it. And when, later, the phase of woman's right to suffrage came up it was to me only a part of the whole, just as natural, just as right, and just as certain to take place.

And whenever I have been urged, as a petitioner, to ask for this privilege for woman, a kind of dazed, bewildered feeling has come over me.

Of whom should I ask this privilege? Who possessed the right to confer it? Who had greater right than woman herself? Was it man, and, if so, where did he get it? Who conferred it upon him? He depended upon woman for his being, his very existence, nurture, and rearing. More fitting that she should have conferred it upon him.

Was it governments? What were they but the voice of the people? What gave them that power? Was it divinely conferred? Alas! No, or they would have been better, purer, more just and stable. . . .

But in one way or another, sooner or later, she is coming to it. And the number of thoughtful and right-minded men who will oppose suffrage will be much smaller than we think and when it is
85 really an accomplished fact all will wonder, as I have done, what the objection ever was.

31

What does Passage 1 suggest about the author's perception of women's suffrage?

A) The author was adamant about the need for women to take on positions of responsibility.
B) The author believed that granting voting rights to women would be detrimental.
C) The author viewed suffrage as a never-ending inconvenience to men.
D) The author was politically engaged overall but ambivalent about the right to vote.

32

Which choice provides the best evidence for the answer to the previous question?

A) Lines 12-14 ("the kindness . . . great")
B) Lines 14-17 ("We know . . . beloved")
C) Lines 33-36 ("This is . . . one")
D) Lines 42-47 ("Where . . . earth")

33

As used in line 22, "extravagant" most nearly means

A) ephemeral.
B) eclectic.
C) generous.
D) outrageous.

34

As used in line 25, "importunity" most nearly means

A) belief.
B) opportunity.
C) persistence.
D) sacrifice.

35

The primary purpose of lines 27-31 ("There . . . advantage") is to

A) imply that suffrage might have negative consequences in the future.
B) reinforce an argument for the importance of women's suffrage.
C) emphasize the proactive and self-congratulatory spirit of American men.
D) encourage women to enjoy and celebrate a specific political victory.

36

Which choice best indicates that the sentiments expressed by the author of Passage 2 were NOT universally accepted by the people of her era?

A) Lines 51-54 ("I believe . . . beings")
B) Lines 55-58 ("There . . . free")
C) Lines 65-68 ("And whenever . . . me")
D) Lines 73-75 ("He depended . . . him")

37

What is the main purpose of the questions in lines 69-72 of Passage 2?

A) To reinforce the notion that women should not wait to be granted that which is rightfully theirs

B) To portray a society that does not permit discrimination based on gender

C) To depict women's suffering due to their marginalized role in the society depicted by the author

D) To introduce views which were not prevalent during the author's lifetime

38

It can reasonably be inferred from the final paragraph of Passage 2 that the author believes that

A) there is little hope for women to triumph in their fight to obtain fundamental political rights.

B) many men will emerge as opponents of women's suffrage.

C) women will eventually undergo a dramatic change of attitude and renounce efforts to obtain the right to vote.

D) people of future generations will not fathom the initial problems linked to women's suffrage.

39

Both passages discuss the topic of

A) the benefits of traditional and stabilizing social roles for women.

B) the relations between men and women with respect to political rights.

C) the immediate discord that would result from granting women the right to vote.

D) an idealized yet unlikely reality in which women participate in everyday politics.

40

The crucial difference between the authors of Passage 1 and Passage 2 is that

A) they discuss disparate events in relation to the same topic.

B) one author has personal experience of marriage while the other does not.

C) they disagree on a fundamental issue in women's civic participation.

D) they come from unmistakably different social and educational backgrounds.

41

The author of Passage 1 is firmly convinced that granting women the right to vote would

A) result in the dissolution of current governments, whereas the author of Passage 2 conjectures that new reforms beyond suffrage for women are unlikely.

B) disrupt domestic conventions, whereas the author of Passage 2 predicts that men will be largely accepting of a changed situation.

C) make men ultimately subservient to women, whereas the author of Passage 2 welcomes radical alterations to rigid gender roles.

D) have international consequences, whereas the author of Passage 2 believes that the women's suffrage movement is not as wide-ranging as its critics imagine.

Test 6

Questions 42-52 are based on the following passage and supplementary material.

This passage is adapted from "In Search of Missing Worlds, Hubble Finds a Fast Evaporating Exoplanet," a 2018 news release published* by NASA.

Fishermen would be puzzled if they netted only big and little fish, but few medium-sized fish. Astronomers likewise have been perplexed in conducting a census of star-hugging extrasolar planets. They have found hot Jupiter-sized planets and hot super-Earths (planets no more than 1.5 times Earth's diameter). These planets are scorching hot because they orbit very close to their stars. But so-called "hot Neptunes,"
[10] whose atmospheres are heated to more than 1,700 degrees Fahrenheit, have been much harder to find. Only about a handful of hot Neptunes have been found so far.

In fact, most of the known Neptune-sized
[15] exoplanets are merely "warm," because they orbit farther away from their star than those in the region where astronomers would expect to find hot Neptunes. The mysterious hot-Neptune deficit suggests that such alien worlds are rare, or that
[20] they were plentiful at one time, but have since disappeared.

A few years ago, astronomers using NASA's Hubble Space Telescope found that one of the warmest known Neptunes (GJ 436b) is losing its
[25] atmosphere. The planet isn't expected to evaporate away, but hotter Neptunes might not have been so lucky.

Now, astronomers have used Hubble to nab a second "very warm" Neptune (GJ 3470b) that
[30] is losing its atmosphere at a rate 100 times faster than that of GJ 436b. Both planets reside about 3.7 million miles from their stars. That's one-tenth the distance between our solar system's innermost planet, Mercury, and the Sun.

[35] "I think this is the first case in which this is so dramatic in terms of planetary evolution," said lead researcher Vincent Bourrier of the University of Geneva in Sauverny, Switzerland. "It's one of the most extreme examples of a planet
[40] undergoing a major mass loss over its lifetime. This sizable mass loss has major consequences for its evolution, and it impacts our understanding of the origin and fate of the population of exoplanets close to their stars."

[45] As with the previously discovered evaporating planets, the star's intense radiation heats the atmosphere to a point where it escapes the planet's gravitational pull like an untethered hot air balloon. The escaping gas forms a giant cloud
[50] around the planet that dissipates into space. One reason why GJ 3470b may be evaporating faster than GJ 436b is that it is not as dense, so it is less able to gravitationally hang on to the heated atmosphere. . . .

[55] Uncovering two evaporating warm Neptunes reinforces the idea that the hotter version of these distant worlds may be a class of transitory planet whose ultimate fate is to shrink down to the most common type of known exoplanet,
[60] mini-Neptunes—planets with heavy, hydrogen-dominated atmospheres that are larger than Earth but smaller than Neptune. Eventually, these planets may downsize even further to become super-Earths, more massive, rocky versions of
[65] Earth.

"The question has been, where have the hot Neptunes gone?" said Bourrier. "If we plot planetary size and distance from the star, there's a desert, a hole, in that distribution. That's been
[70] a puzzle. We don't really know how much the evaporation of the atmospheres played in forming this desert. But our Hubble observations, which show a large amount of mass loss from a warm Neptune at the edge of the desert, is a direct
[75] confirmation that atmospheric escape plays a major role in forming this desert."

The researchers used Hubble's Space Telescope Imaging Spectrograph to detect the ultraviolet light signature of hydrogen in a huge
[80] cocoon surrounding the planet as it passed in front of its star. The intervening cocoon of hydrogen filters out some of the starlight. These results are interpreted as evidence of the planet's atmosphere bleeding off into space.

---

*See Page 182 for the citation for this text.

The team estimates that the planet has lost as much as 35 percent of its material over its lifetime, because it was probably losing mass at a faster rate when its red-dwarf star was younger and emitting even more radiation. If the planet continues to rapidly lose material, it will shrink down to a mini-Neptune in a few billion years.

42

The main purpose of the passage is to

A) give plausible explanations about the mass loss of exoplanets.
B) generate interest among members of the public regarding "hot Neptunes."
C) present the possibility of the existence of gaseous alien worlds.
D) discuss the importance of atmospheric properties in planetary geography.

43

Based on the passage, the primary enigma with respect to the "hot Neptunes" is why

A) they have been so frequently found.
B) they are so rare.
C) they are humid.
D) they are warm.

44

Which choice provides the best evidence for the answer to the previous question?

A) Lines 12-13 ("Only about . . . far")
B) Lines 14-15 ("In fact . . . warm")
C) Lines 25-27 ("The planet . . . lucky")
D) Lines 31-34 ("Both planets . . . Sun")

45

What conclusion can be drawn from the passage's discussion of Neptune-sized exoplanets?

A) Hot explanets that resemble Neptune have never existed.
B) There is a reasonable likelihood of locating a Neptune-like world using existing technology.
C) Though there may have been hot exoplanets that resemble Neptune, they are now elusive.
D) There will be an opportunity to locate alien worlds reminiscent of Neptune in the near future.

46

As used in line 28, "nab" most nearly means

A) monitor.
B) arrest.
C) enclose.
D) portray.

47

According to the author, a planet's major mass loss is related to

A) the strong gravitational forces exerted on the planet.
B) the atmosphere pulling away from the planet's gravity.
C) the weak radiation of the planet.
D) the heated core of the planet.

Cumulative Loss of Planetary Mass, Hot Neptune Exoplanet

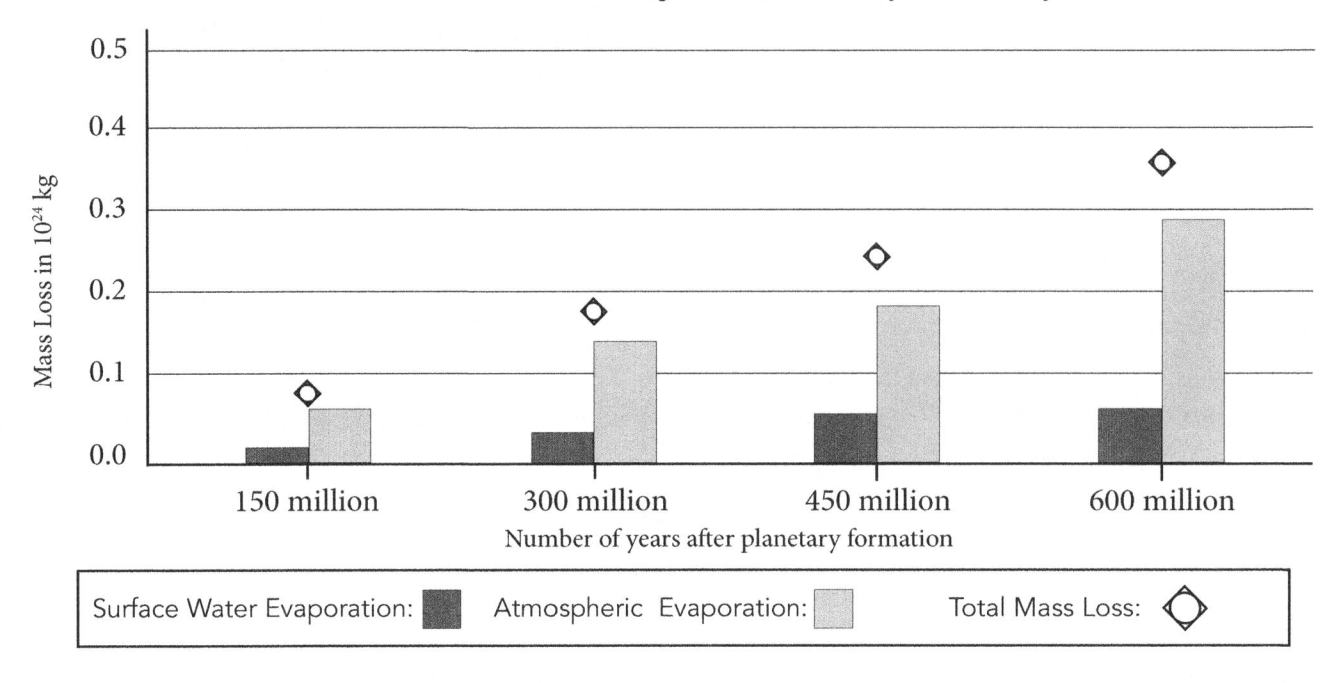

Y-axis: Mass Loss in 10^{24} kg (0.0 to 0.5)
X-axis: Number of years after planetary formation (150 million, 300 million, 450 million, 600 million)

Legend: Surface Water Evaporation ■ | Atmospheric Evaporation ▨ | Total Mass Loss ◇

48

Which choice provides the best evidence for the answer to the previous question?

A) Lines 7-9 ("These planets . . . stars")
B) Lines 28-29 ("astronomers . . . Neptune")
C) Lines 47-49 ("it escapes . . . balloon")
D) Lines 81-82 ("The intervening . . . starlight")

49

As used in line 60, "heavy" most nearly means

A) torrential.
B) overbearing.
C) difficult.
D) weighty.

Test 6

50

For the typical Neptune-like exoplanet depicted in the graph, what period represents the greatest disparity between cumulative atmospheric evaporation and cumulative surface water evaporation?

A) 150 million years from formation
B) 300 million years from formation
C) 450 million years from formation
D) 600 million years from formation

51

One conclusion that can reasonably be drawn from the graph is that, in the first 600 million years after the formation of the given Neptune-like exoplanet,

A) mass loss due to causes other than atmospheric evaporation and surface water evaporation will be negligible.
B) further loss of liquid water will become unlikely after the first 450 years of the exoplanet's existence.
C) the deposits of liquid water on the surface of the planet will have fully disappeared.
D) the atmosphere as a whole will undergo temperature fluctuations while diminishing in total mass.

52

If the hot Neptune exoplanet depicted in the graph is GJ 346b, how would a graph for the lifecycle of GJ 3470b most likely be different?

A) The total amount of atmosphere loss would be greater.
B) The atmosphere loss rate would be greater.
C) The total volume of liquid water evaporated would be roughly the same.
D) The total mass loss would be smaller.

STOP

If you finish before time is called, you may check your work on this section only.
Do not turn to any other section.

Answer Key: Test 6

Passage 1	Passage 2	Passage 3	Passage 4	Passage 5
1. A	11. D	21. A	31. B	42. A
2. C	12. A	22. C	32. D	43. B
3. B	13. C	23. C	33. D	44. A
4. D	14. A	24. B	34. C	45. C
5. B	15. D	25. A	35. A	46. A
6. A	16. B	26. D	36. C	47. B
7. D	17. C	27. B	37. A	48. C
8. A	18. B	28. C	38. D	49. D
9. D	19. B	29. D	39. B	50. D
10. D	20. B	30. A	40. C	51. A
			41. B	52. B

Question Types

Major Issue
1, 11, 42

Passage Details
6-8, 15-16, 21, 23, 29-30, 35, 37-38, 45

Command of Evidence
3-4, 9-10, 12-13, 17, 24-25, 27-28, 31-32, 36, 43-44, 47-48

Word in Context
2, 5, 14, 18, 22, 26, 33-34, 46, 49

Graphics and Visuals
19-20, 50-52

Passage Comparison
39-41

Answer Explanations
Test 6, Pages 154-169

Passage 1, Pages 154-156

1. A is the correct answer.

When the passage begins, Franz is primarily thinking about himself and is worried that he will get in trouble. As the passage progresses, Franz is able to see beyond his own concerns and realizes how the outcome of the war will impact many different spheres of life. Choose A as most appropriate. B can be dismissed since, although the start of the passage does focus on describing the beauty of the setting, the focus of the second half is NOT the physical space of the classroom (as opposed to a series of reactions and repercussions). C and D can also be eliminated since the presence of the Prussian soldiers is only mentioned briefly; moreover, there is no evidence that M. Hamel is a cruel teacher, even though he might be a strict one.

2. C is the correct answer.

In line 28, "bustle" refers to the loud noise created by all of the students getting settled to begin their day. Choose C to reflect this content. A (inappropriately implying ignoring potential danger), B (inappropriately implying enthusiasm or eagerness) and D (inappropriately implying rebellion) all introduce improper contexts and should be eliminated.

3. B is the correct answer.

In lines 75-77, the narrator realizes that the men "were sorry, in the face of military defeat, that they had not gone to school more." The second paragraph refers to how news of the war has gradually indicated that the Prussians were going to be victorious. In the context of the later information about a defeat, this paragraph thus functions as a premonition; choose B as most appropriate. A and D can be eliminated since the content of this paragraph is relevant to the overall passage, and is not used to justify any behavior. C can also be ruled out since the content of the second paragraph is based on factual events, NOT guesses or assumptions.

Answer Explanations, Test 6

4. D is the correct answer.

See the previous answer explanation for analysis of the correct line reference. A describes an assumption made by the narrator, while B describes how events are different from how the narrator had hoped they would be. C gives a description of M. Hamel in the course of explaining that he will no longer be teaching. None of these other answers show why the mention of the French defeats in the second paragraph is linked to further news to come, and therefore they should all be eliminated.

5. B is the correct answer.

In line 52, "strange" refers to the way in which the school seems to depart from its normal mood. Choose B to reflect this content. A (inappropriately implying something hidden or difficult to understand), C (inappropriately implying someone who feels left out or excluded), and D (inappropriately implying something outlandish or comical) all introduce improper contexts and should be eliminated.

6. A is the correct answer.

In lines 37-39, the narrator is clearly nervous about being punished by M. Hamel, and the narrator's allusion to the teacher's "terrible iron ruler" indicates that he sometimes punishes the students by striking them. This content indicates that the teacher is quite strict but NOT necessarily that he is consistently or unjustifiably cruel. A should be selected, and D can thus be eliminated. B and C can be eliminated as outside of the scope of the passage, since nothing in the description reveals the teacher's physical fitness or whether or not he is self-righteous.

7. D is the correct answer.

After the description of the narrator arriving in the classroom and the evocation of the strange atmosphere, the climax of the passage comes with the news that French will no longer be taught in schools. Choose D as the best answer. Be careful not to choose C, since M. Hamel will be ceasing to teach, but NOT due to retirement. A and B can also be eliminated since the presence of townspeople in the classroom is due to these specific circumstances, NOT simply a desire to learn or patient waiting.

8. A is the correct answer.

The final paragraph reveals that the townspeople feel a sense of loss and an awareness that they are transitioning to an uncertain new era. Choose A to reflect this content. B and D can both be eliminated since the focus is on broad geopolitical shifts, NOT on M. Hamel as an individual. C can also be eliminated since education itself (NOT to be confused with the theme of military defeat) has not presented the unwelcome changes which have taken place.

9. D is the correct answer.

In lines 76-78, the narrator observes that the townspeople recognize how hard M. Hamel has worked and want to celebrate that work, even though they are living in uncertain and troubling times. Choose D to reflect this

Answer Explanations, Test 6

content. A and B can both be eliminated since they reflect negative attitudes towards M. Hamel, whereas the townspeople feel very appreciative of him at the end of the passage. C can be eliminated since M. Hamel is being forced to leave the school, NOT retiring voluntarily.

10. D is the correct answer.

See the previous answer explanation for analysis of the correct line reference. A describes the features which the narrator finds strange and confusing, while B summarizes the general mood of everyone in the classroom. C introduces the speech in which M. Hamel will reveal what has happened to cause this sadness. None of these other answers show the townspeople celebrating M. Hamel for his years of service, and therefore they should all be eliminated.

Passage 2, Pages 157-160

11. D is the correct answer.

The passage outlines the valuable skills and learning opportunities that students are likely to gain from attending field school, yet it also describes the ways in which field schools can be cost-prohibitive and inaccessible. The passage ends by suggesting a more cost effective means for students to gain field experience. Choose D to reflect this content. Be careful not to choose A or B, since the author acknowledges the benefits of field school but does not neglect the financial reality and is NOT solely focused on problems associated with field school. C can also be eliminated, since the author acknowledges that many students will want or need paid work, but does NOT evaluate the pros and cons of this option.

12. A is the correct answer.

In lines 69-71, the author explains that "students from low-income backgrounds are less likely to pursue an education in science disciplines where field training is crucial." Choose A to reflect this content. Be careful not to choose D, because the author offers an assessment of a current reality which does NOT reflect a recommendation or connote approval of this reality. B can also be eliminated since paid internships are construed as an option that might prevent a student from pursuing field school, NOT as a way to finance field school. C can be eliminated as illogical since it is factually contradicted by the content of the passage.

13. C is the correct answer.

See the previous answer explanation for analysis of the correct line reference. A explains how participation in field work may impact a student's career choice, while B suggests that fieldwork might help to establish a professional network. D describes how a particular low-cost fieldwork program functions. None of these other answers establish a connection between a student's income level and the likelihood of that student pursuing a science program, and therefore they should all be eliminated.

Answer Explanations, Test 6

14. A is the correct answer.

In line 36, "sentiment" refers to a belief held by professors. Choose A to reflect this meaning. B (inappropriately implying feelings or attachment to an idea), C (implying strategic insight or cunning), and D (implying data used to support a claim or hypothesis) all introduce incorrect contexts and therefore should be eliminated.

15. D is the correct answer.

Up until lines 76-78, the author focuses on explaining why field school is highly valuable but potentially unaffordable for many students. At this point in the passage, the author pivots from describing a problem to identifying a potential solution, but then qualifies the solution by indicating that many students do not know about this option. Choose D to reflect this purpose. A and B can be eliminated since the benefits of field schools have already been described, and since the author does not comment on whether the financial burden of field schools makes them unattractive to students. Be careful not to choose C, since the solution that the author provides is an alternative way to gain field experience and is NOT connected to a traditional field school.

16. B is the correct answer.

In lines 51-55, the author states that "Field schools have many benefits, but are also prohibitively expensive" and then goes on to provide some data about the potentially high costs. Based on this information, a reader can logically infer that the ability to attend field school will be connected to income level; choose B to reflect this content. C can be eliminated since, at the end of the passage, the author identifies alternative ways for a student to gain field experience. A and D can also be eliminated since the author does NOT discuss difficulties in choosing a field school program (focusing instead on challenges around affordability) and also implies that since students attend field schools in spite of the high costs, they most likely DO recognize the value of these programs.

17. C is the correct answer.

See the previous answer explanation for analysis of the correct line reference. A identifies a disconnect between what the author was told during his studies and what he experienced in the structure of his program. B offers a suggestion for how students might finance field school experiences, while D describes a change that would need to take place in order to make certain academic disciplines more accessible. None of these other choices indicate that income can impact a student's ability to attend field school, and therefore all of them should be eliminated.

18. B is the correct answer.

In line 91, "shore up" refers to how opportunities might enable students to gain the experience they need. Choose B to reflect this positive meaning. A (inappropriately implying conquering or imposing power over someone or something), C (inappropriately implying reducing or making something seem less important), and D (inappropriately implying throwing something away) all introduce improper contexts (some of which are negative) and should be eliminated.

Answer Explanations, Test 6

19. B is the correct answer.

The graph shows that between 2013 and 2014, the average cost of field school tuition increased from around $4200 to more than $4500. In the same period, enrollment declined from almost 5000 students to approximately 4600 students. Choose B to reflect these trends. A can be eliminated since this answer contradicts the data displayed in the graph. C and D can also both be eliminated since both tuition costs and enrollment numbers experienced fluctuations until about 2016-2017, when they began to show a steady pattern of increase.

20. B is the correct answer.

The graph demonstrates that BOTH the cost of attending field school and the number of students who do so have been steadily increasing. The author, however, argues that rising costs will make field school inaccessible, a trend which would presumably lead to declining enrollment numbers. B represents a statement which would align with the graph's data yet also contradict the author's viewpoint: grant funding would allow more students to attend even as tuition costs rise, and would contradict the author's view that rising tuition costs will definitively lower the chances of students attending field school. A can be eliminated, since it would align with the graph's data but would support the claims made by the author, which link high incomes to high attendance. C and D can both be eliminated since the graph does not provide any specific data about the income of students who attend and does not explain what factors have led tuition costs to increase.

Passage 3, Pages 160-162

21. A is the correct answer.

The first paragraph states that "In the mid-1980s, advice to consume a low-fat diet became a strategy for weight control." Choose A to reflect this content. B and D can be rejected since there is no mention of participants in the study having a particular profile and since there was not a particular emphasis on the widespread prevalence of heart disease. Be careful not to choose C, since the first paragraph indicates a link between obesity and heart disease, NOT a direct link between fat consumption and heart disease.

22. C is the correct answer.

In line 9, "biological" refers to the innate preference for fatty foods. Choose C to reflect this content. A (inappropriately implying combinations of atoms), B (inappropriately implying uncivilized and violent tendencies), and D (inappropriately implying a particularly strong emotional reaction) all introduce improper contexts and should be eliminated.

23. C is the correct answer.

Lines 46-48 summarize the positive responses reported by participants who followed the high-fat diet. Here, the author's discussion includes data indicating that participants enjoyed the relevant diet and also found it

Answer Explanations, Test 6

economically feasible; choose C to reflect this content. A and B can also be eliminated since the lines focus only on one particular diet and further focus on the reaction of participants, but NOT on the ways in which they benefited. D can be eliminated because it reflects a negative perspective, whereas the content of these lines is positive.

24. B is the correct answer.

In lines 24-31, the author distinguishes between different types of fats, indicating that there are multiple varieties of fatty acids; choose B to reflect this content. A and D can both be eliminated since both of these answers oversimplify the author's ideas and suggest that fatty acids always potentially cause negative effects. C can also be eliminated since it represents an over-generalization that there is only one type of diet which qualifies as healthy.

25. A is the correct answer.

See the previous answer explanation for analysis of the correct line reference. B explains that if participants consistently followed the diet, then physiological changes could be observed. C specifies that not all participants responded to the diet in the same way, and D summarizes an overall consensus on how to achieve a healthy diet. None of these other answers indicate that there are different types of fat, and therefore they should all be eliminated.

26. D is the correct answer.

In line 63, "concept" refers to the theory or idea that differing individuals will respond differently to the same diet. Choose D to reflect this content. A (inappropriately implying a visual representation), B (inappropriately implying an embodied and time-defined representation), and C (inappropriately implying a plot to achieve a particular goal) all introduce improper contexts and should be eliminated.

27. B is the correct answer.

Lines 63-66 state that "These data support the concept that not all people respond to a dietary approach in the same way and there is no one optimal diet for all people." This content shows that analysis of the lipid response reveals that a range of diets may be needed to support optimal health; choose B as appropriate. A can readily be eliminated since the study was investigating high-fat diets, NOT low fat ones. C and D can also be eliminated since Caucasian women did not see an improvement in HDL cholesterol levels, and since the changes in these levels observed in the African-American population were significant.

28. C is the correct answer.

See the previous answer explanation for analysis of the correct line reference. A summarizes the positive response to the diet as articulated by participants, while B explains the different results revealed by different categories of participants. D identifies an existing gap in scientific research. None of these answers argue that no one diet is ideal for everyone, and therefore they should all be eliminated.

Answer Explanations, Test 6

29. D is the correct answer.

The final paragraph presents the viewpoint that most people could improve their health by paying more attention to the specific combination of fats that are being consumed, rather than focusing on rigidly restricting dietary practices. Choose D to reflect this content. A and B can both be eliminated since the author specifically indicates that most people do NOT need to dramatically reduce the total number of calories consumed. C can also be eliminated since the author is reflecting on the potential value of diets that contain specific combinations of fat, NOT very low amounts of fat.

30. A is the correct answer.

The study considered in the passage investigates the results of high fat diets within different populations and ultimately concludes that no uniform diet will achieve optimal health results for every individual. Choose A as the best answer. B and D can both be eliminated since the study indicates changes in HDL cholesterol levels among African American women but NOT that this population necessarily always has high levels to begin with. Likewise, the study clearly indicated that race and gender DID affect responses to dietary changes. C can be eliminated since the study focused on the results of a higher fat diet, NOT a low-fat one.

Passage 4, Pages 163-165

31. B is the correct answer.

Lines 42-47 reveal that, according to the author, granting women the right to vote could be both harmful to women themselves and disruptive to society in general. This content implies that the author views female suffrage as damaging and detrimental; choose B as appropriate. A and C can be eliminated since the author is clearly NOT in favor of women attaining more responsibility and sees suffrage as being damaging to women, NOT inconvenient to men. D can also be eliminated since the author's negative feelings about female suffrage are readily apparent in the passage.

32. D is the correct answer.

See the previous answer explanation for analysis of the correct line reference. A describes the benevolent behavior exhibited by American men, while B highlights how American women have been well-treated and well-regarded. C states that women can feel confident that they will get anything that they ask for. None of these other answers reflect the author's belief that female suffrage will be damaging, and therefore they should all be eliminated.

33. D is the correct answer.

In line 22, "extravagant" refers to demands which are excessive or unreasonable. Choose D to reflect this content. A (inappropriately implying something temporary and lasting only a short time), B (inappropriately

Answer Explanations, Test 6

implying something unusual or unconventional), and C (inappropriately implying something being helpfully offered to someone else) all introduce improper contexts and should be eliminated.

34. C is the correct answer.

In line 25, "importunity" refers to women's tendency to return to the same demands. Choose C to reflect this content. A (inappropriately implying an ideal or a conviction), B (inappropriately implying a chance to do something), and D (inappropriately implying a need to give up something or to do without) all introduce improper contexts and should be eliminated.

35. A is the correct answer.

Lines 27-31 state that groups or individuals achieving a goal can sometimes lead to harm if that goal was not well thought-out to begin with. The implication in the content of the passage is that even though some women may think that they want the right to vote, granting them suffrage could do more harm than good. Choose A as the best reflection of the author's argument. B and D can both be eliminated, since they both imply a positive attitude towards female suffrage, whereas the author clearly has a negative attitude towards women having the right to vote. C can also be eliminated, since the discussion of potential harm occurs in a discussion about women and their demands, NOT about men.

36. C is the correct answer.

Lines 65-68 present the author of Passage 2 feeling a sense of deep confusion when asked to explain why women should have equal rights. The fact that she is being asked to explain and justify her convictions indicates that the author's beliefs were not universally held, so that C is appropriate. A explains how the author herself has always believed in the total equality of women, while B argues that freedom is an inherent human right which does not need to be earned. D argues that since, as children, men depend on women, it would make more sense for them to expect women to grant them political agency. None of these other answers reveal that the author's beliefs were not universally shared during her era (even though some DO raise the author's central beliefs), and therefore they should all be eliminated.

37. A is the correct answer.

In lines 69-72, the author poses a series of rhetorical questions designed to draw attention to the fact that she finds it ridiculous to be expected to justify and earn equality. She does not want women to wait to have their natural rights granted to them by others. Choose A to reflect this content. Be careful not to choose C, since the author does believe that women suffer due to their marginalized position, but this is not the point that she argues through the series of rhetorical questions. B and D can also be eliminated since the author is portraying a society that is deeply unjust and is introducing views which many people would subscribe to, even though the author personally rejects them.

Answer Explanations, Test 6

38. D is the correct answer.

In the final paragraph, the author states that "when [suffrage] is really an accomplished fact all will wonder, as I have done, what the objection ever was." This content implies that she believes that future generations will not understand why suffrage was ever a controversial issue; choose D to reflect this content. A and C can both readily be eliminated since the author believes that universal suffrage will eventually be achieved and that women will never back down in their fight for equality. B can also be eliminated, since the author looks ahead to an era when suffrage will no longer be contentious, without focusing on the resistance it may encounter (and which seems minimal on the basis of the concluding paragraph).

39. B is the correct answer.

Passage 1 and Passage 2 both discuss debates around giving women the right to vote and take opposing positions on whether or not suffrage is a reasonable demand. Given this shared focus, choose B as the best answer. A and C can both be eliminated, since only Passage 1 identifies the benefits of traditional social roles and evokes the threat of disruption due to suffrage. D can also be ruled out, since both passages discuss suffrage as a very real, and possibly even inevitable, prospect in the near future.

40. C is the correct answer.

The author of Passage 1 is firmly opposed to granting women the right to vote, while the author of Passage 2 strongly supports women's right to equal suffrage. Choose C to reflect this crucial difference. B and D can both be dismissed, since neither of the authors discusses her personal life; it is impossible to know either author's marital history or social background based solely on the passages. A can also be eliminated because the authors discuss the same topic, but the difference emerges from their differing overall opinions, NOT the events that these authors focus on.

41. B is the correct answer.

The author of Passage 1 fears that granting women the right to vote will upset social norms and domestic conventions, while the author of Passage 2 assumes that within a short time, female equality will be totally normalized. Choose B to reflect this content. A can be eliminated since, while the author of Passage 1 is fearful of disruption, the dissolution of government is an exaggeration beyond the scope of the passage. C can also be ruled out since Passage 1 does not name a reversal of gender roles as a specific feared outcome, and D can be eliminated because the discussion is focused specifically on the United States.

Answer Explanations, Test 6

Passage 5, Pages 166-169

42. A is the correct answer.

The passage begins by describing the small numbers of hot Neptune planets and then connecting this surprising absence to a loss of planetary mass, and hypothesizing why that loss occurs. Choose A to reflect this content. B and C can be eliminated, since the author is interested in reporting a scientific phenomenon, NOT necessarily in inspiring widespread public interest; moreover, the passage does not introduce speculation about what types of life might exist on other planets. D can also be ruled out since atmospheric properties are mentioned in the passage, but only in the context of a discussion that focuses primarily on the loss of planetary mass.

43. B is the correct answer.

In lines 12-13, the author explains that scientists have only been able to locate a small number of planets that qualify as "hot Neptunes," indicating that such planets are rare. Choose B to reflect this content. A and C can be eliminated because A is factually contradicted by the content of the passage and because humidity (which considers both moisture AND heat) is not fully relevant to the passage (which discusses the question of heat alone). Be careful not to choose D, since the passage does point to the presence of "warm Neptunes" as a surprising discovery, but this fact is distinct from the discussion of the features of the hot Neptunes which have been discovered.

44. A is the correct answer.

See the previous answer explanation for analysis of the correct line reference. B indicates that many medium-sized exoplanets exist but do not qualify as "hot Neptunes." C introduces a hypothesis connecting the scarcity of hot Neptunes to the loss of atmosphere, while D describes the position of a planet which astronomers have recently been observing. None of these other answers indicate the rarity of hot Neptunes, and therefore all should be eliminated.

45. C is the correct answer.

The passage indicates both that it is currently hard to locate exoplanets which resemble Neptune in their size and that there may have once been much higher numbers of these planets. Choose C to reflect this content. A can be ruled out since it is factually contradicted by the content of the passage: some hot Neptunes have in fact been located, even if hot Neptunes are very rare. Both B and D should be eliminated since nothing in the passage indicates that it will become easier to find and observe Neptune-like exoplanets, only that scientists may become better able to explain their scarcity.

46. A is the correct answer.

In line 28, "nab" refers to astronomers' ability to seize the chance to observe a particular exoplanet. Choose A to reflect this meaning. B (inappropriately implying exercising legal measures against someone who committed a crime), C (inappropriately implying putting a fence or boundary around someone), and D (inappropriately

Answer Explanations, Test 6

implying representing someone or something in an artistic or fictional work) all introduce improper contexts and should be eliminated.

47. B is the correct answer.

In lines 47-49, the passage describes how radiation from a nearby star heats the atmosphere of a planet to the point that the atmosphere itself pulls away from the gravity of that planet. Choose B to reflect this content. A can be eliminated since it is the radiation, NOT the gravity, exerted on the planet which triggers this effect. C and D can also be eliminated, since strong, NOT weak, radiation is a factor in this effect and since there is no discussion of what role a heated core might play in the escape of an atmosphere.

48. C is the correct answer.

See the previous answer explanation for analysis of the correct line reference. A explains what conditions make an exoplanet "hot," while B explains that Neptune-sized exoplanets display lower temperatures than exoplanets which are either smaller or larger. D describes the observation which led to scientists concluding that atmosphere was being lost. None of these other answers describe how loss of planetary mass is connected to the behavior of its atmosphere, and therefore they should all be eliminated.

49. D is the correct answer.

In line 60, "heavy" refers to the abundant mass and weight of the atmosphere of certain exoplanets. Choose D to reflect this context. A (inappropriately implying an abundant amount of precipitation), B (inappropriately implying someone who interferes to a great extent), and C (inappropriately implying a task which requires great effort to complete) all introduce improper contexts and should be eliminated.

50. D is the correct answer.

At the mark of 600 million years after formation, the typical hot Neptune exoplanet has lost almost 0.3×10^{24} kilograms of surface water, but less than 0.1×10^{24} kilograms of atmosphere through evaporation. This gap between the evaporation of surface water and the evaporation of atmosphere is at its most disparate at this point in the planet's history; choose D as appropriate. A, B, and C can all be eliminated since they represent points in an exoplanet's history where a gap exists between the amount of water and the amount of atmosphere which has evaporated, but these gaps are smaller earlier in a planet's history.

51. A is the correct answer.

The graph shows that the total mass loss of an exoplanet is close to equal to the sum of the mass lost through atmospheric evaporation and surface water evaporation. It is therefore logical to conclude that any other factors leading to the loss of planetary mass only have a very small effect; choose A as appropriate. B can be dismissed since the graph does show relatively stable levels of surface water evaporation between the 450 and 600 million year marks, but this situation does NOT clearly indicate what might happen after 600 years. C and D can also readily be eliminated since the graph does NOT provide any information about how much surface water remains as some of it evaporates or about the temperature of the atmosphere.

Answer Explanations, Test 6

52. B is the correct answer.

The passage specifies that Neptune (GJ 3470b) "is losing its atmosphere at a rate 100 times faster than that of GJ 436b" (lines 29-31), and a graph based on the lifecycle of the former planet would likely display this trend; choose B to reflect this content. A, C, and D can all be eliminated since nothing in the passage indicates that GJ 3470b has lost more of its atmosphere overall, has a resulting smaller total mass loss, or has experienced a different pattern around surface water loss. Therefore, none of these trends would be likely to appear on a relevant graph.

NOTES

- Passage 2 on Pages 157-158, "It's time for universities to rethink what counts as field school," is adapted from the article of the same name by Liam Zachary and published by the PLOS Early Career Researcher Community blog. 29 May 2015, PLOS ONE. https://blogs.plos.org/thestudentblog/2015/05/29/its-time-for-universities-to-rethink-what-counts-as-field-school/. Accessed 28 July 2019.

- Passage 3 on Pages 160-161, "Let them eat more fat? Researcher argues that a balance of types of fat is the key," is an excerpt from the article of the same name by Heidi Silver and published by The Conversation in partnership with Vanderbilt University. 8 January 2019, The Conversation. https://theconversation.com/let-them-eat-more-fat-researcher-argues-that-a-balance-of-types-of-fat-is-the-key-106409. Accessed 28 July 2019.

- Passage 5 on Pages 166-167, "In Search of Missing Worlds, Hubble Finds a Fast Evaporating Exoplanet," is adapted from the article of the same name published by NASA. 13 December 2018, NASA. https://www.nasa.gov/feature/goddard/2018/in-search-of-missing-worlds-hubble-finds-a-fast-evaporating-exoplanet. Accessed 28 July 2019.

About the Figures: The various visual resources that accompany the passages in this section are primarily meant to facilitate critical thinking skills and may not reflect historical data.

Test 7
Full Reading Section
2020 SAT Practice

Test 7

Reading Test

65 MINUTES, 52 QUESTIONS

Turn to Section 1 of your answer sheet to answer the questions in this section.

DIRECTIONS

Each passage or pair of passages below is followed by a number of questions. After reading each passage or pair, choose the best answer to each question based on what is stated or implied in the passage or passages and in any accompanying graphics (such as a table or graph).

Questions 1-10 are based on the following passage.

This passage is adapted from "The Friend" by Leonid Andreev, a text that appeared in *The Little Stone Angel and Other Stories* (1916, translated by W.H. Lowe).

When late at night he rang at his own door, the first sound after that of the bell was a resonant dog's bark, in which might be distinguished both fear that it might have been a stranger, and joy
[Line 5] that it was his own master, who had arrived.
  Then there followed the squish-squash of galoshes, and the squeak of the key taken out of the lock.
  He came in, and, taking off his wrappers in the
[10] dark, was conscious of a silent female figure close by, while the nails of a dog caressingly scratched at his knees, and a hot tongue licked his chilled hand.
  "Well, what is it?" a sleepy voice asked in a
[15] tone of perfunctory interest.
  "Nothing! I'm tired," curtly replied Vladimir Mikhailovich, and went to his own room. The dog followed him, his nails striking sharply on the waxed floor, and jumped on to the bed. When
[20] the light of the lamp which he lit filled the room, his glance met the steady gaze of the dog's black eyes. They seemed to say: "Come now, pet me." And to make the request better understood the dog stretched out his fore-paws, and laid his head
[25] sideways upon them, while his hinder quarters wriggled comically, and his tail kept twirling round like the handle of a barrel-organ.
  "My only friend!" said Vladimir Mikhailovich, as he stroked the black, glossy coat. As though
[30] from excess of feeling the dog turned on his back, showed his white teeth, and growled gently, joyful and excited. But Vladimir Mikhailovich sighed, petted the dog, and thought to himself, how that there was no one else in the world that would ever
[35] love him.
  If he happened to return home early, and not tired out with work, he would sit down to write, and the dog curled himself into a ball on a chair somewhere near to him, opened one black eye
[40] now and again, and sleepily wagged his tail. And when excited by the process of authorship, tortured by the sufferings of his own heroes, and choking with a plethora of thoughts and mental pictures, he walked about in his room, and
[45] smoked cigarette after cigarette, the dog would

follow him with an anxious look, and wag his tail more vigorously than ever.

"Shall we become famous, you and I, Vasyuk?" he would inquire of the dog, who would wag his
50 tail in affirmation. "We'll eat liver then, is that right?"

"Right!" the dog would reply, stretching himself luxuriously. He was very fond of liver.

Vladimir Mikhailovich often had visitors. Then
55 his aunt, with whom he lived, would borrow china from her neighbour, and give them tea, setting on samovar after samovar. She would go and buy vodka and sausages, and sigh heavily as she drew out from the bottom of her pocket a greasy rouble-
60 note. In the room with its smoke-laden atmosphere loud voices resounded. They quarrelled and laughed, said droll and sharp things, complained of their fate and envied one another. They advised Vladimir Mikhailovich to give up literature and
65 take to some more lucrative occupation. Some said that he ought to consult a doctor, others clinked glasses with him, while they bewailed the injury that vodka was doing to his health. He was so sickly, so continually nervous. This was why he
70 had such fits of depression, and why he demanded of life the impossible. All addressed him as "thou," and their voices expressed their interest in him, and in the friendliest manner, they would invite him to drive beyond the city with them,
75 and prolong the conviviality. And when he drove off merry, making more noise than the others, and laughing at nothing, there followed him two pairs of eyes: the gray eyes of his aunt, angry and reproachful, and the anxiously caressing black
80 eyes of the dog.

1

Over the course of the passage, the narrator discusses the idea that

A) Vladimir Mikhailovich does not betray any interest in his visitors in order to maintain decorum.

B) writing is a dull yet arduous process that involves psychological torture.

C) successful writers need to be supported by forgiving patrons.

D) Vladimir Mikhailovich enjoys a loving and exclusive bond with his dog.

2

In characterizing Vladimir, the narrator indicates that

A) Vladimir will become a revered and a highly successful writer.

B) Vladimir finds the company of his friends soothing.

C) Vladimir's writing process is complex but invigorating.

D) Vladimir wants to live as a recluse with his dog.

3

The main purpose of the first paragraph is to

A) underscore the fact that the main character always returns home late.

B) delineate the main character's living arrangement.

C) emphasize the importance of having a dog guarding the house.

D) hint at the unconditional love between a dog and its owner.

Test 7

4

It can reasonably be inferred that the "silent female figure" in line 10 is

A) a stranger in Vladimir's home.
B) Vladimir's estranged wife.
C) a statue of an idealized woman.
D) Vladimir's aunt.

5

As used in line 43, "plethora" most nearly means

A) plenitude.
B) confusion.
C) chaos.
D) depth.

6

The primary impression created by the narrator's depiction of Vladimir's aunt is that she can be

A) menacing and confused.
B) alienated and indifferent.
C) lonely and hesitant.
D) vexed and disgruntled.

7

Which choice provides the best evidence for the answer to the previous question?

A) Lines 54-57 ("Then . . . samovar")
B) Lines 57-60 ("She . . . note")
C) Lines 69-71 ("This . . . impossible")
D) Lines 77-79 ("there . . . reproachful")

8

The narrator indicates that Vladimir's friends

A) have faith in his genius as a writer.
B) are eager to offer a remedy for his depression.
C) suggest that Vladimir will not become a wealthy writer.
D) have never envied his success despite their own deficiencies.

9

Which choice provides the best evidence for the answer to the previous question?

A) Lines 61-62 ("They . . . laughed")
B) Lines 63-65 ("They . . . occupation")
C) Lines 68-69 ("He . . . nervous")
D) Lines 73-75 ("they . . . conviviality")

10

As used in line 75, "conviviality" most nearly means

A) sociability.
B) frivolity.
C) engagement.
D) submissiveness.

Questions 11-20 are based on the following passage and supplementary material.

This passage is an excerpt from David Markowitz, "Text analysis of thousands of grant abstracts shows that writing style matters," a 2019 article published* by The Conversation in partnership with the University of Oregon.

Is there a financial relationship to what or how people communicate?
Placing a value on words can feel crude or
Line highfalutin—unless you're in academia, where
5 words are often tied to money. More publications can lead to a promotion, and receiving grant aid can fund new research.
  In a paper published on January 30 of 2019, I evaluated the financial value of words based on
10 a sample of funded National Science Foundation grant abstracts. The data indicated that what we researchers say and how we say it can foretell the amount of funding we are awarded. They also show that writing idealized by funders may not
15 always match up with what they actually prefer.
  Prior research shows a relationship between language patterns and the funding of personal online loans. Loan applications that had more complex writing—such as those with more
20 words in the description—were more likely to receive full funding. Loan writers also received money if their text contained high levels of verbal confidence—such as words that convey certainty ("definitely," "always," "clearly").
25 To assess complexity and confidence indicators in the NSF sample, I ran over 7.4 million words through an automated text analysis program. The grants covered all NSF directorates, U.S. locations, and nearly nine years of funding from
30 2010 to 2018.
  Consistent with the online loans data, grant abstracts with more words and more markers of verbal confidence received more award money. In fact, each additional word in the grant abstract
35 is associated with a US$372 increase. The ideal word count across NSF directorates is 681 words. After this threshold, additional words associated with a decrease in award funding.
  Two other results were telling about the NSF
40 data. First, using fewer common words was associated with receiving more award funding, which is inconsistent with the NSF's call and commitment to plain writing.
  Second, the amount of award funding was
45 related to the writing style of the grant. Prior evidence suggests that we can infer social and psychological traits about people, such as intelligence, from small "junk" words called function words. High rates of articles and
50 prepositions, for example, indicate complex thinking, while high rates of storytelling words such as pronouns indicate simpler thinking.
  NSF grant abstracts with a simpler style—that is, grant abstracts that were written as a story with
55 many pronouns—tend to receive more money. A personal touch may simplify the science and can make it relatable.
  The data include only funded grants, and the relationships may not indicate a direct cause and
60 effect. Therefore, such patterns are not a recipe for a marginal proposal to receive funding or a "how-to" guide to outfund the competition.
  Instead, the results demonstrate that real-world language data have rich psychological value.
65 Just counting words can provide new insights into institutional processes such as grant funding allocation.
  Most grant writers believe, and are even told by funders, that a competitive proposal starts with
70 a great idea. This study suggests that another part of grantsmanship may be the proposal's word patterns and writing style. Since most funded grants will contribute knowledge to science, one way to potentially enhance a funded proposal with
75 more award money is to consider how the science is communicated in the writing phase.
  Poet George Herbert suggested, "Good words are worth much, and cost little." The NSF data offer a different perspective: more complex and
80 confident stories tend to cost the NSF a lot. For researchers looking to support their work with more money, word patterns may be an inexpensive place to start.

---
*See Page 212 for the citation for this text.

Study of 73 Grant Applications, Anthropological Studies for 2018

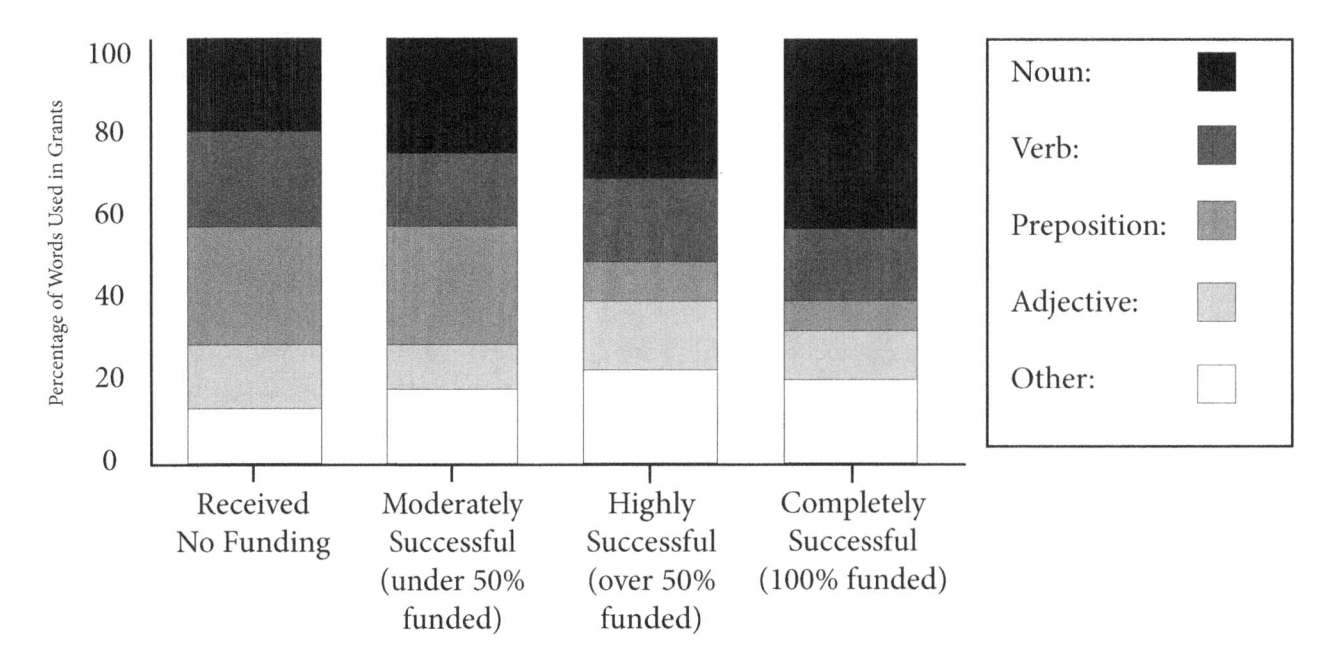

11

As used in line 4, "highfalutin" most nearly means

A) unnecessary.
B) bizarre.
C) pretentious.
D) ridiculous.

12

The passage most strongly suggests that NSF grant abstracts

A) which make science more easily comprehensible get more money.
B) with an abundance of prepositions stand a better chance of garnering funds.
C) composed prior to 2010 were taken into account for a study performed by the author of the passage.
D) should rely on hard data, rather than writing style, as a means of ensuring success.

13

Which choice provides the best evidence for the answer to the previous question?

A) Lines 8-11 ("In a paper . . . abstracts")
B) Lines 28-30 ("The grants . . . 2018")
C) Lines 53-57 ("NSF grant . . . relatable")
D) Lines 63-67 ("Instead . . . allocation")

14

What function does the fourth paragraph (lines 16-24) serve in the passage as a whole?

A) It emphasizes the connection between full funding and the use of particular types of words.
B) It encourages NSF grant applicants to use less complex vocabulary in their submissions.
C) It elaborates on a universally accepted style of grant writing by providing a few examples.
D) It gives a broad yet mostly accurate overview of the history of NSF grant applications.

15

What does the author explicitly cite as the dominant factor in receiving grant funding?

A) Following a set of "how-to" guidelines

B) Ability to communicate highly obscure scientific concepts

C) Displaying verbal confidence on a grant application

D) Maintaining a balance between rather frequently misused words such as prepositions and more common words such as pronouns.

16

One of the grant-writing recommendations set forward in the final two paragraphs of the passage is the idea that

A) having an innovative idea is the deciding factor in getting full funding.

B) there will normally be numerous competitive proposals for any given research grant.

C) fully-funded grants contribute to the speedy development of new scientific procedures.

D) skillfully communicating nuanced ideas can lead to superior funding.

17

Which choice provides the best evidence for the answer to the previous question?

A) Lines 68-70 ("Most grant . . . idea)

B) Lines 70-72 ("This study . . . style")

C) Lines 73-76 ("one way . . . phase")

D) Lines 77-79 ("Poet . . . perspective")

18

As used in line 74, "enhance" most nearly means

A) reinforce.

B) modernize.

C) harden.

D) accumulate.

19

According to the graph, an application that uses a relatively small (roughly 10%) number of adjectives would be

A) likely to receive at least partial funding.

B) unlikely to receive any funding whatsoever.

C) difficult to assign to a single predicted funding category.

D) likely to receive full funding regardless of other category measures.

20

Which additional piece of information would be most useful for assessing the graphs alongside the statements provided in lines 44-57 ("Second . . . relatable")?

A) Which categories in the graph featured the most one- or two-syllable words

B) How much money, on average, the fully-funded grants considered in the graph received

C) Whether the graph classifies pronouns under "Nouns" or "Other"

D) What the single most common preposition used in the 73 applications relevant to the graph was

Questions 21-31 are based on the following passage and supplementary material.

This passage is adapted from Emilie Reas, "The supremely intelligent rat-cyborg," a 2016 article that originally appeared* on the PLOS Neuro Community blog.

When Deep Blue battled the reigning human chess champion, the world held its breath. Who was smarter . . . man or machine? A human victory would confirm the superiority of human intelligence, while a victory for Deep Blue would offer great promise for the potential applications of artificial intelligence to benefit mankind. And with the defeat of Garry Kasparov by an algorithm, the debate heated over what constitutes intelligence and whether computers can possess it. But perhaps the answer to the man-versus-machine debate isn't so black and white. Perhaps both synthetic and biological systems have unique, complementary strengths that, when merged, could yield an optimally functioning "brain"—a supremely intelligent cyborg, if you will. In their new PLOS ONE paper, Yipeng Yu and colleagues tested this possibility, comparing the problem-solving abilities of rats, computers, and rat-computer "cyborgs."

Six rats were trained over the course of a week to run a series of unique mazes. The rats were implanted with microelectrodes in their somatosensory cortex and medial forebrain bundle, which releases dopamine to the nucleus accumbens and is a key node of the brain's reward system. They were enticed to reach the maze target by the fragrance of peanut butter, a sip of water (they were mildly dehydrated), and stimulation of the medial forebrain bundle once they solved the puzzle. After training, the researchers tested the rats on 14 new mazes, monitoring their paths, strategies, and time spent solving the mazes.

To compare the performance of the rats to that of a computer, the research team developed a maze-solving algorithm implementing left-hand and right-hand wall-following rules. This algorithm completed the same 14 mazes run by the rats.

Rat cyborgs integrated the computational powers of organic and artificial intelligence systems. Rats completed the same set of mazes, but this time with the assistance of the computer algorithm. By stimulating the rats' left and right somatosensory cortex to prompt them to move left or right, the algorithm intervened when the rats needed help, directing them to traverse unique paths and avoid dead ends and loops.

Performances for the rats, computer, and rat-cyborgs were compared by evaluating how many times they visited the same location (steps), how many locations they visited, and total time spent to reach the target. Although the cyborgs and computers took roughly the same number of steps, the cyborgs took fewer than the rats, a sign of more efficient problem solving. Furthermore, the cyborgs visited fewer locations than computers or rats and took less time than the rats to solve the mazes. Across the various maze layouts, the number of steps and locations covered were strongly correlated between the types of beings (rats and cyborgs, rats and computer, cyborgs and computer). Thus, a maze that was challenging for a rat was similarly challenging for the computer and for the rat's cyborg counterpart.

These findings from Yu and colleagues suggest that optimal intelligence may not reside exclusively in man or machine, but in the integration of the two. By harnessing the speed and logic of artificial computing systems, we may be able to augment the already remarkable cognitive abilities of biological neural systems, including the human brain. The prospect of computer-assisted human intelligence raises obvious concerns over the safety and ethics of such an application. Are there conditions under which a human "cyborg" could put humans at risk? Is altering human behavior with a machine tantamount to "playing god" and a dangerous overreach of our powers?

Despite these concerns, such computer-assisted intelligent systems are already available and in surprisingly wide-spread use. . . . But

*See Page 212 for the citation for this text.

85 where does one draw the line between harmless lifestyle enhancement and dangerous mind-control? Yu and colleagues' findings suggest that, at least for now, we need not fear takeover by super-smart robots; perhaps instead it's time
90 to embrace the computing abilities of machines as complementary—and beneficial—to our own natural powers of intelligence.

21

The primary purpose of the first paragraph is to

A) present a new approach to understanding intelligence.

B) suggest that human intelligence might be superior to artificial intelligence.

C) initiate a debate about the mode of intelligence that will dominate the world in the future.

D) outline how artificial intelligence will be profoundly beneficial to humankind.

22

Which choice most effectively indicates that the combination of artificial and natural factors may yield optimal outcomes?

A) Lines 3-7 ("A human . . . mankind")
B) Lines 8-11 ("And . . . it")
C) Lines 13-16 ("both . . . cyborg")
D) Lines 21-22 ("Six . . . mazes")

23

As used in line 48. "traverse" most nearly means

A) convey.
B) run past.
C) embark on.
D) move across.

24

Which of the following was NOT a feature of the experiment designed by Yu and colleagues?

A) A firm conceptual distinction between "steps" and "time" in measuring outcomes

B) Incentives for the non-cyborg test subjects

C) A competitive format to prompt rat cyborgs to outperform non-cyborg rats

D) Algorithmic navigation for both live and computerized test subjects

25

According to the information in the fifth paragraph (lines 50-66), what is considered "a sign of more efficient problem solving"?

A) Completing an assignment by undertaking the smallest number of moves

B) Being able to calculate a variety of possible outcomes when only one outcome is readily apparent

C) Providing several plausible solutions to interrelated problems

D) Systematically eliminating competitors similar to oneself

26

As used in line 80, "tantamount" most nearly means

A) superior to.
B) as tantalizing as.
C) synonymous with.
D) derivative from.

Figure 1: Turns Needed to Solve a 15-Turn Maze

Test Subject	Trial 1	Trial 2	Trial 3	Trial 4	Trial 5
Rat 1	34	31	31	28	24
Rat 2	36	34	28	25	22
Rat 3	33	33	31	25	20
Cyborg Rat 1	25	25	21	18	17
Cyborg Rat 2	25	24	21	18	17
Cyborg Rat 3	25	25	20	17	17
Computer 1	28	23	18	15	15
Computer 2	27	22	19	15	15

Figure 2: Brain Activity of Rat Test Subjects

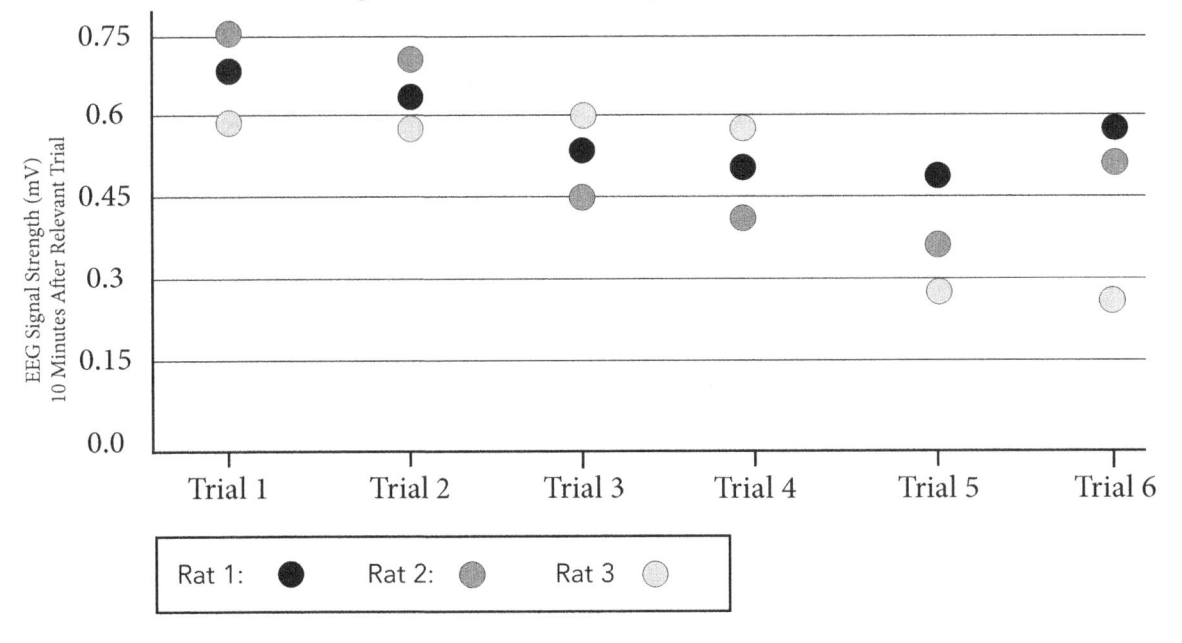

27

What implication for society is suggested by Yu and colleagues' findings?

A) That the future of intelligence involves both artificial and biological systems
B) That AI may be responsible for the downfall of human civilization in the future
C) That a variety of ethical problems will ultimately not outweigh the economic importance of AI
D) That human intelligence will eventually cease to play a role in developing optimal artificial intelligence

28

Which choice provides the best evidence for the answer to the previous question?

A) Lines 54-57 ("Although . . . solving")
B) Lines 79-81 ("Is altering . . . powers?")
C) Lines 84-87 ("But where . . . control?")
D) Lines 89-92 ("Perhaps . . . intelligence")

29

The data in Figure 1 indicate that, for the eight test subjects under observation,

A) the computers may navigate more efficiently than the cyborgs navigate.
B) the rat-cyborgs will invariably outperform the rats beyond Trial 5.
C) the computers took less time to solve the maze than the rats took.
D) exposure to cyborg algorithms will increase a rat's overall intelligence.

30

Compared to BOTH of the other rats considered in Figure 2, rat 3 exhibited anomalous brain activity in

A) Trial 3.
B) Trial 4.
C) Trial 5.
D) Trial 6.

31

In relation to the project explained in the passage, the research that yielded the data in the two figures could be derived from

A) an independent project that built upon Yu's investigations, since Yu voiced little interest in purely computerized maze navigation.
B) a single stage of Yu's research, since Yu's team tested rats, cyborgs, and computers in multiple mazes.
C) an extension of Yu's inquiry, since Yu only considered a single rat test subject despite tracing multiple types of data.
D) a corrective experiment designed by Yu's own team, since the figures only loosely suggest a symbiotic relationship between animals and technology.

Questions 32-42 are based on the following passages.

Passage 1 is adapted from President James K. Polk, Message to the United States Congress urging a declaration of war against Mexico. Passage 2 is adapted from Theodore Parker, speech delivered at Faneuil Hall. Polk's address took place on May 11 of 1846, while Parker's took place on February 4 of the following year.

Passage 1

The strong desire to establish peace with Mexico on liberal and honorable terms, and the readiness of this Government to regulate and adjust our boundary and other causes of difference with that power on such fair and equitable principles as would lead to permanent relations of the most friendly nature, induced me in September last to seek the reopening of diplomatic relations between the two countries. Every measure adopted on our part had for its object the furtherance of these desired results. In communicating to Congress a succinct statement of the injuries which we had suffered from Mexico, and which have been accumulating during a period of more than twenty years, every expression that could tend to inflame the people of Mexico or defeat or delay a pacific result was carefully avoided. An envoy of the United States repaired to Mexico with full powers to adjust every existing difference. But though present on the Mexican soil by agreement between the two Governments, invested with full powers, and bearing evidence of the most friendly dispositions, his mission has been unavailing. The Mexican Government not only refused to receive him or listen to his propositions, but after a long-continued series of menaces has at last invaded our territory and shed the blood of our fellow-citizens on our own soil.

. . . The grievous wrongs perpetrated by Mexico upon our citizens throughout a long period of years remain unredressed, and solemn treaties pledging her public faith for this redress have been disregarded. A government either unable or unwilling to enforce the execution of such treaties fails to perform one of its plainest duties.

Our commerce with Mexico has been almost annihilated. It was formerly highly beneficial to both nations, but our merchants have been deterred from prosecuting it by the system of outrage and extortion which the Mexican authorities have pursued against them, whilst their appeals through their own Government for indemnity have been made in vain.

Passage 2

The honor and dignity of the United States are in danger. I love my country; I love her honor. It is dear to me almost as my own. I have seen stormy meetings in Faneuil Hall before now, and am not easily disturbed by a popular tumult. But never before did I see a body of armed soldiers attempting to overawe the majesty of the people, when met to deliberate on the people's affairs. Yet the meetings of the people of Boston have been disturbed by soldiers before now, by British bayonets, but never since the Boston massacre on the 5th of March, 1770! Our fathers hated a standing army. This is a new one, but behold the effect! Here are soldiers with bayonets to overawe the majesty of the people! They went to our meeting last Monday night, the hireling soldiers of President Polk, to overawe and disturb the meetings of honest men. Here they are now, and in arms!

We are in a war; the signs of war are seen here in Boston. Men, needed to hew wood and honestly serve society, are marching about your streets; they are learning to kill men, men who never harmed us, nor them—learning to kill their brothers. It is a mean and infamous war we are fighting. It is a great boy fighting a little one, and that little one feeble and sick. What makes it worse is, the little boy is in the right, and the big boy is in the wrong, and tells solemn lies to make his side seem right. He wants, besides, to make the small boy pay the expenses of the quarrel.

The friends of the war say, "Mexico has invaded our territory!" When it is shown that it is we who have invaded hers, then it is said, "Ay, but

80 she owes us money." Better say outright, "Mexico has land, and we want to steal it!"

This war is waged for a mean and infamous purpose, for the extension of slavery. It is not enough that there are fifteen Slave States, and
85 3,000,000 men here who have no legal rights—not so much as the horse and the ox have in Boston: it is not enough that the slaveholders annexed Texas, and made slavery perpetual therein, extending even north of Mason and Dixon's line, covering
90 a territory forty-five times as large as the State of Massachusetts.

32

As used in line 6, "equitable" most nearly means

A) impartial.
B) innocent.
C) serious.
D) noble.

33

From the discussion of international relations in Passage 1, it can be inferred that Polk himself believes that

A) the governments of Mexico and the United States both refused to reopen diplomatic relations.
B) Mexico was responsible for the failure to establish peace between Mexico and the United States.
C) commerce with Mexico should proceed as it did at an earlier time.
D) the United States government judiciously refused to listen to Mexico's propositions.

34

Which choice provides the best evidence for the answer to the previous question?

A) Lines 1-9 ("The strong . . . countries")
B) Lines 10-11 ("Every measure . . . results")
C) Lines 18-20 ("An envoy . . . difference")
D) Lines 24-29 ("The Mexican . . . soil")

35

One of the central points made by the author of Passage 2 is that

A) the impending war is between unequal opponents.
B) it is necessary for loyal soldiers to defend their country.
C) Boston has never willingly participated in a war.
D) the impending war is the lesser of two evils.

36

As used in line 77, "friends" most nearly means

A) relatives.
B) acquaintances.
C) sponsors.
D) proponents.

37

In Passage 2, the author claims that the real reasons for going to war against Mexico are

A) monetary and dishonorable.
B) perfectly acceptable and commonplace.
C) too complex to understand.
D) connected to a valid sense of nationalism.

38

Which choice provides the best evidence for the answer to the previous question?

A) Lines 47-50 ("I love my . . . tumult")
B) Lines 58-60 ("This is . . . people!")
C) Lines 65-68 ("We are . . . streets")
D) Lines 80-83 ("Better . . . slavery")

39

In lines 77-78, the author of Passage 2 refers to a sentiment present in Passage 1 in order to

A) show that the two authors harbor the same opinion.
B) address the ostensibly false claims made in Passage 1.
C) highlight the differences between the United States and Mexico.
D) emphasize the importance of diplomatic relations.

40

Which choice best describes the relationship between Passage 1 and Passage 2?

A) Passage 2 strongly opposes a thesis that is presented in Passage 1.
B) Passage 1 reaches conclusions comparable to those explained in Passage 2.
C) Passage 1 paints a more realistic historical image than can be found in Passage 2.
D) Passage 2 assentingly develops the ideas espoused in Passage 1.

41

What is the main difference between the standpoints of the author of Passage 1 and the author of Passage 2?

A) The author of Passage 1 finds the war with Mexico an expression of innately vicious human tendencies, and the author of Passage 2 does not.
B) The author of Passage 2 is willing to overlook the consequences of the war Mexico, and the author of Passage 1 is not.
C) The author of Passage 1 is unconcerned about the effects of slavery, whereas the author of Passage 2 believes that the threat posed by slavery has been overestimated.
D) The author of Passage 2 strongly opposes the war with Mexico, whereas the author of Passage 1 deems the war necessary.

42

Which topic is addressed in Passage 2 and not in Passage 1?

A) The prevalence of slavery in the United States
B) Commerce with Mexico
C) Mexico's invasion of the United States
D) The lack of diplomatic cooperation between the United States and Mexico

Questions 43-52 are based on the following passage.

This passage is adapted from "How Hurricanes Michael, Florence May Have Spread Nonnative Species," a 2018 news release from the United States Geological Survey.

Hurricane Florence's floodwaters and Hurricane Michael's storm surge caused obvious devastation to natural areas, but a subtler set of harms is harder to see. Potentially destructive nonnative aquatic species, such as fast-growing plants that can choke waterways and hungry snails that can attack crops, can fan out across the landscape in the storms' waters, spreading unseen and becoming hard to eradicate.

To help land managers find and manage these flood-borne newcomers before they get established, scientists at the U.S. Geological Survey have created two preliminary online maps, one for each hurricane. These early "storm tracker" map sets show that more than 160 nonnative aquatic plant and animal species had the potential to spread during the 2018 hurricane season.

Nationwide, more than 1,280 freshwater aquatic species have been reported as found beyond their home ranges. Some have caused no obvious ill effects on their new habitats. Others, like the zebra mussels introduced into the Great Lakes, have caused damage to fisheries, shipping, water utilities, and other industries.

Storm surges and floodwaters can quickly spread nonnative aquatic species into waterways where they weren't found before. The USGS's innovative storm tracker maps were first produced in 2017 after Hurricane Harvey made landfall on Texas' Gulf Coast and became useful tools for land managers. Scientists with the USGS Nonindigenous Aquatic Species Program have made six storm trackers so far: four for the 2017 hurricanes Harvey, Irma, Maria, and Nate, and the preliminary trackers for the 2018 hurricanes Florence and Michael.

"These powerful hurricanes affected wide expanses of open spaces, including farmlands, forests, wetlands, and wildlife refuges," said USGS fishery biologist Pam Fuller, who leads the program. "It's very difficult for land managers to search all the places where flooding or storm surge occurred. Our results can help them concentrate on areas where nonnative aquatic species are most likely to appear."

For example, in the Florida Panhandle Michael's storm surge had the opportunity to spread curly pondweed, a South American aquatic plant that out-competes native species and can form dense mats that can foul boat propellers, said USGS research biologist Matthew Neilson, one of the storm tracker developers. Nonnative giant apple snails, which feed heavily on native plants and can become pests in rice fields, also could have been spread by the hurricane's waters.

In North Carolina, floodwaters from Hurricane Florence potentially spread two Mississippi Basin catfish species, blue catfish and flathead catfish, which feed on native pan fish like sunfish. The flathead is the subject of an eradication campaign in nearby Georgia, Neilson said.

"It's important to note that the storm tracker shows where a nonnative species has been found, but it doesn't show how abundant a species was before the hurricane," said USGS research biologist Wesley Daniel, a storm tracker developer. "And the more abundant a species is, the more likely it is to be picked up and carried along on floodwaters and start a new population somewhere else. So the tracker can show which species had the potential to spread, but it can't show which ones were the most likely to spread."

The Gainesville, Florida-based research group maintains the Nonindigenous Aquatic Species database, the nation's most complete record of freshwater plant and animal species found outside their native range, and used it to develop these preliminary maps within a few days of each hurricane's passage. From the database, the researchers identified all the nonnative plant

and animal species known to occur along the hurricane's path. Then they used storm surge and rainfall forecasts to identify places where lakes,
85 rivers, streams, and other waterways merged, giving aquatic species the opportunity to spread.

In the coming weeks, the team will incorporate more information collected by USGS hydrologists, including measurements from USGS
90 streamgages and thousands of high water marks left on the landscape. That data will be used to develop revised maps, available in three to six months, showing precisely where the natural or human-made barriers between watersheds were
95 breached.

43

The main purpose of the passage is to

A) clearly show that hurricanes have far-reaching consequences on natural habitats.
B) describe the devastation to natural areas caused by storm surges.
C) inform the readers of the versatile nature of online mapping technology.
D) depict the complexity of animal interactions in at-risk ecosystems.

44

As used in line 3, "devastation" most nearly means

A) grief.
B) destruction.
C) pilfering.
D) scarcity.

45

In lines 3-4, the phrase "a subtler set of harms" refers to

A) the secondary type of disruption to ecological balance.
B) the spread of disease among different aquatic species.
C) a problem which the U.S. Geological Survey faces.
D) the creation of online maps that display hurricane damage.

46

The passage clearly states that storm trackers

A) do not provide information on the number of species in a given area prior to a hurricane.
B) are predominantly used by farmers checking over their farmlands.
C) provide all the necessary information on particular species both before and after a hurricane.
D) need to be upgraded in the near future for optimal functionality.

47

Which choice provides the best evidence for the answer to the previous question?

A) Lines 14-18 ("These . . . season")
B) Lines 26-28 ("Storm . . . before")
C) Lines 63-66 ("It's important . . . hurricane")
D) Lines 74-80 ("The Gainesville . . . passage")

Test 7

48

The third paragraph (lines 19-25) primarily serves to

A) emphasize the negative effects of nonnative aquatic species.
B) explicate the concept of a "habitat" for the sake of providing background.
C) point out the damage inflicted on the environment by a few different industries.
D) discuss the importance of home ranges.

49

Which choice best reflects the difference between the comments from Pam Fuller (line 41) and Wesley Daniel (line 67)?

A) Fuller questions the protocol that surrounds a specific type of emergency; Daniel defends that same protocol as fundamentally sound.
B) Fuller explains the extent of a problem and presents a possible solution; Daniel highlights the limitations of a specific method.
C) Fuller presents anecdotal evidence in support of a policy recommendation; Daniel draws upon different evidence to justify the same conclusion.
D) Fuller outlines a course of action that she acknowledges to be divisive; Daniel casts doubt on recommendations such as Fuller's by appealing to a group of authorities.

50

The passage strongly suggests that according to the "storm tracker" maps

A) future large storms will not cause problems for fisheries.
B) there will be more than 160 flood-borne newcomer species during hurricane season.
C) geologists will persist in creating online maps as ecological crises become more intense.
D) it is unlikely that nonnative aquatic species will appear during the hurricane season.

51

Which choice indicates that online maps may be revised to reflect new information?

A) Lines 57-60 ("In North Carolina . . . sunfish")
B) Lines 60-62 ("The flathead . . . Georgia")
C) Lines 80-83 ("From the database . . . path")
D) Lines 91-95 ("That data . . . breached")

52

As used in line 95, "breached" most nearly means

A) crossed.
B) ruptured.
C) elevated.
D) flooded.

STOP

If you finish before time is called, you may check your work on this section only.
Do not turn to any other section.

Answer Key: Test 7

Passage 1	Passage 2	Passage 3	Passage 4	Passage 5
1. D	11. C	21. A	32. A	43. A
2. C	12. A	22. C	33. B	44. B
3. B	13. C	23. D	34. D	45. A
4. D	14. A	24. C	35. A	46. A
5. A	15. C	25. A	36. D	47. C
6. D	16. D	26. C	37. A	48. A
7. D	17. C	27. A	38. D	49. B
8. C	18. A	28. D	39. B	50. B
9. B	19. C	29. A	40. A	51. D
10. A	20. C	30. D	41. D	52. B
		31. B	42. A	

Question Types

Major Issue
1-2, 35, 43

Passage Details
3-4, 14-15, 21, 24-25, 45, 48-50

Command of Evidence
6-9, 12-13, 16-17, 22, 27-28, 33-34, 37-38, 46-47, 51

Word in Context
5, 10, 11, 18, 23, 26, 32, 36, 44, 52

Graphics and Visuals
19-20, 29-31

Passage Comparison
39-42

Answer Explanations
Test 7, Pages 184-199

Passage 1, Pages 184-186

1. D is the correct answer.

The passage begins with a discussion of the dog patiently waiting for Vladimir and experiencing "joy" (line 4) that his master has arrived home. It is further revealed that the dog and Vladimir have a close relationship in the dog's behavior in jumping on Vladimir's bed and in Vladimir's exclamation that the dog is "[his] only friend" (line 28). Further, the passage goes on to describe the various interactions between man and dog, including those in lines 48-53 in which Vladimir seems to speak with his dog as though it were a person. The passage ends with the phrase "caressing black eyes of the dog" (lines 79-80), further showing the relationship between the two characters and justifying D as the best choice. B correctly suggests that Vladimir is in some psychological pain, though it is not revealed in the passage that this pain is the result of the writing process. The passage only hints at the notion that writers need financial support in the final paragraph, since it is revealed that Vladimir is being advised to "take to some more lucrative occupation" (line 65). This makes C, like A, something not discussed explicitly by the narrator or discussed over the course of the passage but rather only mentioned in the final paragraph.

2. C is the correct answer.

The narrator discusses Vladimir's writing process in lines 41-47. Here, the narrator explains that Vladimir is "excited by the process of authorship" (line 41) and that he is "choking with a plethora of thoughts and mental pictures" (line 43-44), suggesting that the writing process is both complex but invigorating, so that Vladimir "walked about his room, and smoked cigarette after cigarette" (lines 44-45). C is thus appropriate, while A can be eliminated based on the phrase "highly successful," since the final paragraph of the passage suggests that Vladimir's friends want him to pursue some other profession. B can be eliminated based on information in the final paragraph, in which it is made clear that Vladimir often finds his friends more of an annoyance than a soothing presence. However, the narrator does not go so far as to suggest that Vladimir wants to live alone with his dog, so that D can be eliminated.

Answer Explanations, Test 7

3. B is the correct answer.

The first paragraph serves primarily to give insight into the living arrangement of Vladimir. Here, it is revealed that Vladimir returns home late at night but must "ring at his own door" (line 1), suggesting that he does not live alone. He is greeted by his dog, who barks in joy at his master's arrival, so that B is the best answer. A incorrectly presumes that Vladimir returns late each night, for which there is no evidence. Though there is some suggestion in this paragraph that the dog would bark at the arrival of a stranger, the paragraph does not suggest that having such a guard dog is important, making C a trap answer. While D might be tempting since this unconditional love is hinted at later in the passage, there is no direct evidence of this theme in the first paragraph itself.

4. D is the correct answer.

The direct reference to Vladimir's aunt does not occur until the final paragraph (line 54-55): "Then his aunt, with whom he lived . . . " Drawing on this detail, a reader can infer that the figure in his home is his aunt, since it is known that the aunt is Vladimir's housemate. D is appropriate, while A should be eliminated since the narrator reveals that Vladimir's dog would have been fearful if it had "been a stranger" (line 4) who arrived. Trap answers B and C can be immediately disregarded as irrelevant to the passage, since there is no mention of Vladimir being married or of any statuary in his aunt's home.

5. A is the correct answer.

The word "plethora" refers to a plenitude or a large quantity of "thoughts and mental pictures." The phrase "choking with" (line 43) suggests that Vladimir's thoughts and mental pictures are in a very large quantity since there are so many that he is choking upon them. Choose A to reflect this content. While B and C correctly suggest that Vladimir is in a frazzled state, Vladimir's situation is not rightly characterized as confusion or chaos since the description more strongly indicates that Vladimir is engaged in a fit of creativity. D is problematic because the thoughts create a negative "choking" reaction in Vladimir that would be inappropriate to the positive connotation of "depth," which can indicate wise or respected thinking.

6. D is the correct answer.

Though there is evidence throughout the final paragraph that Vladimir's aunt makes a fuss at the arrival of guests by "borrow[ing] china" (line 55) from neighbors and "sigh[ing] heavily" (line 58) when entertaining them, the best evidence is in lines 77-79. Here, it is revealed that Vladimir's aunt's eyes are "angry and reproachful," showing that she is vexed and disgruntled. D is thus the best choice. Though negative, other answers raise inappropriate concepts: A indicates that the aunt does not know what is going on (when in fact she comprehends and disapproves), while B and C wrongly identify her feelings about her own situation (NOT about Vladimir's) as explanations of her negativity.

7. D is the correct answer.

See the previous answer explanation for analysis of the correct line reference. Trap answers A and B can be eliminated based on lack of evidence that the aunt is menacing or threatening, confused, or indifferent since she seems to give indication of her unhappiness at the arrival of guests. C describes Vladimir perhaps, since he might be characterized as lonely at times. However, there is no reason to make a similar inference about his aunt, as it seems that she is entertaining his friends with some regularity.

8. C is the correct answer.

When Vladimir's friends visit, they often tell him to stop writing and to "take to some more lucrative occupation" (line 64-65). Such a lucrative occupation is one that earns more money, so it would seem as though Vladimir is currently not earning much from his writing pursuits and does not seem to have hopes of doing so in the future in the opinion of his friends. C reflects this choice, while A, B, and D all wrongly present the friends in a primarily positive manner as APPROVING of Vladimir's career or at least as seeking to help.

9. B is the correct answer.

See the previous answer explanation for analysis of the correct line reference. A can be eliminated based on its lack of correlation with the lucrativeness of Vladimir's chosen profession. This choice merely describes the jovial and friendly nature of the visit. C provides evidence of Vladimir's physical condition, not his financial one. Trap answer D, like correct answer B, further elaborates upon the nature of the relationship between Vladimir and his friends but does NOT provide any evidence for Vladimir's financial status.

10. A is the correct answer.

The word "conviviality" means "sociability." This meaning can be determined based on the context of the sentence in which Vladimir's friends "expressed their interest in him, and in the friendliest manner" (lines 72-73). This content makes A an appropriate choice. While the term "prolong" (line 75) might suggest something frivolous in a manner that might seem to justify B, the interaction described is far more one of friendship and social interaction than engaging in frivolous behavior. Trap answer C suggests correctly that there is social interaction or engagement, but "conviviality" has a positive connotation that makes "engagement" an insufficient synonym. While there is some indication that Vladimir's friends give him unwanted advice, it would seem that Vladimir is an active agent in his own life, making D implausible because the relationship between Vladimir and his friends cannot rightly be described as one of submission.

Passage 2, Pages 187-189

11. C is the correct answer.

In line 4, "highfalutin" refers to language which is unnecessarily complex, or perhaps situationally inappropriate. Choose C to reflect this meaning. A (inappropriately implying language which did not need to be present at all), B (inappropriately implying language which is simply strange or confusing), and D (inappropriately implying language that might trigger mockery or ridicule) all introduce improper contexts and therefore should be eliminated.

Answer Explanations, Test 7

12. A is the correct answer.

In lines 53-57, the author explains that "NSF grant abstracts with a simpler style—that is, grant abstracts that were written as a story with many pronouns—tend to receive more money. A personal touch may simplify the science and can make it relatable." Choose A to reflect this content. B can be eliminated since the content of the passage implies that proposals with more prepositions are actually LESS likely to get funded, while C can be dismissed because the author specifies that the relevant study only included grants submitted between 2010 and 2018. D can also be eliminated because the entire study focused on analyzing the relationship between funding and writing style, implying that writing style is a strong contributing factor in grant funding.

13. C is the correct answer.

See the previous answer explanation for analysis of the correct line reference. A summarizes the research goal of a recently published paper, while B explains the details of the sample which was used in the study. D explores the implications and value of the research that was conducted. None of these other answers show a connection between relatable content and successful funding, and therefore they should all be eliminated.

14. A is the correct answer.

The fourth paragraph summarizes previous research on language choices in grant proposals, concluding that complexity and confidence seemed to be factors in whether or not a project received funding. This content suggests that there is a connection between funding and certain types of language, an idea which had already been established prior to the author's study. Choose A as appropriate. B and C can be eliminated since the passage suggests that complex language is MORE likely to lead to funding and does NOT provide specific examples from actual grants. D can also be ruled out since the paragraph summarizes previous studies, NOT the entire history of grant writing.

15. C is the correct answer.

In lines 21-24, the author notes that "Loan writers also received money if their texts contained high levels of verbal confidence, such as words that convey certainty ("definitely," "always," "clearly")"; choose C to reflect this content. A and D can be readily eliminated since there are no specific guidelines offered for grant applications and since the passage indicates that pronouns and prepositions are two different categories of words, NOT that they are often misused. Be careful not to choose B, since authors who use a relatable "storytelling" style DO seem to be more likely to receive funding, but this reality does not necessarily imply that these authors are simplifying complex science as a result.

16. D is the correct answer.

In lines 73-76, the author argues that strategically using language to communicate complex ideas can make a project more likely to receive funding. Choose D as appropriate. Be careful not to choose B because the passage does imply that there will be multiple competitive proposals, but this fact is NOT a grant writing recommendation or a primary idea in the passage. A and C can also be eliminated since the passage implies that innovative ideas are not the only factor leading to funding and does NOT specify a connection between a grant and what happens to a project after it is funded.

17. C is the correct answer.

See the previous answer explanation for analysis of the correct line reference. A identifies a possibly mistaken belief which may be preventing individuals from receiving funding, while B offers an alternative perspective drawn from the results of the study considered in the passage. D contrasts a quotation from a well-known figure with the findings of the study. None of these other answers support the idea that clearly communicating complex ideas can increase the odds of receiving funding, and therefore they should all be eliminated.

18. A is the correct answer.

In line 74, "enhance" refers to how award money can benefit or bolster a compelling scientific proposal. Choose A to reflect this meaning. B (inappropriately implying rendering something up to date or aligned with current technology), C (inappropriately implying rendering something tougher or more resilient), and D (inappropriately implying the action of acquiring and storing items) all introduce improper contexts and therefore should be eliminated.

19. C is the correct answer.

The graph indicates that the percentage of words in a grant proposal in the adjectives category does not have a clear effect on the odds of a proposal receiving funding. For example, proposals which were moderately successful and proposals which were completely successful had roughly the same percentage of words classified as adjectives. Choose C to reflect the fact that, because there does not appear to be a strong correlation between adjective usage and funding, it would be difficult to predict how this proposal would be received. Given the lack of correlation indicated by the graph, A, B, and D can all readily be eliminated, since they rely on the assumption that a correlation can be documented between adjective usage and the odds of receiving funding.

20. C is the correct answer.

Lines 44-57 explain that proposals that include a high percentage of pronouns were more likely to receive funding, but the graph does not include a category for pronouns. In order to better assess to what extent the graph aligns with the results of the study, it would be helpful to know how data about pronoun usage were categorized. Choose C as appropriate. A can be eliminated since type of word, NOT length of word, was explored in both the study and the graph, while B can be eliminated since the focus is simply on the likelihood of a proposal receiving some funding, NOT on the specifics of how much funding (as a monetary figure) was received. D can also be ruled out since which specific preposition is used is less important than the percentage of words which can be classified as prepositions.

Answer Explanations, Test 7

Passage 3, Pages 190-193

21. A is the correct answer.

The first paragraph begins by setting the stage for conflict between biological (human and animal) intelligence and artificial intelligence, but then pivots to suggest that "both synthetic and biological systems have unique, complementary strengths that, when merged, could yield an optimally functioning "brain" " (lines 13-16). The primary purpose of the paragraph is to introduce a theory about a new kind of intelligence which is neither exclusively biological nor exclusively artificial; choose A as appropriate. B and D can both be dismissed since the passage does not articulate a preference for either type of intelligence, or specifically indicate the value of artificial intelligence. C can also be eliminated since the author proposes a synthesis of both types of intelligence, NOT a competition between them.

22. C is the correct answer.

Lines 13-16 explain that the ideal form of intelligence might combine the unique features of artificial and natural factors; choose C as appropriate. A explains how different outcomes from a chess challenge might indicate the strengths of different types of intelligence, while B focuses on a debate that arose after the outcome of that challenge was determined. D explains how the experiment which constitutes the focus of the study was conducted. None of these other answers highlight the potential fusion of artificial and biological intelligence, and therefore they should all be eliminated.

23. D is the correct answer.

In line 48, "traverse" refers to the rats following or moving along particular pathways in the maze. Choose D to reflect this meaning. A (inappropriately implying shifting an object from one location to another), B (inappropriately implying moving past something at a rapid speed), and C (inappropriately implying the beginning of a journey or action) all introduce improper contexts and therefore should be eliminated.

24. C is the correct answer.

The passage specifies that the experiment designed by Yu involved the steps of incentivizing the rats with rewards, tracking both the number of times that the rats visited a specific location AND the total time it took them to complete the maze, and providing algorithmic assistance to both rats (creating the "rat-cyborg" hybrid) and computer intelligence. The only element NOT mentioned in the passage is a competition between rats and rat-cyborgs; choose C. The other answers reflect elements which were specified as parts of the experiment, and therefore they should be eliminated.

25. A is the correct answer.

The fifth paragraph specifies that "the cyborgs took fewer [steps] than the rats, a sign of more efficient problem solving" (lines 56-57). Choose A to reflect this content. B and C can be eliminated since there was no way for researchers to calculate and monitor whether the rats were calculating possible outcomes or providing multiple solutions. The only things which could be measured were how many steps the rats took, and how long it took them to complete the maze. D can also be ruled out since the rats were completing the maze individually and did not have the opportunity to intervene against competitors.

26. C is the correct answer.

In line 48, "tantamount" refers to one idea being equivalent to, or the same as, another. Choose C to reflect this meaning. A (inappropriately implying one thing being better than another), B (inappropriately implying something being seductive or tempting), and D (inappropriately implying something originating from the idea of something else) all introduce improper contexts and therefore should be eliminated.

27. A is the correct answer.

Lines 89-92 propose that "perhaps instead it's time to embrace the computing abilities of machines as complementary—and beneficial—to our own natural powers of intelligence," implying that future advances in intelligence most likely rest on combining artificial and biological intelligence. Choose A to reflect this content. B and C can both be readily eliminated since they emphasize the economic and ethical implications of artificial intelligence—topics which lie outside of the scope of the passage. D can be eliminated since the passage clearly indicates that human intelligence will always have a role in future technologies and optimization.

28. D is the correct answer.

See the previous answer explanation for analysis of the correct line reference. A summarizes how the computers, cyborgs, and rats all experienced different results in completing the maze, while B raises a rhetorical question to introduce a potential argument. C also uses a question to reflect on a potential fear which might be triggered by advances in artificial intelligence. None of these other answers argue that optimal intelligence can be generated by combining artificial and biological intelligence, and therefore they should all be eliminated.

29. A is the correct answer.

Figure 1 shows that the computers at first required more turns to solve the maze than the cyborg rats did, but that, over multiple trials, the computers began to consistently complete the maze with fewer turns than the cyborg rats. This data indicates that the computers may be capable of navigating more efficiently than the cyborgs; choose A as appropriate. B can be eliminated since data are only presented for five trials, and therefore it is not possible to know how the different subjects would perform beyond the fifth trial. C can also be eliminated since the figure does NOT present any information about completion times, only about the number of turns required. D should be eliminated since the data reflect only a rat's ability to solve a particular challenge, NOT a given rat's overall intelligence.

30. D is the correct answer.

In Trial 6, Rats 1 and 2 both showed an increase in their EEG signal strength, whereas in all previous trials the signal strength had either declined or remained relatively stable. Rat 3, however, did not display this increase

Answer Explanations, Test 7

in signal strength, indicating the possibility of anomalous brain activity. Choose D as appropriate. In all of the other trials, Rat 3 showed brain activity which seemed consistent with the brain activity displayed by the other rats, and therefore the other answers should be eliminated.

31. B is the correct answer.

The two figures provide data about different subjects completing the same maze multiple times and about the subject's brain activity after doing so. Yu's research involved different subjects completing different mazes, so that the research documented in the figures could plausibly be drawn from data collected about one particular maze. Choose B to reflect this content. A and C can both be readily dismissed, since Yu's team studied computerized, cyborg, and rat subjects, and also tested multiple rat subjects. D can also be eliminated since there is no evidence of a need for a corrective experiment, or a need to prove a relationship between animals and technology.

Passage 4, Pages 194-196

32. A is the correct answer.

In line 6, "equitable" refers to principles which are applied equally to different parties. Choose A to reflect this meaning. B (inappropriately implying someone being unwitting or unknowing), C (inappropriately implying gravity or significance), and D (inappropriately implying high standards of integrity) all introduce improper contexts and therefore should be eliminated.

33. B is the correct answer.

In lines 24-29, the author states that, in reference to an envoy from the United States, "The Mexican Government not only refused to receive him or listen to his propositions, but after a long-continued series of menaces has at last invaded our territory and shed the blood of our fellow-citizens on our own soil." This content implies that the author sees Mexico as having failed to maintain peace; choose B as appropriate. A and D can both be eliminated since these choices imply that the United States bears some responsibility for the conflict, whereas the author sees the fault as resting solely with the Mexican government. C can also be eliminated since the author does NOT specifically discuss commerce between the two nations.

34. D is the correct answer.

See the previous answer explanation for analysis of the correct line reference. A describes an action that the author took in order to mend the relationship between America and Mexico and explains the motivation for doing so. B asserts the sincerity behind these efforts, while C describes one strategy employed in an effort to re-establish diplomatic relations. None of these other answers reflect the author's belief that Mexico failed to cooperate in efforts to reestablish peace, and therefore these false answers should be eliminated.

… Answer Explanations, Test 7

35. A is the correct answer.

The author of Passage 2 compares the war between America and Mexico to "a great boy fighting a little one, and that little one feeble and sick" (lines 71-72). This statement implies that the author sees the war as taking place between unfairly matched parties; choose A as appropriate. B and C can be eliminated since the author is NOT urging individuals to defend their country by participating in the war, and since the author refers to conflicts in which Boston has participated in the past. D can also be eliminated since the author does NOT contrast the American-Mexican war with any other possibility, and (because the speech is designed as an argument AGAINST the war) is NOT resigned to American participation in this conflict.

36. D is the correct answer.

In line 37, "friends" refers to people who argue in favor of America participating in the war. Choose D to reflect this meaning. A (inappropriately implying someone connected by blood or by a family relationship), B (inappropriately implying people who know each other slightly but not well), and C (inappropriately implying someone who provides money or other material support to a project or cause) all introduce improper contexts and therefore should be eliminated.

37. A is the correct answer.

In lines 80-83, the author angrily explains, "Better say outright, "Mexico has land, and we want to steal it!" This war is waged for a mean and infamous purpose, for the extension of slavery." This content shows that the author believes that American participation in the war is driven by greed and is unethical. Choose A as appropriate. B and D can both readily be eliminated since these answers imply that the author has a positive view of American motivations, whereas his view is clearly negative. C wrongly indicates that the author would be indecisive, when in fact he argues that the reasons for war against Mexico are understandable and unjust.

38. D is the correct answer.

See the previous answer explanation for analysis of the correct line reference. A describes the author's personal feelings and past experiences, while B raises a critique regarding the presence of military force. C summarizes the current state of affairs and the problems that it may cause. None of these other answers reflect the author's belief about why America has gotten involved in a war with Mexico, and therefore they should all be eliminated.

39. B is the correct answer.

In lines 77-78, the author notes that some people who are in favor of the war will argue that Mexican forces invaded American territory. This is indeed an argument made by the author of Passage 1, and this comment by the author of Passage 2 shows that he sees such a contention as a false argument. Choose B as appropriate. A and C can be eliminated since the two authors have opposing opinions about the war, and since the argument refers to American motivations, NOT the differences between two countries. D can also be eliminated since the author is less concerned with diplomatic relations than with criticism of the war.

Answer Explanations, Test 7

40. A is the correct answer.

Passage 1 argues that it would be justifiable for America to declare war on Mexico, while Passage 2 vehemently opposes the war. Choose A, since the perspective presented in Passage 1 is opposed to the arguments present in Passage 2. B and D can be dismissed since these answers imply that there is alignment between the two passages, whereas the two passages present strongly opposed views. C can also be dismissed since no additional information is provided to enable assessment of the historical validity of either passage.

41. D is the correct answer.

Passage 1 argues that it would be justifiable for America to declare war on Mexico, while Passage 2 vehemently opposes the war. Choose D as appropriate. Both A and B can be eliminated since they misrepresent the viewpoints of the authors: the author of Passage 1 is in favor of the war, and the author of Passage 2 is opposed to it. Be careful not to choose C, since the connection between slavery and the war only appears in Passage 2 and is NOT discussed in Passage 1.

42. A is the correct answer.

Passage 2 explicitly raises the topic of American slavery, since the author sees slavery as a factor leading to support for the Mexican-American war (lines 82-91). Passage 1 does not discuss slavery and focuses instead on diplomatic tensions between the United States and Mexico. Choose A to reflect this content. B, C, and D can all be eliminated since all of these topics are addressed only in Passage 1 and NOT in Passage 2.

Passage 5, Pages 197-199

43. A is the correct answer.

By describing how hurricanes can contribute to the spread of nonnative species, the passage highlights a typically unrecognized consequence of severe storms. Choose A to reflect this content. Be careful not to choose B or D, since, while storm surges are discussed in the passage, they are NOT presented as a direct force of destruction. Likewise, both invasive animal and plant species are discussed in the passage, and therefore D should be eliminated. C can be ruled out since online maps are only mentioned in the passage on account of one specific purpose that they can serve (identifying where nonnative species are most likely to be found).

44. B is the correct answer.

In line 3, "devastation" refers to the harm and environmental damage caused by tropical storms. Choose B to reflect this meaning. A (inappropriately implying a sense of emotional loss), C (inappropriately implying property being seized by someone other than the owner), and D (inappropriately implying a limited amount of resources) all introduce improper contexts and therefore should be eliminated.

Answer Explanations, Test 7

45. A is the correct answer.

In lines 3-4, "a subtler set of harms" refers to types of damage which are not immediately apparent in the wake of a storm, and may take longer to detect or have may ripple effects which combine with other factors to cause damage. In this particular case, the harm explored in most detail is the transfer of nonnative species to different areas. Choose A to reflect this content. Be careful not to choose B, since the spread of disease could be a consequence of nonnative species appearing in different areas, but this possibility is NOT the only destructive effect discussed in the passage. C and D can readily be eliminated since the "harms" refer to a consequence of tropical storms, not to a problem faced by a specific government department or to a type of technology.

46. A is the correct answer.

Lines 63-66 specify that "It's important to note that the storm tracker shows where a nonnative species has been found, but it doesn't show how abundant it was before the hurricane." Choose A to reflect this content. C can be eliminated since it is factually contradicted by the content of the passage (which specifies how the data provided by the storm tracker is limited). B and D can also be ruled out since the passage mentions a variety of users who benefit from the tracker technology, and since there is no mention of the tracker technology (which is mostly depicted as useful) becoming obsolete.

47. C is the correct answer.

See the previous answer explanation for analysis of the correct line reference. A describes the type of information that storm tracker maps are able to provide, while B explains the link between storms and the spread of nonnative species. D describes the creators of the storm tracker maps and the data that they drew on in order to create the maps. None of these other answers acknowledge a key limitation in the storm tracker technology, and therefore they should all be eliminated.

48. A is the correct answer.

The third paragraph provides context by explaining the negative consequences that may be caused by a nonnative species spreading into a new territory. Choose A to reflect this content. Be careful not to choose B or C, since the paragraph does describe damage but focuses on damage inflicted by invading species, NOT man-made industries. Here, the author also does NOT go into detail about the concept of habitats. D can be eliminated since the paragraph talks about what can happen when a species expands outside of its typical home range, NOT why a home range is important in general.

49. B is the correct answer.

In line 41, Fuller identifies a problem and the circumstances which make that problem hard to solve, while in line 67, Daniel mentions that storm tracker technology does have one important limitation. Choose B to reflect this relationship between the two quotations. A and C can be ruled out since ONLY Fuller identifies a problem and does not propose any protocols or policy recommendations to resolve it. D can also be ruled out

Answer Explanations, Test 7

since Daniel acknowledges a limitation but does NOT attempt to challenge or discredit the usage of storm tracker technology.

50. B is the correct answer.

The author states that "These early "storm tracker" map sets show that more than 160 nonnative aquatic plant and animal species had the potential to spread during the 2018 hurricane season." Choose B to reflect this content. A can be eliminated since storm tracker maps may help to curtail post-storm problems, but NOT eliminate them entirely. C can be eliminated since nothing in the passage specifically predicts the creation of more maps or connects the rise in maps (which mostly help with ANALYSIS of events) to increasing ecological crises. D can also be ruled out since the whole passage implies that nonnative species ARE likely to appear in new regions during hurricane season, a reality that led to the creation of storm tracker technology.

51. D is the correct answer.

Lines 91-95 explain a planned future attempt to improve the maps and make them more accurate and useful by incorporating new information. Choose D to reflect this content. A and B can be ruled out since these answers focus on a specific example of a destructive invasive species and on the measures taken to control that species. C describes how researchers used existing data to generate a predictive tool. None of these other answers reflect an intention to update existing storm tracker maps, and therefore they should all be eliminated.

52. B is the correct answer.

In line 95, "breached" refers to how barriers between waterways may become ineffective and allow water from a different environment to spill over, potentially carrying new species along. Choose B to reflect this meaning. A (inappropriately implying someone or something moving from one location to another), C (inappropriately implying someone or something occupying a new position that is higher up than the previous position), and D (inappropriately implying a liquid spilling out of the boundaries intended to contain it) all introduce improper contexts and therefore should be eliminated.

NOTES

- Passage 2 on Page 187, "Text analysis of thousands of grant abstracts shows that writing style matters," is an excerpt from the article of the same name by David Markowitz and published by The Conversation in partnership with the University of Oregon. 31 January 2019, The Conversation. https://theconversation.com/text-analysis-of-thousands-of-grant-abstracts-shows-that-writing-style-matters-108662. Accessed 28 July 2019.

- Passage 3 on Pages 190-191, "The supremely intelligent rat-cyborg," is adapted from the article of the same name by Emilie Reas and published by the PLOS Neuro Community blog. 4 March 2016, PLOS ONE. https://blogs.plos.org/neuro/2016/03/04/the-supremely-intelligent-rat-cyborg/. Accessed 28 July 2019.

- Passage 5 on Pages 197-198, "How Hurricanes Michael, Florence May Have Spread Nonnative Species," is adapted from the article of the same name published by the United States Geological Survey. 14 November 2018, USGS. https://www.usgs.gov/news/how-hurricanes-michael-florence-may-have-spread-nonnative-species. Accessed 28 July 2019.

About the Figures: The various visual resources that accompany the passages in this section are primarily meant to facilitate critical thinking skills and may not reflect historical data.

Test 8

Full Reading Section

2020 SAT Practice

Test 8

Reading Test

65 MINUTES, 52 QUESTIONS

Turn to Section 1 of your answer sheet to answer the questions in this section.

DIRECTIONS

Each passage or pair of passages below is followed by a number of questions. After reading each passage or pair, choose the best answer to each question based on what is stated or implied in the passage or passages and in any accompanying graphics (such as a table or graph).

Questions 1-10 are based on the following passage.

This passage is adapted from the short story "To Rest" by Winnie Khaw (copyright 2019 Winnie Khaw). In this excerpt, the narrator, a 23-year-old woman named Hanna is grappling with the death of her fiance Dan.

When I dream about Dan, the events are always the same: I'm driving our old, gigantic car, and there's a man walking around by the side of the road, holding up a cardboard sign stating "Please Pick Me" and ending with a smiley face. It's sweltering today, and I slow the car to a stop and open the door.
    "Come on in. Going my way?"
    "Sure." He grins. "Where're you headed?" Dan asks, sliding into the seat next to me.
    "Nowhere in particular," I admit, about to twist the dial to another channel. "Fine. Neverland," I joke.
    "That's exactly my destination. Small world, huh, Hanna?"
    I clear my throat and decide I can leave the current station playing a bit longer. The static won't continue forever. "Well. We should move on," I say.
    Dan slouches in his seat, trying to get comfortable. "By all means. Let's go."
    "I've seen you around here for a while," I tell him after several minutes of silence, keeping my eyes on the road.
    "I was waiting for someone."
    "To pick you?" I joke, gesturing at the cardboard sign at his feet.
    "Guess you won the lottery." He's found an expired ticket under the seat while fidgeting. His response fills my stomach with butterflies, and automatically I glance over at him to see sunlight haloing his dark head while he gazes back with a flippant smile and punning eyes. "And I'd like to offer my services as a mechanic to the lucky winner."
    I remember our childhood friendship: Dan and I climbing up the loft, hay in our hair, hiding from Mom's sight. We laughed softly as Mom huffed around the barn looking for me and then finally left, muttering. And then there was adulthood: a few weeks after Dan proposed, and then showed me the behemoth vehicle he'd put together for our

future, another car with faulty brakes lost control and drove into Dan's, killing him instantly.

    The GPS informs me that I'm driving into cliff territory. After a time, during which I force myself to keep my hands on the wheel and Dan says nothing and a heavy fall of rain suddenly sets on and only lets up slightly, I find myself on the edges of the road. Looking down, I can see the ground beneath gradually receding as I climb further up the mountain. There's a perilous turn coming up.

    "Don't panic," Dan says. I had almost forgotten his presence. I startle and whip my head around, but he has put a gentle hand on my cheek, stopping me. "You'll get past this turn."

    "I don't know if I can," I moan, my fingers clutching at each other.

    "Isn't it time you laid your ghosts to rest?" he asks. I can see the brilliance of sunset through the window filtering past his pupils and suddenly I don't remember if his eyes were dark gray or blue.

    I step on the brake, and the car comes to an obedient stop. Even then, the front wheels scatter pebbles over the cliff into eternity. I lean forward against the steering wheel, breathing hard; finally, I back up and bring the car to a secure stop.

    Dan finally speaks. It's odd to hear him after so much silence. "Well, you can't bring me with you to Neverland," he says wryly, holding up the expired ticket, and then he's gone, leaving only the scrap of paper on the passenger's seat. No, the cardboard sign, "Please Pick Me," which Dan had used to propose, still lies crumpled on the car floor, and I look at it until I wake up.

1

Over the course of the passage, the main focus of the narrative shifts from

A) the happiness Hannah felt during her moments with Dan to a near-death situation.

B) providing an example of trust to showing how Dan paid the ultimate price for his innocence.

C) reflecting on a reoccurring scenario to connecting the end of a dream with reality.

D) a character's attempts to deal with grief to an example of her personal growth.

2

The description of Hanna and Dan's early interactions (lines 1-21) indicates that Hanna is

A) not in a hurry.

B) eager to make room for Dan in the car.

C) certain of her destination.

D) nervous about having Dan as a passenger.

3

Which choice provides the best evidence for the answer to the previous question?

A) Lines 5-7 ("Please . . . door")

B) Lines 9-10 ("Sure . . . me")

C) Lines 11-12 ("Nowhere . . . channel")

D) Lines 16-21 ("I clear . . . go")

Test 8

4

As used in line 33, "flippant" most nearly means

A) disrespectful.
B) playful.
C) energized.
D) nonsensical.

5

The main purpose of the paragraph that takes up lines 36-44 is to

A) display a past conflict that was quickly resolved.
B) connect Hanna's dream to specific recollections.
C) establish Hanna's mother as a symbolic presence.
D) suggest that Dan's demise was random yet unavoidable.

6

Which choice most effectively emphasizes the theme that Dan is not a normal hitchhiker?

A) Lines 14-15 ("That's . . . Hanna")
B) Lines 40-43 ("And . . . future")
C) Lines 45-50 ("The GPS . . . road")
D) Lines 64-66 ("I step . . . eternity")

7

Based on the passage, Dan's statement "Isn't it time you laid your ghosts to rest?" (line 60) implies that ghosts represent

A) Hanna's memory of her extended family.
B) Hanna's fear of cliffs.
C) Hanna's inability to drive safely.
D) Hanna's concern that the sun will set before she makes her way down the mountain.

8

The author's use of the term "brilliance" (line 61) most directly suggests that

A) the sunset looked beautiful in the mirror.
B) the natural landscape reflects Dan's own virtues.
C) the view from the cliffside unusually distinct.
D) the light from outside the car impeded Hanna's ability to drive.

9

The author of the passage employs the phrase "he's gone" (line 72) in order to show that Dan had

A) vanished since he was an illusion in Hanna's dream.
B) passed away from the impact of the vehicle's emergency brakes.
C) opened the door and left all his belongings in the vehicle.
D) abandoned Hanna due to her inability to overcome fear.

10

The author includes a description of the vehicle's interior (lines 73-76) primarily to

A) clarify that Hanna was having a nightmare.
B) prove that the vehicle was not damaged.
C) reiterate that Dan will visit Hanna in another dream.
D) describe Hanna's feeling of emptiness due to Dan's untimely death.

Questions 11-20 are based on the following passage.

This passage is adapted from President Gerald R. Ford, Address on Foreign Policy, delivered to a joint session of Congress on April 10, 1975.

Tonight it is my purpose to review our relations with the rest of the world in the spirit of candor and consultation which I have sought to maintain with my former colleagues and with our countrymen from the time that I took office. It is the first priority of my Presidency to sustain and strengthen the mutual trust and respect which must exist among Americans and their Government if we are to deal successfully with the challenges confronting us both at home and abroad.

The leadership of the United States of America since the end of World War II has sustained and advanced the security, well-being, and freedom of millions of human beings besides ourselves. Despite some setbacks, despite some mistakes, the United States has made peace a real prospect for us and for all nations. I know firsthand that the Congress has been a partner in the development and in the support of American foreign policy, which five Presidents before me have carried forward with changes of course but not of destination.

The course which our country chooses in the world today has never been of greater significance for ourselves as a nation and for all mankind. We build from a solid foundation. Our alliances with great industrial democracies in Europe, North America, and Japan remain strong with a greater degree of consultation and equity than ever before.

With the Soviet Union we have moved across a broad front toward a more stable, if still competitive, relationship. We have begun to control the spiral of strategic nuclear armaments.

After two decades of mutual estrangement, we have achieved an historic opening with the People's Republic of China.

In the best American tradition, we have committed, often with striking success, our influence and good offices to help contain conflicts and settle disputes in many, many regions of the world. We have, for example, helped the parties of the Middle East take the first steps toward living with one another in peace.

We have opened a new dialogue with Latin America, looking toward a healthier hemispheric partnership. We are developing closer relations with the nations of Africa. We have exercised international leadership on the great new issues of our interdependent world, such as energy, food, environment, and the law of the sea.

The American people can be proud of what their Nation has achieved and has helped others to accomplish, but we have from time to time suffered setbacks and disappointments in foreign policy. Some were events over which we had no control; some were difficulties we imposed upon ourselves.

We live in a time of testing and of a time of change. Our world—a world of economic uncertainty, political unrest, and threats to the peace—does not allow us the luxury of abdication or domestic discord.

I recall quite vividly the words of President Truman to the Congress when the United States faced a far greater challenge at the end of the Second World War. If I might quote: "If we falter in our leadership, we may endanger the peace of the world, and we shall surely endanger the welfare of this Nation."

President Truman's resolution must guide us today. Our purpose is not to point the finger of blame, but to build upon our many successes, to repair damage where we find it, to recover our balance, to move ahead as a united people. Tonight is a time for straight talk among friends, about where we stand and where we are going.

Test 8

11

It can be inferred from the speech that Gerald Ford believes that

A) China is a trusted ally of the United States.

B) the United States played a crucial role in maintaining amicable relations between Middle Eastern countries.

C) the Soviet Union and Japan are both on equally comfortable diplomatic terms with the United States.

D) the world is experiencing a bout of economic uncertainty as a result of shaky leadership in the United States.

12

Over the course of the passage, the main focus of Ford's speech shifts from

A) exercising his power as President to agreeing with President Truman's remarks from years earlier.

B) providing a stern warning concerning American leadership to heralding foreign intervention in domestic policy.

C) establishing sincerity towards the audience to clarifying the position of the United States in world affairs.

D) building rapport with his audience to reflecting on the successes of United States foreign policy.

13

As used in line 3, "candor" most nearly means

A) openness.

B) analysis.

C) expertise.

D) determination.

14

The main purpose of the second paragraph (lines 12-23) of Ford's speech is to

A) describe the importance of American foreign policy in world affairs.

B) explain the development of democratic foreign policy since World War II.

C) provide an argument in support of the intervention of the United States in World War II.

D) highlight the consistencies of foreign policy during the previous three decades.

15

The term "course" (line 24) most likely refers to

A) the approach to foreign policy adopted by the United States.

B) a means of choosing the best leadership to ensure the prosperous future of the country.

C) determining the outcome of positive relations with the Soviet Union.

D) President Ford's own appointment to the position of Secretary of State.

16

Which choice supports the idea that the United States did not previously enjoy a healthy relationship with China?

A) Lines 24-26 ("The course . . . mankind")

B) Lines 31-34 ("With . . . armaments")

C) Lines 35-37 ("After . . . China")

D) Lines 38-42 ("In the. . . world")

17

According to President Ford, which of the following countries was a democracy in 1975?

A) Germany
B) Poland
C) Brazil
D) Japan

18

Which choice provides the best evidence for the answer to the previous question?

A) Lines 27-30 ("Our . . . before")
B) Lines 42-44 ("We have . . . peace")
C) Lines 45-47 ("We have . . . partnership")
D) Lines 47-48 ("We are . . . Africa")

19

Why does Ford mention that "The American people can be proud" (line 52)?

A) To instill patriotic sentiments in the audience
B) To conclude that American foreign policy has been effective
C) To prepare the audience to acknowledge the shortcomings of American foreign policy
D) To show his support for American foreign policy

20

Ford includes a quote from Harry Truman (lines 67-70) primarily to

A) express respect for a former president whose ideology was not compatible with Ford's own.
B) reinforce the perspective that world peace rests on the success of the United States.
C) unveil a novel opinion regarding the position of the United States in world affairs.
D) provide an example of how setbacks were surmounted in a different era of United States history.

Questions 21-31 are based on the following passage and supplementary material.

This passage is adapted from "Blood test shows promise for early detection of severe lung-transplant rejection," a 2018 news release* from the National Institutes of Health.

Researchers have developed a simple blood test that can detect when a newly transplanted lung is being rejected by a patient, even when no outward signs of the rejection are evident. The test could make it possible for doctors to intervene faster to prevent or slow down so-called chronic rejection—which is severe, irreversible, and often deadly—in those first critical months after lung transplantation. Researchers believe that this same test might also be useful for monitoring rejection in other types of organ transplants. The work was funded by the National Heart, Lung, and Blood Institute (NHLBI), part of the National Institutes of Health....

"This test solves a long-standing problem in lung transplants: detection of hidden signs of rejection," said Hannah Valantine, M.D., co-leader of the study and lead investigator of the Laboratory of Organ Transplant Genomics in the Cardiovascular Branch at NHLBI. "We're very excited about its potential to save lives, especially in the wake of a critical shortage of donor organs."

The test relies on DNA sequencing, Valantine explained, and, as such, represents a great example of personalized medicine, as it will allow doctors to tailor transplant treatments to those individuals who are at highest risk for rejection.

Lung transplant recipients have the shortest survival rates among patients who get solid organ transplantation of any kind—only about half live past five years. Lung transplant recipients face a high incidence of chronic rejection, which occurs when the body's immune system attacks the transplanted organ. Existing tools for detecting signs of rejection, such as biopsy, either require the removal of small amounts of lung tissue or are not sensitive enough to discern the severity of the rejection. The new test appears to overcome those challenges.

Called the donor-derived cell-free DNA test, the experimental test begins with obtaining a few blood droplets taken from the arm of the transplant recipient. A special set of machines then sorts the DNA fragments in the blood sample, and in combination with computer analysis determines whether the fragments are from the recipient or the donor and how many of each type are present. Because injured or dying cells from the donor release lots of donor DNA fragments into the bloodstream compared to normal donor cells, higher levels of donor DNA indicate a higher risk for transplant rejection in the recipient.

In the study, 106 lung transplant recipients were enrolled and monitored. Blood samples collected in the first three months after transplantation underwent the testing procedure. The results showed that those with higher levels of the donor-derived DNA fragments in the first three months of transplantation were six times more likely to subsequently develop transplant organ failure or die during the study follow-up period than those with lower donor-derived DNA levels. Importantly, researchers found that more than half of the high-risk subjects showed no outward signs of clinical complications during this period.

"We showed for the first time that donor-derived DNA is a predictive marker for chronic lung rejection and death, and could provide critical time-points to intervene, perhaps preventing these outcomes," Valantine said. "Once rejection is detected early via this test, doctors would then have the option to increase the dosages of anti-rejection drugs, add new agents that reduce tissue inflammation, or take other measures to prevent or slow the progression."

In 2010, Valantine was part of a research team that pioneered the first blood test to diagnose organ rejection. The now widely-used test, called the AlloMap, analyzes the expression of 20 genes in a transplant recipient's blood sample to determine whether the patient's immune system is launching an attack. The following year, Valantine

*See Page 242 for the citation for this text.

and her colleagues showed for the first time that a cell-free DNA blood test could be useful for monitoring early signs of rejection. However, those early studies of the cell-free DNA test only identified signs of "acute" transplant rejection, which is easily reversed. The current study shows that high cell-free DNA levels during the first three months after transplant predicts chronic rejection. If validated, this blood test could become a routine tool used to monitor transplant patients at very early stages of rejection, the researchers said.

21

The main purpose of the passage as a whole is to

A) promote the application of donor-derived cell-free DNA testing to detect lung transplant rejection at early stages.

B) explain how scientific advances have contributed to distinguishing fatal and non-fatal lung transplant rejection.

C) discuss the variety of methods that can be used to replace biopsy removal in determining lung transplant issues.

D) report on the benefits of employing the AlloMap when dealing with at-risk lung transplant patients.

22

The author's recommendations in the passage are premised on the idea that

A) lung transplants should be undertaken with caution.

B) the AlloMap is more effective than biopsies at detecting early signs of rejection.

C) researchers are getting closer to eliminating the risk of lung transplant rejection.

D) biopsies are unreliable at detecting lung transplant rejections.

23

Which choice provides the best evidence for the answer to the previous question?

A) Lines 28-31 ("Lung transplant . . . five years")
B) Lines 38-39 ("The new . . . challenges")
C) Lines 79-83 ("The now . . . attack")
D) Lines 89-92 ("The current . . . rejection")

24

How do the words "severe," "irreversible," and "deadly" in the first paragraph (lines 1-14) help to establish the tone of the paragraph?

A) They create a candid tone that describes the drawbacks of having a lung transplant.

B) They create an authoritative tone that indicates that the author has the credentials to issue a warning on the repercussions of having lung replacement surgery.

C) They create a serious tone that elucidates the author's intention in highlighting the significance of the new research test.

D) They create a skeptical tone that suggests that the author is unsure whether the lung transplant procedure is truly effective and safe.

25

The commentary from Hannah Valantine serves to

A) provide expert input to validate an account of the development of the blood test.

B) introduce an official researcher from the NHLBI whose ideas overturn earlier assumptions.

C) show the potential benefits of a new type of testing that is relevant to future lung transplants.

D) make the claim that an innovative test will perfectly diagnose lung transplant issues.

Transplant Rejections* in the United States

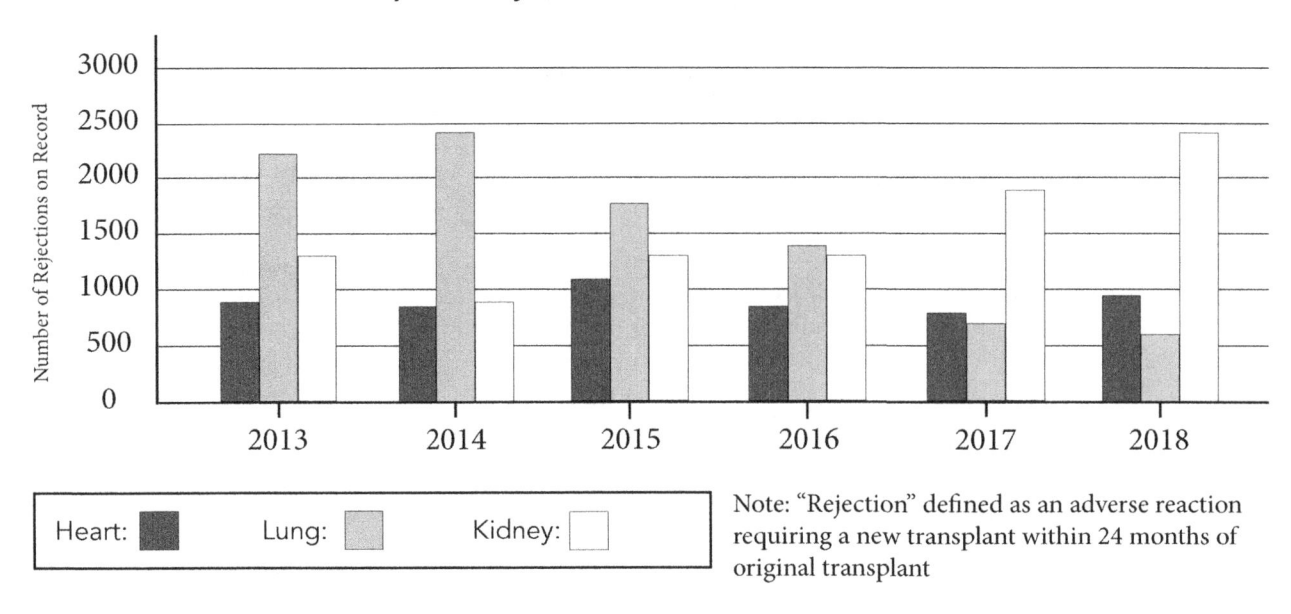

Bar graph showing Number of Rejections on Record for Heart, Lung, and Kidney transplants from 2013 to 2018:

- 2013: Heart ~900, Lung ~2200, Kidney ~1300
- 2014: Heart ~850, Lung ~2400, Kidney ~900
- 2015: Heart ~1100, Lung ~1750, Kidney ~1300
- 2016: Heart ~850, Lung ~1400, Kidney ~1300
- 2017: Heart ~800, Lung ~700, Kidney ~1900
- 2018: Heart ~950, Lung ~600, Kidney ~2400

Note: "Rejection" defined as an adverse reaction requiring a new transplant within 24 months of original transplant

---

26

Which choice provides the best evidence for the answer to the previous question?

A) Lines 11-14 ("The work . . . Health")
B) Lines 15-17 ("This test . . . Valantine")
C) Lines 77-79 ("In 2010 . . . rejection")
D) Lines 86-89 ("However . . . reversed")

27

As used in line 23, "sequencing" most nearly means

A) discovery.
B) pattern.
C) arrangement.
D) method.

28

The information in the second-to-last paragraph (lines 67-76) can best be characterized as

A) a conclusion about whether the donor-derived cell-free DNA test should be used.
B) a statement of scientific consensus as to how lung transplant rejection could be detected earlier.
C) a final argument about whether the new blood test is a superior method of detection.
D) a synopsis of study outcomes for the new blood test.

29

Which of the following quantities from the graph represents the lowest number of rejections?

A) Lung, 2013
B) Lung, 2014
C) Kidney, 2017
D) Kidney, 2018

30

The graph as a whole supports the conclusion that

A) the number of kidney transplant rejections consistently increased year-over-year.

B) the number of lung transplant rejections consistently decreased year-over-year.

C) the number of heart transplant rejections remained constant year-over-year.

D) no organ transplant rejection type displayed a perfectly consistent year-over-year pattern of increase, decrease, or consistency.

31

Which information would most effectively place the graph in the context of the claims presented in lines 28-34 ("Lung transplant . . . organ")?

A) How many instances of rejection resulted in death between 2013 and 2019

B) Whether the data in the graph originated from the NHLBI

C) How many of the types of organ transplant rejection considered in the graph were investigated through blood testing

D) Whether Hannah Valantine and her fellow researchers considered the graph when constructing their inquiry

Questions 32-42 are based on the following passage and supplementary material.

This passage is an excerpt from Andrew Graham, "Why governments are so bad at implementing public projects," an article originally published* by The Conversation in 2019.

As Canada's federal government starts looking for a replacement for its failed payroll system and the Ontario provincial government launches yet another major shake-up of its health-care system, it's useful to remind decision-makers of a long history of failures in major public sector implementations.

Research from around the world shows a consistent pattern of failures in public sector policy and project implementation. Yet we continue to embark upon implementation built on bias and faulty logic. So maybe it's time to better understand the architecture of failure and what can be done to overcome it.

Recent publications from Australia, Canada, the United Kingdom, and the United States deliver some consistent messages. "The Blunders of Government" delves into the many restarts of the UK National Health Service. The "Learning from Failure" report details major project failures in Australia. In the U.S., "A Cascade of Failures: Why Government Fails, and How to Stop It" reports similar themes. In Canada, the auditor general's latest reports on the Phoenix pay system echo the common basis for implementation failure. It's not often that an auditor uses the phrase "incomprehensible," but there it is.

When distilling all this research and all these investigations, certain themes are common to them all. First and foremost in the public sector, announcement was equated with accomplishment. This is the equivalent of thinking that just cutting the ribbon is enough. A corollary of this is that most projects get lots of attention by both political and bureaucratic leaders at first, but that attention fades as the boring, detail-oriented work begins and the next issue, crisis, or bright shiny object comes along.

*See Page 242 for the citation for this text.

In many cases, there is a cultural disconnect
in the project design that prevents bad news
from making it to those at the top of the chain of
command, minimizes problems that are
often warning signs, and deliberately downplays
operational issues as minor.

What can be called the "handover mentality"
often takes over between a project's designers and
the people who have to actually implement it and
get it up and running. It's best characterized by the
phrase "We design it. You make it work."

The next element is that when things go
wrong, those who speak up about the problems
are dismissed, discounted, or just plain punished.
This leads to groupthink, a failure to challenge
assumptions and a desire to just go along, even
when danger signs are in full sight.

Policy designers and those who must
implement government projects or infrastructure
are often guilty of what's known as optimism
bias ("What could possibly go wrong?") when,
in fact, they should be looking at the end goal.
They should be working backwards to identify not
only what could go wrong but also how the whole
process will roll out. Instead, they focus on the
beginning—the announcement, the first stages.

We hear the word "complexity" a lot
when examining government project failures.
Indeed, most of the problems examined in the
aforementioned research pointed to the increasing
complexity in failed implementations that went
well beyond IT, and the failure to map those
complexities out.

But that complexity increases the risks of
some moving part of a government project
malfunctioning and shutting down the entire
system. People get busy and distracted. If a policy
is just the flavour of the week and something else
becomes popular next week, the project starts to
lose momentum, needed attention, reaction, and
adaptation to inevitable challenges. The gears
start to slip. Then there is the churn of officials.
At both the political and bureaucratic level, this
is a consistent theme in projects failing or in
governments responding poorly to crises as they
arise.

The champions of a policy simply move on,
and their successors are left to decide how much
energy to put into someone else's pet project.
Similarly, the rapid turnover of senior managers in
government often leaves well-intentioned people
to respond to emergencies in areas where they
have little experience.

32

The main purpose of the passage is to

A) survey tendencies that explain why public sector projects fail.

B) promote the creation of bureaucratic groups to alleviate public sector project failures.

C) report previous examples of public sector project failures.

D) compare countries that enjoy relatively high levels of success in public sector implementation and supply these solutions to the Canadian government.

33

One of the author's central ideas is that

A) governments are incompetent at producing successful public projects.

B) most public projects are ultimately unsuccessful due to neglect at early stages.

C) successful announcements are an important part of initiating public sector projects.

D) public project management roles would be better if left to the discretion of private companies.

Test 8

Spending on Public Sector Projects

Figure 1: United States

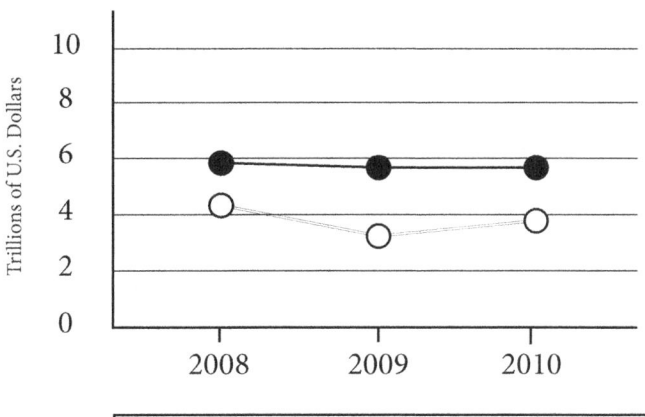

[Line graph showing Trillions of U.S. Dollars from 2008-2010. Including failed projects: ~6 across all years. Excluding failed projects: ~4 in 2008, ~3 in 2009, ~4 in 2010.]

Figure 2: United Kingdom

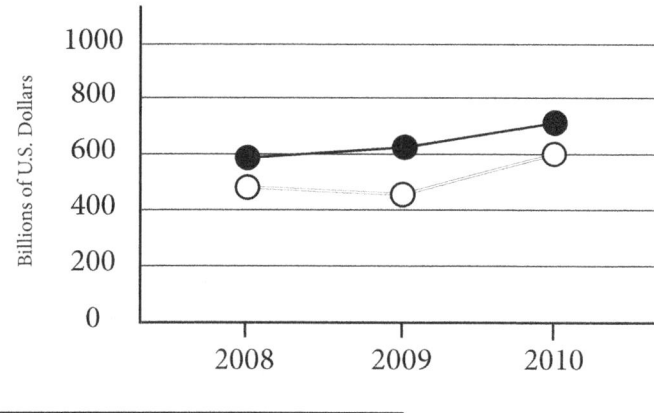

[Line graph showing Billions of U.S. Dollars from 2008-2010. Including failed projects: ~580 in 2008, ~620 in 2009, ~700 in 2010. Excluding failed projects: ~470 in 2008, ~450 in 2009, ~590 in 2010.]

Excluding failed projects: ─○─   Including failed projects: ─●─

34

The author of the passage argues that public sector failure

A) occurs in regions of North America other than the United States.
B) can unfailingly be traced to insufficient planning and oversight.
C) has increased in severity despite efforts to allocate resources more efficiently.
D) naturally escalates as a government becomes more intricate.

35

Which choice provides the best evidence for the answer to the previous question?

A) Lines 8-10 ("Research . . . implementation")
B) Lines 19-23 ("The "Learning . . . themes")
C) Lines 23-27 ("In Canada . . . it is")
D) Lines 67-71 ("Indeed . . . out")

36

The author's discussion of "Recent publications" (lines 15-27) is primarily concerned with establishing a connection between

A) the United Kingdom and United States in public sector project implementation.
B) different countries which had neglected public service projects.
C) different countries which had similarly witnessed failing payroll systems.
D) different countries which had dealt with unsuccessful public projects by using comparable tactics.

37

As used in line 28, "distilling" most nearly means

A) purging.
B) skimming.
C) extracting.
D) reforming.

38

The author of the passage discusses the role of miscommunication in public projects in order to

A) highlight the initial stage of government project failures.

B) provide evidence that a typical modern bureaucracy is incapable of change.

C) promote new terminology that can clarify bureaucratic failures.

D) prove that current public sector hierarchy is incompatible with successful projects.

39

Which choice provides the best evidence for the answer to the previous question?

A) Lines 39-44 ("In many . . . minor")
B) Lines 48-49 ("It's best . . . work")
C) Lines 50-52 ("The next . . . punished")
D) Lines 75-79 ("If a policy . . . challenges")

40

It can be reasonably inferred that "handover mentality" (line 45) was a phrase generally intended to

A) explain the steps of project management in the public sector.

B) characterize the danger of groupthink in public sector project management.

C) promote a more lucrative system of project management in the public sector.

D) encourage government workers to delegate difficult portions of a project to other teammates.

41

Taken together, the graphs indicate that the United Kingdom

A) experiences a lower rate of public sector project failure due to the relative size of its economy.

B) has successfully instituted reform measures to safeguard against project failure in a manner that has not been attempted in the United States

C) funded fewer failed public sector projects than the United States did between 2008 and 2010.

D) spent significantly less on public sector projects between 2008 and 2010 than the United States spent in the same period.

42

If the two figures were generated by the U.S. and the U.K. governments, respectively, it would be reasonable to conclude that

A) modern governments are gradually abandoning the "handover mentality" explained in the passage.

B) the passage does not adequately account for impact that an economic crisis can play in terms of public sector project failure.

C) the tendency to downplay or dismiss bad news that is cited in the passage is not a universal trait of political systems.

D) a deficit of expertise, as mentioned in the passage, explains a large number of project failures.

Questions 43-52 are based on the following passages.

Passage 1 is adapted from Emily Hare, "Four new species of zombie ant fungi—another step forward for open-access taxonomy" (2011). Passage 2 is adapted from Nicola Stead, "Taking a piece of home with you: Farming fungi in a new Azteca ant colony" (2018). Both of these articles were initially published* by EveryONE, the community blog of PLOS One.

Passage 1

Zombie fungi have always ranked high on my list of irresistibly interesting yet disturbing organisms. Though these fungi infect a wide range of arthropod hosts, today's victim is the ant. When an ant is infected, members of its colony rapidly dump the victim as far away from the colony as possible. The reason for this harsh treatment soon becomes clear. The fungus manipulates the ant's behavior, causing it to climb to a prime location for spore dispersal before killing the ant. What comes next has the makings of a low-budget sci-fi flick. The fungus slowly emerges from the ant's head, culminating in a fruiting body from which deadly spores emerge.

In an article published today in PLoS ONE, researchers Harry Evans, Simon Elliot, and David Hughes describe four new Brazilian species of zombie fungi. The characterization of these morbidly fascinating organisms is a worthy feat in its own right. However, this article also marks another milestone for both mycologists and PLoS ONE. This is the first paper to publish new fungal species names in an online journal in compliance with the rules and recommendations of the International Code of Botanical Nomenclature (ICBN), the body that governs the naming of new plant and fungal species.

This is a very important step for taxonomists in the transition from print to online-only publishing. In 2010, Sandra Knapp published a pioneering paper in PLoS ONE of four new plant species, which we also highlighted in an EveryONE post. By doing so, she provided the first test-case for how new plant species can be published online whilst adhering to the strict botanical code.

Passage 2

Moving to a new home is usually accompanied with a long to-do list, from painting the walls to unpacking boxes. For young queen Azteca ants, however, one important job is to start growing fungus. Many tropical ant species are famous for their mutualistic relationship with fungi, carefully cultivating and farming different fungi species to use as food or building materials or even to trap prey. However, when and how the fungiculture is started is still a mystery. Do new queens culture fungi that just happen to be around in their new home at the time of colonization? And how soon after their arrival do queens start flexing their agriculture prowess? To answer these questions, Veronika Mayer from the University of Vienna and some of her colleagues set off to the tropics of Costa Rica on the hunt for young Cecropia plants that make ideal new homes for young queen ants.

In total, they sampled 64 plants, finding 212 foundress queens at various stages of colonizing small chambers within the plant stem. In two instances, the researchers were lucky enough to catch the colonization process from start to finish. They watched as the young queens bored their way into the hollow stems of the Cecropia trees and then scraped away the white parenchyma lining the stems to plug the hole. In addition to using the parenchyma to patch up the hole, the queens were also observed carefully amassing little piles of parenchyma within the cavity itself.

To see if these piles contained fungus and, if so, what type of fungus, the researchers collected 52 samples of the parenchyma to look for traces of fungal hyphen and to extract DNA. They found that fungus was only present in parenchyma samples taken from chambers where a queen was also present. Unfortunately, the researchers couldn't trace foundress ants back to their mother colonies to directly compare the fungal species, but they were able to compare DNA sequences obtained from new colonies to DNA sequences obtained from a sample of established colonies. The team found a great deal of overlap between the two, suggesting that the new queens used very similar fungal species as used in established

*See Page 242 for the citations for these texts.

colonies. Given the similarity with established colonies and the fact that the fungi found only represent a small percent of all fungi species, it seems likely that fungi are transported in some
85 way by queens from their mother colony. When Mayer and her colleagues examined the contents of the infrabuccal cavity of four foundress ants, they also found traces of fungal spores and hyphens. Like hamsters, these ants may be
90 capable of squirreling away and transporting fungal elements that could be useful for setting up a little fungi farm.

43

Over the course of Passage 1, the main focus of the author's discussion shifts from

A) showing the reader how ants behave to summarizing scientific advances as recorded by PLoS ONE journalists.

B) providing evidence that ants treat other infected ants harshly to surveying research developments across academic journals.

C) describing colony treatment of fungi-infected ants to recording taxonomy progress as presented in the PLoS ONE online journal databases.

D) developing an understanding of fungi-infected ant behavior to building interest in online science journalism.

44

In Passage 1, the term "zombie fungi" (line 1) is used in reference to

A) the behaviors that ants display when infected with a particular type of fungi.

B) a low-budget sci-fi flick that showcases fungi-infected ants.

C) ants that are dying from a disease that also affects once-malignant fungi.

D) how an entire ant colony reacts to infected ants.

45

As used in line 41, "mutualistic" most nearly means

A) beneficial.

B) experienced.

C) sympathetic.

D) common.

46

Why does the author of Passage 2 begin by mentioning "Moving to a new home" (line 36)?

A) To establish a setting that might be unknown to the reader

B) To begin outlining the close relationship between ants and fungi

C) To provide details as to how ants use other species to construct new homes

D) To show how ants transport fungi wherever they travel

47

According to the author of Passage 2, the presence of similar fungi species in disparate locations can be best explained by

A) mushroom cultivation by humans.

B) the beneficial relationship between ants and specific fungus species.

C) fungus varieties being present in the parenchyma.

D) the fungi being transported by queen ants from these insects' colonies of origin.

Test 8

48

Which choice provides the best evidence for the answer to the previous question?

A) Lines 40-44 ("Many . . . prey")
B) Lines 59-62 ("They . . . hole")
C) Lines 69-72 ("They . . . present")
D) Lines 81-85 ("Given . . . colony")

49

Which choice supports the idea that fungi can be fatal to ants?

A) Lines 3-4 ("Though . . . ant")
B) Lines 8-10 ("The fungus . . . ant")
C) Lines 18-20 ("The characterization . . . right")
D) Lines 85-89 ("When . . . hyphens")

50

The authors of both passages would most likely agree with which of the following statements concerning fungi?

A) Overall, the relationship between ants and fungi is a net-gain for ants despite some liabilities.
B) Ants and fungi are beneficial to each other in various ways.
C) Fungi are well-known as a pathogen that targets ants.
D) Fungi and ants are consistently found in some of the same ecosystems.

51

Which choice best describes the overall relationship between Passage 1 and Passage 2?

A) Passage 2 continues describing the co-dependent relationship of ants and fungi outlined in Passage 1.
B) Passage 1 is a prerequisite that anticipates information provided in Passage 2.
C) Passage 2 presents a relationship between ants and fungi that fundamentally contrasts with that described in Passage 1.
D) Passage 2 uses new evidence that expands on and cautiously challenges the research explained in Passage 1.

52

One of the central ideas set forward by the author of Passage 2 but NOT by the author of Passage 1 is that

A) some types of fungi are fatal to ants.
B) many ants benefit from intentionally growing fungus.
C) fungiculture can occur without action from a queen ant in her native ecosystem.
D) new research proves that ostensibly toxic fungi is beneficial for food, building materials, and prey attraction for ants.

STOP
If you finish before time is called, you may check your work on this section only.
Do not turn to any other section.

Answer Key: Test 8

Passage 1	Passage 2	Passage 3	Passage 4	Passage 5
1. C	11. B	21. A	32. A	43. C
2. A	12. C	22. B	33. B	44. A
3. C	13. A	23. B	34. A	45. A
4. B	14. D	24. C	35. C	46. B
5. B	15. A	25. A	36. D	47. D
6. A	16. C	26. B	37. B	48. D
7. B	17. D	27. C	38. A	49. B
8. A	18. A	28. D	39. A	50. D
9. A	19. B	29. C	40. B	51. C
10. D	20. B	30. D	41. D	52. B
		31. A	42. C	

Question Types

Major Issue
1, 11-12, 21, 32-33, 43

Passage Details
5, 7-8, 10, 14, 19-20, 28, 36, 46

Command of Evidence
2-3, 6, 16-18, 22-23, 25-26, 34-35, 38-39, 47-49

Word in Context
4, 9, 13, 15, 24, 27, 37, 40, 44-45

Graphics and Visuals
29-31, 41-42

Passage Comparison
50-52

Answer Explanations
Test 8, Pages 214-229

Passage 1, Pages 214-216

1. C is the correct answer.

The passage focuses on describing a dream which the narrator has repeatedly. At the end of the dream, her fiancée is gone, and this ending mirrors the reality of his absence after his death. Choose C to reflect this content. A and B can be eliminated because there is no evidence that the narrator experiences a dangerous situation (since she is mostly dreaming) and because there is no evidence that Dan's death (the result of a car accident) was linked to him being overly trusting. Be careful not to choose D, because while the description of the dream does show a character wrestling with her grief, there is no context OUTSIDE of the dream to indicate her growth.

2. A is the correct answer.

In lines 11-12, Hanna reveals that when Dan asks her about her destination, she responds "Nowhere in particular." This lack of specific destination indicates she is not in a rush; choose A as appropriate. C can be eliminated because Hanna directly communicates that she does not have a specific destination in mind. B overstates Hanna's reaction to Dan (letting him in the car but not showing strong enthusiasm), while D is wrongly negative about a situation that Hanna quickly accepts.

3. C is the correct answer.

See the previous answer explanation for analysis of the correct line reference. A describes a contextual feature of the dream and an action that Hanna takes within it. B describes a brief exchange and offers evidence that Dan feels warmly towards Hanna. D describes an awkward moment as the couple settles into the car journey. None of these other answers indicate that Hanna is unhurried, and therefore they should all be eliminated.

Answer Explanations, Test 8

4. B is the correct answer.

In line 33, "flippant" refers to Dan's warm and light-hearted demeanor. Choose B to reflect this meaning. A (inappropriately implying that Dan is behaving in a way that is not aligned with the context), C (inappropriately implying that Dan has become more alert or excited), and D (inappropriately implying that Dan's actions or words do not make logical sense) all introduce incorrect contexts and therefore should be eliminated.

5. B is the correct answer.

The paragraph that occupies lines 36-44 moves quickly—clarifying that Dan and Hanna have known each other since childhood, describing a shared memory, and then explaining when and how Dan died. The primary purpose of this content is to draw a connection between the way Dan died (in a car accident) and the content of the recurring dream experienced by Hanna. Choose B as appropriate. A and C both wrongly focus on content from early in the paragraph (the tensions involving Hanna's mother) and thus wrongly mistake a detail for the function of the paragraph as a WHOLE. D wrongly focuses on content that is only found later in the passage (the accident) without clearly addressing the central matters of recollections and their context.

6. A is the correct answer.

In lines 14-15, Dan refers to Hanna by name, even though she has not yet introduced herself. This detail indicates that he is not a typical hitchhiker (often a person unfamiliar to the driver); choose A as appropriate. B focuses on explaining that Hanna and Dan were engaged, while C describes how the driving conditions gradually become more perilous. D describes an action undertaken by Hanna and the dangerous situation in which she undertakes it. None of these other answers reveal that Dan is not a typical hitchhiker (since some focus mainly on Hanna), and therefore they should all be eliminated.

7. B is the correct answer.

Dan's comment about Hanna laying her ghosts to rest comes just after she reveals she is not sure that she can handle driving on a road that runs through cliffs. This content implies she may have a fear of cliffs; choose B as appropriate. A and C can both be eliminated since there is no evidence in the passage to indicate that Hanna has a difficult relationship with her family (a topic raised only briefly and without especially strong negative tones in lines 36-40), or that she is unable to drive. D is overly specific and should be eliminated as a misinterpretation of a neutral scenic detail.

8. A is the correct answer.

In line 61, the narrator describes Hanna observing a "brilliant" sunset, content which seems to imply that the setting sun is very striking and beautiful. Choose A to reflect this content. B can be eliminated since, while Dan is presented in a positive way in the passage, it is an unsupported stretch to assume that the beauty of the sunset is somehow linked to that description. C and D can both be eliminated, since nothing in the passage implies that the beauty of the sunset is influenced by Hanna's location on the cliffs or that the setting sun is impacting her driving ability.

Answer Explanations, Test 8

9. A is the correct answer.

In line 72, Dan abruptly vanishes, signaling that, at this point in Hanna's dream, he disappears. Choose A to reflect this content. B and C both indicate actions that might be undertaken if the scenario described were occurring in reality (rather than in a dream), but since the action takes place in a dream space, logical explanations are not required. D extrapolates beyond the scope of the passage to wrongly describe a conflict between characters who are actually on good terms and should therefore be eliminated.

10. D is the correct answer.

The passage ends with a description of the inside of Hanna's car, emphasizing the sudden lack of Dan's presence. This description creates a heightened sense of loss and shows that this dream reflects Hanna's grief: choose D as appropriate. A and B can be eliminated since the dream is not necessarily a nightmare, and since the purpose of the description is not to reveal the status of the car (despite the passage's frequent use of scenic details). C can also be eliminated since there is no evidence that Dan will come back; in fact, the description seems to reflect Hanna's grief that she will never see him again.

Passage 2, Pages 217-219

11. B is the correct answer.

In lines 42-44, President Ford states that Americans "have, for example, helped the parties of the Middle East take the first steps toward living with one another in peace." This content implies that he believes that America played a role in bolstering good relationships between Middle Eastern countries; choose B as appropriate. A can be dismissed because Ford alludes to a tentatively positive relationship with China, which indicates that the two countries have historically NOT been on good terms. C and D can also be eliminated since Japan is discussed in different terms than the USSR is (implying that terms are NOT the same with both countries) and because Ford emphasizes the positive leadership that America is providing.

12. C is the correct answer.

The speech opens with Ford assuring his audience that he is going to be sincere, before moving into a discussion of foreign relations. Choose C to reflect this content. A can be eliminated since the speech does NOT initially focus on Ford demonstrating his power, while B can be eliminated because Ford focuses on relationships with other countries, NOT on how those countries intervene in America's domestic affairs. Be careful not to choose D, since Ford's initial intent is more specific than simply establishing rapport, and since he acknowledges the limitations as well as the successes of U.S. foreign policy.

13. A is the correct answer.

In line 33, "candor" refers to Ford's intention to be open and transparent in his communication. Choose A to reflect this meaning. B (inappropriately implying reflection and thought), C (inappropriately implying

Answer Explanations, Test 8

extensive knowledge), and D (inappropriately implying commitment) all introduce incorrect precise contexts despite the seemingly appropriate positive tones and therefore should be eliminated.

14. D is the correct answer.

The paragraph that includes lines 12-23 provides a summary of how America has contributed to global affairs since the end of the second World War, acknowledging both failures and successes but arguing that America has maintained consistency and stability. Choose D to reflect this content. Be careful not to choose A or B, since the importance of American foreign policy is implied but is NOT the main focus of the paragraph. C can also be eliminated since the paragraph discusses events from AFTER World War II, not during.

15. A is the correct answer.

In line 24, "course" refers to the series of actions America may enact as part of its foreign policy. Choose A to reflect this content. B can be eliminated because Ford is not discussing potential changes in leadership, while C can be eliminated as overly specific (since Ford is interested in countries other than the USSR). D can also be eliminated since Ford speaks generally, without mentioning that he has held a specific position in the U.S. government.

16. C is the correct answer.

Lines 35-37 explain that there has been a long history of animosity between China and America, even as Ford celebrates a recent improvement in that relationship. Choose C as appropriate. None of the other answers specifically reference China (although these answers do GENERALLY raise the topic of international relations), and therefore they can all be eliminated.

17. D is the correct answer.

In lines 27-30, Ford references positive relationships with certain democratic states and includes Japan in the relevant list. This content suggests that, in 1975, Japan was a democratic nation; choose D as appropriate. None of the other countries listed as possible answers are specifically mentioned in the passage. The reference to "Europe" in lines 27-30 should not be misread as evidence for A or B (since Germany and Poland are not DIRECTLY named), while Ford's frequent focus on North America would not necessarily include a South American country such as Brazil.

18. A is the correct answer.

See the previous answer explanation for analysis of the correct line reference. B offers a statement about American efforts to promote peace and then references a specific example. C describes how the relationship between America and Latin America has shifted, while D alludes to optimistic hopes about a future relationship with Africa. None of these other answers indicates Japan's status as a democratic state, and therefore they should all be eliminated.

Answer Explanations, Test 8

19. B is the correct answer.

Ford provides a generally positive perspective on what America has been able to accomplish with its foreign policy. As a result of this perspective, he suggests that the American people can feel proud on behalf of their country; choose B as appropriate. A and D can be eliminated since Ford largely assumes that the American people already have patriotic feelings, and because he has strongly communicated his support for American foreign policy throughout the passage. Be careful not to choose C, since Ford does pivot to acknowledging some shortcomings immediately after the relevant statement. However, his primary purpose is to praise American foreign policy, NOT to prepare his audience for the limitations that he will acknowledge.

20. B is the correct answer.

Ford quotes Truman's words about the importance of strong American leadership in order to ensure overall global security. Thus, Ford chooses these words to support his argument that world peace is largely determined by American foreign policy; choose B as appropriate. A and D can be eliminated since Ford and Truman offer similar perspectives and since Ford's words do not describe an approach to overcoming obstacles. Be careful not to choose C, since Ford's purpose in quoting Truman is more specific than simply showing an opinion about American foreign policy, and B better reflects his purpose.

Passage 3, Pages 220-223

21. A is the correct answer.

The passage primarily focuses on explaining how the donor-derived cell-free DNA test can help doctors to detect lung transplant rejection sooner, and the author applauds the test's utility in detecting and potentially treating a serious medical problem. Choose A to reflect this content. Be careful not to choose B, which mistakes the idea of detecting rejection for the idea of FATAL transplant rejection (a possibility that, though negative, the passage does not clearly consider at length). C and D can also be eliminated since only one method of detection is discussed in contrast to biopsy, and since the Allo Map test offers value to all lung transplant recipients, NOT just high risk ones.

22. B is the correct answer.

In lines 38-39, the author explains that "The new test appears to overcome those challenges," referring to how the Allo Map test is not restricted by the limitations that apply to biopsy-based testing. Choose B as appropriate. A and C can readily be eliminated since the author wants to see lung transplant recipients enjoy longer lifespans, NOT advocate for fewer lung transplants to be performed; moreover, the author explains how lung transplant rejection might be detectable sooner, NOT eliminated altogether. D can also be eliminated since biopsy-based testing can help to provide indications that rejection may occur, but is less sensitive and more invasive than DNA-based testing methods are.

Answer Explanations, Test 8

23. B is the correct answer.

See the previous answer explanation for analysis of the correct line reference. A explains that lung donor recipients have a high rejection rate and low predicted life expectancy, while C describes the original example of a donor-derived cell-free DNA test and how it functioned. D describes how the latest study indicates further applications for DNA-based testing. None of these other answers contrast Allo Map testing with biopsies, and therefore they should all be eliminated.

24. C is the correct answer.

The use of language in the first paragraph makes it clear to a reader that very serious problems can be associated with the rejection of lung transplants and that the author is gravely concerned about these implications. This effect makes it apparent that the author is invested in finding a resolution to these problems; therefore, the author will be invested in improvements which make it possible to diagnose and treat rejection more effectively. Choose C as appropriate. A, B, and D should all be eliminated since they all inaccurately imply that the author has a negative view of lung transplants.

25. A is the correct answer.

In lines 15-17, the author quotes a recognized expert in praising a new testing method for solving a problem which had previously made it difficult to detect and treat transplant rejection until it was too late. This positive evaluation validates the value of the blood test to the reader; choose A as appropriate. B can be eliminated since the quotation from Valantine is used to support the argument that the author has already started to make, NOT to introduce a new line of argumentation. C and D can be rejected since Valantine does NOT assert that this testing will improve lung transplants themselves (just the monitoring of previously transplanted organs) or that this test (though promising) will be perfect in detecting problems.

26. B is the correct answer.

See the previous answer explanation for analysis of the correct line reference. A identifies the body which provided funding for the study discussed in the passage, while C describes Valantine's role in the early development of blood tests used to detect potential organ donation. D identifies why earlier forms of DNA-based testing were somewhat limited in their utility and indicated room for improvement. None of these other answers reflect Valantine's opinion on the efficacy and utility of DNA-based testing methods to screen for potential rejection, and therefore they should all be eliminated.

27. C is the correct answer.

In line 23, "sequencing" refers to the order in which DNA is arranged. Choose C to reflect this content. A (inappropriately implying something being located or identified for the first time), B (inappropriately implying a specific grouping which shows a visible strategy behind it), and D (inappropriately implying a chosen strategy or approach) all introduce improper meanings and should be eliminated.

Answer Explanations, Test 8

28. D is the correct answer.

The second-to-last paragraph summarizes what the study has shown about the new blood test; choose D as appropriate. A can be eliminated since the answer is too broad and imprecise; the paragraph does imply that the test should be used, but that is NOT the primary purpose of the content. B and C can also be eliminated since the paragraph shows one researcher summarizing the results of a specific study but does NOT indicate widespread consensus or a definitive claim about the new blood test.

29. C is the correct answer.

In 2017, fewer than 2000 transplanted kidneys were recorded as rejected. Choose C, since all of the other answers represent data points for which 2000 or more rejections were recorded. A and B can be rejected since, in 2013 and 2014, between 2000 and 2500 lungs were recorded as rejected. D can be rejected since, in 2018, the number of kidneys recorded as rejected rose to almost 2500 and was greater than the number rejected in 2017.

30. D is the correct answer.

For all types of organ transplants documented on the graph, rejection numbers rose and fell inconsistently, with no steady pattern of increase or decrease. Choose D to reflect this content. A can be rejected since the number of kidney transplant rejections fell between 2013 and 2014, while B can be rejected because the number of lung transplant rejections increased between 2013 and 2014. C can also be rejected since the number of heart transplant rejections rose between 2014 and 2015.

31. A is the correct answer.

Lines 28-34 indicate that lung transplant recipients face a high risk of death due to organ rejection. However, the data in the graph only show adverse reactions resulting from organ rejection and do not document whether recipients survived or not. In order for the graph to support the claim in lines 28-34, data about mortality rates due to organ rejection would need to be present; choose A as appropriate. B can be rejected since the information provided in lines 28-34 applies to all lung transplant recipients, not just to those studied by a particular body, and C can be eliminated since blood testing can only affect detection, not mortality rates for those already subject to detection. D can be eliminated as illogical, since the graph and the information in this segment of the passage extend beyond Valantine's specific study.

Passage 4, Pages 223-226

32. A is the correct answer.

The passage focuses on arguing that it is common for public sector projects to fail, and substantiates this argument using examples and explanations from a number of different countries. Choose A to reflect this

Answer Explanations, Test 8

content. Be careful not to choose C, since the passage does mention some reports which cite examples of previous failures but does NOT use past examples as the primary focus. B and D can also be eliminated since the author does NOT specify any particular solutions which might make public sector projects more effective and does NOT cite any countries where public sector projects enjoy high success rates.

33. B is the correct answer.

In lines 35-36, the author argues that "attention fades as the boring, detail-oriented work begins," making a case for projects often being neglected in their crucial early stages and connecting this neglect to their eventual failure. Choose B to reflect this content. Be careful not to choose A, since the author focuses on a government's ability to execute a project, NOT ability to develop the concept for one. C and D can also be eliminated since the author is less interested in the form of an announcement than in whether or not that announcement is followed by strategic actions and does NOT go as far as to make recommendations for how these projects could be better executed.

34. A is the correct answer.

In lines 22-24, the author cites an example in which an external auditor was highly critical of the Canadian government's implementation of the Phoenix pay system. The use of this example reveals that failures in project implementation occur in governments outside of the United States; choose A as appropriate. Be careful not to choose B, since the author does suggest that failures are often traceable to problems with planning and oversight, but it is an overstatement to say that this is always the case. C and D can also be ruled out since the author identifies a pattern of public sector projects repeatedly failing but does NOT make an argument that a pattern can be detected whereby these failures increase in frequency or severity.

35. C is the correct answer.

See the previous answer explanation for analysis of the correct line reference. A articulates the author's central claim that public sector projects often fail, while B identifies two examples of documents produced by national governments documenting their failed projects. D addresses complexity of the projects as a factor which might be contributing to the failure of projects. None of these other answers describe failures occurring in regions other than the United States, and therefore they should all be eliminated.

36. D is the correct answer.

Lines 15-27 describe how different countries, including Canada, the U.S., the U.K., and Australia all responded to failed projects by publishing documents describing these failures, in hopes of preventing the same mistakes from occurring again. Since this content describes multiple countries responding to project failure in the same way, choose D as appropriate. A can be dismissed since the focus of the excerpt is broader than A indicates, and the content itself also focuses on what happens after a project fails, NOT on when it is implemented. B and C can be eliminated since the projects which failed are not all payroll-related, and since the cause of failure cannot be confirmed to have always been neglect.

Answer Explanations, Test 8

37. B is the correct answer.

In line 28, "distilling" refers to briefly reviewing and finding common themes within many different documents. Choose B to reflect this meaning. A (inappropriately implying that a source of tension or an impurity has been eliminated), C (inappropriately implying removing a trace amount of an object or information from a larger whole), and D (inappropriately implying that a problem has been addressed) all introduce improper meanings and should be eliminated.

38. A is the correct answer.

In lines 39-44, the author explains that the mode of communication often used in public sector projects often creates problems; this mode does not serve to effectively advance a given project because it minimizes problems at the early stages, when they could still be resolved if they were acknowledged and taken seriously. Choose A to reflect this content. B and C can be eliminated since the author does NOT introduce any new terminology and instead describes how bureaucracies currently operate without analyzing whether they are capable of change. D can also be eliminated since the author's argument rests on the belief that governments could operate public sector projects more successfully if such endeavors operated differently.

39. A is the correct answer.

See the previous answer explanation for analysis of the correct line reference. B describes a rigidly divided mentality which often contributes to project failure, while C describes the response which people who criticize projects are often met with. D describes an outcome of project failure which may occur when a project drags on for a long time and people become invested in other initiatives instead. None of these other answers connect miscommunication to failures in the early stages of project development, and therefore they should all be eliminated.

40. B is the correct answer.

The author uses the phrase "handover mentality" with negative and critical connotations, as a way to draw attention to the way in which collective actions and groupthink can increase the rate of failure in public sector projects. Choose B as appropriate. A and C can be dismissed since the author does NOT give a detailed breakdown of current project management processes and does NOT offer alternatives to these processes. D can be dismissed as illogically positive since the phrase refers to workers being disinterested in projects, not to delegating strategically to ensure a project's success.

41. D is the correct answer.

The graph showing spending on public projects in the U.S. is measured in trillions of dollars, while the graph showing comparable spending in the U.K. is only measured in billions. This fact indicates that, between 2008 and 2010, the U.K. spent far less on public sector projects than the U.S. did; choose D as appropriate. A can be eliminated since the graph does show that the U.K. did experience a lower rate of project failure but cannot confirm WHY that trend occurred, while B can be eliminated since significant project failure still occurred

Answer Explanations, Test 8

in the U.K. C can also be eliminated since the graph only shows the dollars which were lost due to failed projects, not the total number of projects or the percentage which failed.

42. C is the correct answer.

The graph provides transparent data indicating that billions of dollars are being lost every year due to failed public sector projects; if these graphs were produced by governments, such a fact would indicate a willingness to own up to their failures rather than a desire to hide them. This transparency would contradict the author's argument that governments tend to downplay and hide failed projects; choose C as appropriate. A and B can be dismissed since nothing in the graphs entails data about projects being transferred between different government employees, and since the passage does NOT discuss any implications related to an economic crisis. D can be dismissed because the graph only offers data about the costs of public sector project failure, NOT evidence as to the causes of these failures.

Passage 5, Pages 227-229

43. C is the correct answer.

Passage 1 begins with a discussion of ant behavior after ants have been infected by a zombie fungus and then moves to describing a milestone in which a new species name first appeared in an online (rather than print) publication. Choose C to reflect this content. A can be eliminated since the second half of the passage focuses on online journals broadly rather than on PLoS ONE specifically. B can be eliminated because the passage does not primarily focus on how ants behave towards one another (even though such a detail is mentioned in lines 4-8), while D can be eliminated because the author's goal is to report a shift in scientific inquiry, NOT to encourage audience interest in scientific publications.

44. A is the correct answer.

In this passage, the term "zombie fungi" refers to ants exhibiting particular behaviors after becoming infected by certain species of fungi. Choose A as appropriate. B can be taken as a faulty reference since no ACTUAL film has been made documenting this behavior, while C can be eliminated because the fungi infect the ants, rather than both being infected by a shared disease. D can be eliminated since the term refers to the behavior of the infected ants, NOT the reaction of the rest of the colony.

45. A is the correct answer.

In line 41, "mutualistic" refers to how some ants and fungi behave in ways which benefit one another. Choose A to reflect this meaning. B (inappropriately implying knowledge), C (inappropriately implying an emotional investment), and D (inappropriately implying a frequent occurrence) all introduce incorrect contexts and therefore should be eliminated.

Answer Explanations, Test 8

46. B is the correct answer.

The author of Passage 2 uses the reference to moving house in order to set the stage for describing how ants and fungi can interact. Choose B to reflect this content. A can be eliminated since the idea of moving house is likely familiar to most readers (so that this reference makes a scientific topic understandable), while C can be eliminated because the relationship between ants and fungi does NOT include using species near ants to build new homes. D can also be eliminated since it does not seem to be the case that ants consistently carry fungus around with them (even though queen ants find fungus useful).

47. D is the correct answer.

Lines 81-84 describe the hypothesis that queen ants may transport fungi with them from their home colonies, which may account for why the same species of fungi can be found in different locations. Choose D as appropriate. A can be eliminated since the passage does NOT discuss human cultivation of fungi (despite references to human housekeeping for the sake of analogy). Be careful not to choose B, which is overly broad and general; D more specifically explains the role ants play. The presence of fungus in the parenchyma does NOT in itself explain why the same species would be found in similar locations, so that C can be eliminated.

48. D is the correct answer.

See the previous answer explanation for analysis of the correct line reference. A states that some ant species deliberately cultivate fungi and explains why they do so; B describes the process of how a foundress queen went about creating a new colony. C describes a conclusion that researchers arrived at after collecting and testing samples. None of these other answers reflect the theory that queens transport fungi samples with them, and therefore they should all be eliminated.

49. B is the correct answer.

Lines 8-10 specify that a zombie fungus eventually kills the ant that it infects; choose B, since this content reveals that fungi can be fatal to ants. A explains that a zombie fungus can infect species other than ants, while C marks a transition between discussing one topic and introducing another. D describes another piece of evidence that ants may be transporting fungi. None of these other answers describe a case in which a fungus can kill an ant (since OTHER fungus activities or traits are mentioned), and therefore they should all be eliminated.

50. D is the correct answer.

Passage 1 describes a relationship in which fungi threaten ants, while Passage 2 describes a relationship in which fungi and ants provide mutual benefits to one another. For either of these relationships to exist, ants and fungi have to be found in the same setting; choose D as the best answer. A and B can both be eliminated since these statements would only be true in the context of Passage 2 and NOT in the context of Passage 1. C can also be eliminated because it is only true in the context of Passage 1.

Answer Explanations, Test 8

51. C is the correct answer.

Passage 1 describes a relationship in which fungi threaten ants, while Passage 2 describes a relationship in which fungi and ants provide mutual benefits to one another. Since these relationships contrast with one another, choose C as appropriate. A can be eliminated because Passage 1 describes an antagonistic, not a mutualistic, relationship between ants and fungi. B and D can be eliminated since the two passages describe entirely different events and research, and no direct relationship (despite consideration of similar organisms) is established between their content.

52. B is the correct answer.

The author of Passage 2 acknowledges that ants benefit from the presence and cultivation of fungus, while the author of Passage 1 does not discuss this possible relationship. Choose B to reflect this content. A can be eliminated since a discussion of the destructive effects of fungi is present only in Passage 1 and NOT in Passage 2. C can be eliminated since this statement is not necessarily supported by either passage, while D can be eliminated because this choice factually contradicts the content of Passage 1.

NOTES

- Passage 3 on Pages 220-221, "Blood test shows promise for early detection of severe lung-transplant rejection," is adapted from the article of the same name published by the National Institutes of Health. 23 January 2019, NIH. https://www.nih.gov/news-events/news-releases/blood-test-shows-promise-early-detection-severe-lung-transplant-rejection. Accessed 28 July 2019.

- Passage 4 on Pages 223-224, "Why governments are so bad at implementing public projects," is an excerpt from the article of the same name by Andrew Graham and published by The Conversation in partnership with Queens University, Ontario. 13 February 2019, The Conversation. https://theconversation.com/why-governments-are-so-bad-at-implementing-public-projects-111223. Accessed 28 July 2019.

- Passage 5, Reading 1 on Page 227, "Four new species of zombie ant fungi—another step forward for open-access taxonomy," is adapted from the article of the same name by Emily Hare and published by EveryONE, the community blog of the research journal PLOS ONE. 2 March 2011, PLOS ONE. https://blogs.plos.org/everyone/2011/03/02/four-new-species-of-zombie-ant-fungi-another-step-forward-for-open-access-taxonomy/. Accessed 28 July 2019.

- Passage 5, Reading 2 on Pages 227-228, "Taking a piece of home with you: Farming fungi in a new Azteca ant colony," is adapted from the article of the same name by Nicola Stead and published by EveryONE, the community blog of the research journal PLOS ONE. 22 February 2018, PLOS ONE. https://blogs.plos.org/everyone/2018/02/22/fungiculture-azteca-ants/. Accessed 28 July 2019.

About the Figures: The various visual resources that accompany the passages in this section are primarily meant to facilitate critical thinking skills and may not reflect historical data.

Made in the USA
Monee, IL
28 June 2023